The Sexual State

THE SEXUAL STATE

How Elite Ideologies Are Destroying Lives and
Why The Church Was Right All Along

Jennifer Roback Morse, PhD

TAN Books
Charlotte, North Carolina

Contents

Acknowledgments

I thank Sue Ellen Browder for numerous helpful conversations about structuring the book. I thank all my audiences who have listened to or read parts of this material while it was in preparation. I particularly thank the participants of the Ruth Institute Literary Salon, the students assembled by the Alliance Defending Freedom, and the audiences of the Acton University over the years.

I also thank my friends and colleagues at the Ruth Institute, who conversed with me about these concepts, literally for years. Associate Director Jennifer Johnson has been an especially helpful dialogue partner over the years.

I thank the Earhart Foundation for financial support specifically for the writing of this book. I am especially grateful to Ingrid Gregg, the president of the Earhart Foundation, for her support and patience.

I thank all the friends and benefactors of the Ruth Institute. Thanks to their support, I have been able to spend the time needed to develop these ideas, share them with others, and best of all, refine them to make them accessible to a wide audience. Without all of you posing questions, sharing heartfelt stories, writing encouraging notes, and sending your checks large and small, I could not have worked out the ideas in this book.

Finally, I would like to thank my husband, Rob Morse, for his love and support over the years of our journey of marriage and parenthood. He made it possible for me to leave academic life. This allowed me both full-time motherhood and independent thought. I could not have written this book without both of those gifts. Thank you, honey.

A Note on the Timeliness of Data

I supplement many of the arguments in this book with the results of scientific research. Some readers may wonder: is this data too old to be useful? Is this study really current? Let me address that concern here, at the beginning of the book, since this question may arise in multiple places throughout the text.

Ask yourself why you think the age of the study matters. If the study is referring to a technological fact, then the date on which the study was performed may indeed matter. When I make claims about the dangers associated with some forms of hormonal contraception, it is theoretically possible that the pharmaceutical companies have made improvements in their products. In that case, my claim would no longer stand.

If, instead, the study is referring to a social fact, the date of the study may or may not be relevant. Children need their parents. People bond with their sex partners and with their children. Men and women are different. These are facts of human nature. Technology will not and cannot change these facts.

You may think that enough social change will overwrite

these facts. If you think so, the burden of proof is on you, not me. I think it is frankly immoral to undertake a program of social change which depends for its success on having enough power to change human nature.

If the data in question refers to one of these perennial questions of human nature, an older study is actually quite valuable. In fact, a very early study showing that women are troubled by their abortions or that children suffer from the divorce of their parents is a damning indictment of the Sexual Revolution. Those "old" and "obsolete" studies show that we knew from the beginning that something was not going according to ideological plan. We had reason to know that people were suffering. We ignored that evidence.

Finally, I hope people will be reading this book for many years. If you pick up this book ten years after it was written, none of the studies will be "current" if by "current" you mean "recent" or "the latest." If my hypothesis is correct, the age of the studies will not be a problem. The events that transpire between the time of this writing and the time you read this book should confirm my proposition that the Sexual Revolution has been a big mistake and that certain people are hanging on to it for dear life, regardless of the evidence, including social science evidence.

PART ONE

The Sexual State

Chapter 1

The Misery of Modern Life

The greatest disease in the West today is not TB or leprosy; it is being unwanted, unloved, and uncared for. We can cure physical diseases with medicine, but the only cure for loneliness, despair, and hopelessness is love. There are many in the world who are dying for a piece of bread but there are many more dying for a little love. The poverty in the West is a different kind of poverty—it is not only a poverty of loneliness but also of spirituality. There's a hunger for love, as there is a hunger for God.

—Saint Teresa of Calcutta, *A Simple Path*

This book is about the ideology of the Sexual Revolution, the havoc it has created in the lives of its victims, and why we have been unable to make the connection between the two up until now. Once you see the connections, you'll never be the same.

Let me introduce you to a few people who have been harmed by the Sexual Revolution. Elise is an actual little girl. Todd and Annette are composites of many people I have known. Perhaps you know similar people.

Elise is a six-year-old who lives with her grandmother and whose mother had a baby with someone other than Elise's father.

"I hate Thanksgiving. I hate it when my mom comes with her new baby and her new boyfriend. I don't feel like eating. Why do I have to live with my grandma? How come they are all fussing over the stupid new baby? Why doesn't my mom love me? Why does that dumb new baby get to live with her and I don't?

"I hate Christmas. I could just bust up this idiotic Christmas tree. Why can't I go home with my mom? Why does that loser baby get to live with her mom and dad and I don't? I don't even have a dad, I guess. I hate all this 'Baby's First Christmas' crap. I don't care about any of the stupid presents. Where is my dad? Why doesn't he love me? Why doesn't my mom love me? Why doesn't anybody want me?

"My grandma is nice, I guess, but I want my mom. I'm mad at my mom, but she isn't here. She went back to her house with her boyfriend and their baby. Grandma is here. I'm going to make life hell for Grandma. I think I'll break something. Maybe scream. Maybe throw stuff. Maybe Grandma will tell my mom to come and get me and take me back to her house to live with her where I belong."

Elise can't put all this into words of course. She expresses herself with her actions precisely because she cannot express her feelings with words. Her grandma (who is an acquaintance of mine) tells me that Elise is angry and acts out after every family holiday get together. For about a week after family holidays, she wets her bed every night, every time.

Todd is a thirty-something pipe fitter whose wife moved out and left him with three small children to care for.

"I love my kids. I'd do anything for them. My wife left the family without a word, without any warning, four years ago. I had no idea where she was and did not hear anything from her. Now she has come back. She says she has 'found herself.' She also 'found' a new boyfriend who has a better job than I do. The kids are happy to see her, but they don't trust her love. They want to believe she will be there for them, but how can they believe it?

"She took me to court over custody. I worked up a whole detailed statement for the court. I explained why I should continue to keep the kids, stating that I am willing to give her reasonable visitation, explaining that we had no contact with her at all for four years. No birthday cards, no phone calls, nothing. The judge took five minutes to decide that the mother should have custody and I should get visitation. I have to pay child support. My ex-wife is not marrying the new boyfriend, because she doesn't want his income counted, but she is living with him.

"My twelve-year-old son is old enough that he can remember when his mom used to live with us. He said, 'Dad, I hate it that mom is in bed with another man. You should be in bed with her.'

"My eight-year-old daughter has lost her appetite and is losing weight. My younger son is angry at school. The teacher called me and said he is acting up at school. I told him I couldn't do much about it: he is living with his mother now. I tried to talk to my wife—I guess I should say his mother; she isn't exactly my wife anymore is she? Anyhow,

I tried to talk to her. She said not to worry. He will get over it. He will adjust. And he will be going to a new school soon anyhow, and everyone will forget all about him punching other kids and breaking stuff at the old school.

"I know 'real men' aren't supposed to cry. But I am heart-broken and just plain broke, financially and otherwise."

Lynette is a fifty-something unmarried childless lawyer.

"I thought I could 'have it all.' After all, the men get to be fathers and have careers. I poured myself into my career. I always thought I would get married and have children. But I wanted to pay off my law school debt and make partner at the firm first.

"By the time I did all that, I realized I was almost forty. So I tried to focus more on dating and finding a husband. I really didn't want to be a single mother. And I really didn't want to go through life alone. So I created a six-month plan for finding a husband. But it didn't work out. I couldn't really find a suitable guy. I don't know why.

"When I was forty, I decided to do IVF (in vitro fertil-ization) with donor sperm. No one told me how unlikely a pregnancy is if you are over forty. After multiple cycles, and two miscarriages, I finally gave up when I was forty-three. Only then did I find a study that said that women aged for-ty-one to forty-two, using their own fresh eggs, have only a 5.8 percent chance of having a live baby and that women aged forty-three to forty-four have a 2.7 percent chance per initiated cycle. The IVF clinic gave me higher numbers.[1]

---

[1]   Sarah Dingle, "IVF doctors misleading women about success rates, industry experts say," ABC News, May 29, 2016, http:// www.abc.net.au/news/2016-05-30/ivf-doctors-misleading-patients-about-success-rates-experts-say/7457750.

Only after I read that study did I realize that their 'success rates' were pregnancies, not live births. My two miscarriages counted as 'successes' in their eyes.

"No one told me I would want a baby so much. It seems so unfair. Some of the men in my firm are fathering children, even when they are my age. And the ones who aren't having kids don't seem to care. I looked at the childless men in my firm and concluded that having kids was an optional add-on to a successful life. I had no idea that being a childless woman would feel so different to me than being a childless man seems to feel to the guys.

"I'm seeing my sisters with kids who are pretty much grown up now. I see my younger relatives getting married and starting families. I used to look down on them because they were not ambitious about their careers or education. Maybe the joke is on me. My career is great, and I should be happy. But I feel empty."

~ ~ ~

It is the best of times; it is the worst of times. Despite all our technological and medical success, life in the modern world is lonely, trying, and long. For example, an article called "The Age of Anxiety? Birth Cohort changes in Anxiety and Neuroticism, 1952-1993" shows that children's anxiety and neuroticism have increased between 1952 and 1993. The average child in the 1980s reported more anxiety than child psychiatric patients in the 1950s. A study called "The Paradox of Declining Female Happiness" shows that women's happiness declined both absolutely and relative to men between the 1970s and the turn of the century.[2]

Let me tell you about a few more people I know. I imagine you know people like these.

Ben

Ben is married and has three children. When Ben was thirty-five, his father decided to divorce his mother for another woman. His father began spending holidays with his new wife and her children and grandchildren. He lost interest in Ben and his siblings and their children. Ben tells me, "My mom lost her husband. I lost my father. My children lost their grandfather."

But Ben's father is free.

Bethany and Joe

Bethany's husband, Joe, is a pornography addict. He lost interest in her and their children. He divorced her. He moved in with another woman. Their children visit him and his live-in girlfriend. He no longer has any respect for the religion in which he and Bethany had their children baptized.

Bethany told me, "Raising my children with the values I thought their father and I shared has become a constant

---

2   See Jean Twenge, "The Age of Anxiety? Birth Cohort changes in Anxiety and Neuroticism, 1952-1993," *Journal of Personality and Social Psychology* 79, no. 2 (December 2000): 1007–21. See also Justin Wolfers and Betsy Stevenson, "The Paradox of Declining Female Happiness," *American Economic Journal* 1, no. 2 (2009): 190–225.

struggle. When Joe and I married, I never expected that I would be sending our children to stay with a man who is a constant pornography user and who is living with a girlfriend. The Joe I married would not have stood for such a thing. And now he has become that thing.

"Earning a living and supporting and caring for the kids is tough. I'm living a day-to-day grind at the time of my life when I thought I would be most enjoying my children. I don't know what I would do without the moral and practical support of my parents. They moved closer so they could help me."

But Joe is free.

Katrina and Michael

Katrina is a good Catholic woman with three children. Her husband, Michael, divorced her when their youngest was in high school. The boy began acting out in rages and breaking things, not unusual for children of divorce.

Michael traveled a lot for his job. While overseas, he met another woman with whom he became enamored. She was the reason for the divorce.

Katrina told me, "It turned out that Michael had a brain tumor. I took care of him when he was in the hospital and recovering. His new girlfriend was nowhere to be seen. He was not entirely in his right mind, but when he got out of the hospital, he was still adamant about the divorce. He bought me out of my half of our house and moved his new girlfriend and her family members into our family home. They got green cards out of the deal somehow. I'm now living with my in-laws. They are mortified by their son's behavior. They are still very dear to me. And I'm still dear to them. That really means a lot to me."

If Michael had made a will while he had a brain tumor, a disinherited relative could have challenged it in probate court in a heartbeat. Divorce is different. He wanted a divorce. He dissipated all the accumulated wealth of his marriage, broke up his family, broke his wife's heart, and broke his son's spirit. He got his divorce.

But Michael is free.

Tom and Genevieve

Tom's mother was married and divorced twice. Neither of these men was Tom's father. Tom has one half-sister. Neither of his mother's husbands was her father either. Tom has never really had much of a relationship with his father.

Tom married a woman named Genevieve, whose mother's first husband was sterile. So she and her husband adopted a child from a foreign country. Later, they decided to have another child through anonymous donor conception. That was Genevieve.

When Genevieve was eight, her mother and her husband divorced. The husband wanted shared custody of the adopted child but not of Genevieve. Genevieve's mother remarried and had a son with her second husband.

Genevieve told me, "I wish I knew my father. I searched and found him. But he is dead. My mother has a hard time understanding why I want to know about my father. She feels that I should be grateful to be alive and stop worrying about my father. But he is half of who I am."

Tom told me, "We want to have a large family. Neither Genevieve nor I have a relationship with a father. Neither of us has a full-blooded sibling. We want our children to have the experience of brotherhood and sisterhood."

But their parents were free.

~ ~ ~

Here are a few more brief snapshots of people I know. Everyone in this first group has something in common.

- The depressed teenage girl who can't figure out why she is unhappy over her hook-ups. The adults in her life taught her that having as much sex as she wants will make her feel empowered.

- The college woman jaded about her sex life. She doesn't expect much in the way of attention or commitment. She only expects to be a "friend with benefits." But she wonders why he gets the "benefits" and she doesn't get much friendship.

- The young man who doesn't want to be a "player." He would like to have a relationship with a girl that isn't based on sex. But the girls around him seem to expect sexual come-ons from him. And the guys around him are strutting. He knows he isn't gay, but still, he quietly wonders if there is something wrong with him.

- The unmarried woman whose contraception fails. She would have preferred not to be a single mother. But the child's father won't commit or is not a suitable marriage partner. She doesn't want an abortion: she wants her child. She was taught that as long as she used "protection," she could have sex without negative consequences.

- The men who have sex with men, abbreviated in the medical literature as MSM. The normal public health protocols designed to protect people from the spread of sexually transmitted infections have never been applied to MSM. Standard public health measures for sexually transmitted infections usually include things like partner notification, mandatory testing, and public awareness campaigns to encourage people to have fewer sexual partners. Anal sex, a common sexual practice among MSM, is so dangerous that the US surgeon general declared it "simply too risky to practice." This statement is seldom publicized. As a result of this pattern of neglect, MSM acquire STIs at substantially increased rates over other groups.[3]
- The cohabiting woman who spends years in a relationship with a boyfriend who won't commit.
- The woman who had an abortion years ago. All the reasons she gave herself for exercising her "right to choose" have come to sound hollow to her. No one takes her and her regrets seriously: not her counselors, not her friends, not her boyfriends (who all too often

---

3   "Condoms and Sexually Transmitted Diseases . . . especially AIDS," FDA pamphlet published in December 1990, http://web.archive.org/web/20090508183048/http:/www.fda.gov/oashi/aids/condom.html.

become ex-boyfriends), and sometimes, not even her pastor.

- The woman who experiences side effects from her contraception. Headaches, weight gain, loss of libido, and irritability are among the more common complaints. The less common problems are more serious: increased risk of heart attacks, strokes, glaucoma, diabetes, and cancer. Some of these "acceptable risks" have been directly implicated in the deaths of several women. Yet no one in power seems interested in justice for these victims.

- The man who literally believes he is "entitled" to sex. The college rapist takes the campus hook-up culture one step further and just takes what he wants.

- The child molester: he, too, takes what he wants. Sometimes an abortion allows him to cover his tracks and go right back to abusing his female victim. Sometimes he has access to male victims through organizations that are supposed to support sexual minority youth. We are now beginning to be told that the child molester just has a different "sexual orientation," a preference for "intergenerational sex."

- Speaking of victims, the women and children who have been sexually assaulted, seduced, or otherwise exploited by the rapist or child molester.

- Pornography addicts. They lose contact with real people and real intimacy as they become preoccupied with fantasy masturbation. They may become unable to respond sexually to a live person without a pornography video playing in the background. Addicts believe themselves to be entitled to sexual stimulation and orgasm. In fact, the mark of true addicts is they think they'll die if they don't get the high. Like Joe.

- The family of the pornography addict. They may lose their spouse, their parent, their brother or sister or friend, who becomes increasingly unavailable to them and unrecognizable by them. Like Bethany and her children.

- The increasingly pornographic culture, with sexually stimulating images used to sell everything from alcohol to cars to window blinds. Even if children somehow avoid seeing explicit pornography on the Internet, everyone is exposed to scantily clad women on billboards while driving down the freeway.

- The women and men with sexually transmitted infections. Some of these infections are deadly; others can cause sterility. All of them are caused by non-monogamous sex on the part of one or both partners. This serious public health problem has increased steadily in the past fifty years.

- The man who discovers, years after the fact, that he is a father. Perhaps he learns that an old girlfriend had a baby and didn't tell him or she had an abortion and didn't tell him. In either case, he grieves the loss of his child once he learns about his or her existence.

What do all these people have in common? Sex. They or someone close to them have accepted certain ideas about sex. They believe it's about freedom and fun instead of babies and bonding. Net result: a lot of hurting and lonely people.

The radical separation of sex from procreation that is peculiar to our time has finally come full circle. We started with having sex without babies. Now we can have babies without sex. In fact, we can have babies without ever having a relationship with the child's other parent, without even having met them in some cases.

Children of these arrangements, like Genevieve, may long for their missing parent, may feel odd about money changing hands as part of their conception, and may fear encountering an unknown half-sibling. The children of assisted reproduction techniques are at greater risk for preterm birth, low birth weight, cerebral palsy, and a variety of rare genetic imprinting disorders.

We'll be hearing more and more about these issues as these children become adults. They'll have thoughts and feelings of their own. Being "wanted" by their social parents won't necessarily be enough to answer all the questions they have and deal with the losses they sustain.

Perhaps the most obvious cause of that loneliness St. Teresa of Calcutta talks about is the lack of permanence in relationships. People now more or less take it for granted that love will not last a lifetime even though the vast majority of people long for lifelong love. Consider the following people.

- Children of divorce. In their minds, they wonder if they're to blame for their parents' divorce.
- Single mothers, not by choice, but by default. Marriage is so uncommon in some communities that people don't view it as a realistic option for themselves.

They become unmarried mothers because they don't want to give up motherhood. They can't figure out how to get suitable men to commit to them and their children and be appropriate husbands and fathers.

- The young professionals who postpone marriage until their thirties so they can complete their education and establish themselves in their careers. Why don't they get married in their early twenties and work with their spouses to jointly pursue their educations and career goals? Their perfectly rational fear of divorce prevents them. Like Lynette.

- The children of divorce: used as pawns in divorce courts, asked to perjure themselves by one parent against the other.

- The new mother who would like to stay home with her baby but is afraid her husband might not stay married to her. She goes back to work and works longer than she wants to. When she drops her baby off at daycare, tears stream down both their faces.

- The reluctantly divorced: those millions of unseen men and women whose marriages ended against their will. The law offers no protection to the spouse who wants to stay married and has kept their marriage vows. In fact, the law takes sides with the party who wants the marriage the least. Like Katrina.

- The despairing divorced father driven out of his home and now living in a Spartan apartment by himself, seeing his children perhaps every other week. Like Todd.

- The child of a "multi-party fertility" situation who has no relationship with her father, whom her mother never married. Her mother has another child with another man. Her mother and new boyfriend are more interested in the child they had together. The original child feels like a leftover from the old relationship. Like Elise.

- The jilted wife whose husband abandons her for a younger woman.

- The children of divorce, shuttling between two houses week after week, never completely a part of either family.

- Fathers falsely accused of child abuse as a strategic move in contested custody cases. There is, as far as I can tell, no penalty for making a false accusation in family court. As a matter of fact, some divorce professionals hold child abuse accusations in reserve as the "nuclear option" to be explored as a strategic possibility.

People can't count on permanence in even the most basic biological and sexual relationships. The net result is fear of rejection, loss of identity, and loneliness. Another source of confusion that ultimately contributes to loneliness is that we don't fully know ourselves and our needs. We're biological beings, mammals, divided into two sexes, male and female. This seems like an obvious and straightforward notion, yet in modern times, we have trouble with this basic concept.

You may think the drive toward incorporating the transgender ideology into American law is a relatively recent development that came upon us suddenly. On the contrary, the drive to de-gender everyone has been going on for a long time. Here are a few people and situations you may recognize or perhaps relate to.

- The cohabiting woman who would like to get married but who can't get her boyfriend to commit. Society has taught her that men and women are identical in their desires for sex, love, marriage, and children. She can't figure out why she wants marriage and children so much more than he does.

- The married couple struggling because they've been taught that men and women are really the same: no differences worth mentioning. The man can't understand why his wife doesn't pursue him sexually and make him feel wanted. The woman can't understand why her husband doesn't talk to her more in the bedroom. Without realizing it, they are expecting the other to act and react as they would. They can't figure out why their sex lives are so complicated and unsatisfying.

- The teenage girl who gives in to sex she doesn't want because she wants to please her boyfriend. She's been taught that girls and boys both like sex. She doesn't want to reveal that she likes it differently from the boy or that she would be satisfied to do without it altogether. In fact, she might prefer to abstain from sex.

- The couple in conflict over when and whether to have children. For some couples, this conflict may be the first time it seriously dawns on them that men and women truly are different. Each couple must work this out completely from scratch since society gives them little guidance.

- The parents in conflict over how to raise their children. The mother wants the children to be comfortable. The father wants them to behave. The mother and father have trouble appreciating and respecting the different but equally necessary perspectives of their spouse. After all, they have been repeatedly told that the differences between men and women are not real but socially constructed. They can't quite entertain the idea that mothers and fathers actually are different, think and feel differently, and bring different strengths and weaknesses to the parenting enterprise.

- The children in schools that expect the boys and girls to have identical needs for physical exercise or aptitudes for sitting quietly at their desks.

- The young woman who would like to become a mother, stay home with her children, and entrust herself to her husband to care for the family's financial needs. This woman finds it difficult to express these desires in public.

- The mother who does stay home with her children and entrusts herself to her husband. When people ask her what she does, she says, "I'm just a mom," as if that was nothing significant. She feels she is supposed to be pursuing meaningful employment outside the home, just like a man.

- The man who would like his wife to stay home with their kids and trust him to take care of the family financially. He doesn't feel it's his place to express that desire to her. He fears she'll think he's imposing sexual stereotypes on her.

- The woman who would like to take simple pleasure in the innocent activities of daily life that may be stereo-typically feminine: cooking, sewing, arranging flow-ers. She feels uncomfortable admitting how much she enjoys these activities, especially if she has an advanced degree.
- The woman who thought she could pursue a career on identical terms as men and still have a family. Like Lynnette.

There's a lot of angst in the twenty-first-century West, in the richest, most technologically advanced society the world has ever known. We are rich but unsatisfied. We pride our-selves on our scientific sophistication, but we cannot face the most basic biological facts about our species. We are enamored of our social media, but we are alone more than ever. We have more sex with more people than any society in the history of the world. But we long for intimacy and true friendship. Most of us know there is something deeply wrong with our culture, but we can't quite put our finger on what it is or what to do about it.

CHAPTER 2

Conflict and Confusion: What Is the Sexual Revolution and How Are People Trying to Deal With It?

Why are so many people hurting? I think most people can recognize that the people I described in the previous chapter are suffering from the changes in sexual mores which are generally called the "Sexual Revolution." But identifying the core ideas or "philosophies" behind those attitudes and behaviors presents a challenge. "Experts" and public intellectuals offer wildly different interpretations of the Sexual Revolution, its causes, its desirability, and its consequences. The net result: an intellectual and interpretive nightmare for the average person. We can hardly be surprised if ordinary people trying to manage their jobs, their homes, and their families can't figure out what to do.

In this chapter, I define the Sexual Revolution. I break the Sexual Revolution down into three basic ideas. Doing so will hopefully make this complex and unwieldy subject more understandable and mentally manageable. I will also describe some of the most common responses people offer to the Sexual Revolution.

The Ideology of the Sexual Revolution

The Sexual Revolution consists of ideas as well as the policies that put those ideas into practice. The three main ideas of the Sexual Revolution are that a good and decent society should:

1. separate sex from childbearing: the Contraceptive Ideology;
2. separate both sex and childbearing from marriage: the Divorce Ideology;
3. eliminate all distinctions between men and women except those that individuals explicitly embrace: the Gender Ideology.

The Contraceptive Ideology

The first revolutionary idea is that a good and decent society ought to separate sex and childbearing from each other. I call this the **Contraceptive Ideology**. The Contraceptive Ideology presents itself as the champion of freedom and gender justice. Caring for unwanted children is an unjust demand on women. Sexual activity without a live baby as a result is an entitlement for men and women alike.

According to this vision, people need and are entitled to sexual activity: that is the underlying idea. A person deprived of sex has a life scarcely worth living. Do I exaggerate? Perhaps a bit. I've never heard an ordinary person actually put it quite so bluntly. However, the United Nations has said something nearly that stark. The United Nations Population Fund asks and answers this question on its "Frequently Asked Questions" page on its website under the heading "What is reproductive health?" "Reproductive health can be defined as a state of well-being related to one's sexual and reproductive life. It implies, according to the ICPD Programme of Action, 'that people are able to have a satisfying and safe sex life and that they have the capability to reproduce and the freedom to decide if, when and how often to do so' (para. 7.2)"[1]

The UN never quite explains who has the responsibility to provide a person with a "safe and satisfying sex life." As for having the "capability to reproduce and the freedom to decide if, when and how often to do so:" a person who judges that the time is not right for a baby has the option of not having sex. Pretty simple. No need for a whole "Programme of Action."

Evidently, it's not that simple. Somehow, the UN doesn't expect people to go without sex, even temporarily or for serious reasons like avoiding pregnancy or STIs. Your parents and your pastor might expect you to forgo sex once in a while, but evidently the United Nations Population Fund doesn't expect it.

Let's ask ourselves if there are any downsides associated with this set of views? Any risks? Is anyone harmed by the

---

[1]   "Frequently Asked Questions," United Nations Population Fund, accessed July 27, 2016, http://www.unfpa.org/frequently-asked-questions#rh.

attempt to build a whole society around the twin ideas that we ought to separate sex from childbearing and that a normal person cannot live a fulfilling life without sexual activity? I refer you back to the first list of lonely and jaded souls in the previous chapter. Think about Joe and Bethany and the others listed there. Allow yourself to consider people you have known who have tried to live according to the Contraceptive Ideology. Then tell me this is a harmless set of ideas.

The Divorce Ideology

The second revolutionary idea is that a good and decent society ought to separate sex and babies from marriage. Of course, if people want to get married and have babies together and stay together for a lifetime, society considers that perfectly OK. But society does next to nothing to encourage or support this increasingly unusual lifestyle choice. Certainly, no one is required to keep sex and babies together inside one lasting, lifelong marriage.

I call this the **Divorce Ideology**. Non-marital cohabitation, no-fault divorce, and non-marital sex and childbearing are all particular instances of the general idea that sex and childbearing can be separated from marriage. Separating sex and childbearing from marriage can take place by having children without ever getting married. Or it can take place by breaking the marriage apart after children are born within it. In either case, the child's need for parents is set aside for the sake of something else, or someone else.

Lurking in the background of the Divorce Ideology are two insidious ideas. First, children don't need steady relationships with their parents. Second, adults do not have particularly serious rights or responsibilities toward their children. The kids will be fine as long as the adults in their lives are happy. Losing access to one's child isn't serious or hurtful to a parent. Abandoning one's child for further sexual adventure or personal satisfaction isn't particularly painful for the spouse or children left behind.

Is there anything harmful worth considering here? I refer you back to the second list of sad souls along with Todd, Elise, Ben, Katrina, Tom, and Genevieve. All these people have problems that flow directly from the idea that sex and babies without marriage is not only socially acceptable but an entitlement.

Some of these people are truly victims. The children of divorce did nothing to deserve the sorrow they feel from having their low-conflict family[2] redefined right out from

---

[2]   Sociologists make a distinction between a low-conflict marriage and a high-conflict marriage. A high-conflict marriage is one with violence, continuous violent arguing, or substance abuse. These marriages would have roughly qualified for divorce under most fault-based regimes. Children in high-conflict marriages are sometimes better off if their parents separate because it diminishes the day-to-day conflict the children experience. However, children in low-conflict marriages benefit from their parents remaining married. In their minds, the separation of their parents makes no sense. These are the children who suffer the most from their parents' divorce. We could say that the way we handle the low-conflict marriage is the main difference between the fault-based divorce regime and the no-fault regime. See Paul Amato and Alan Booth, *A Generation at Risk: Growing up in an Era of Family Upheaval* (Cambridge: Harvard University Press, 1997), see esp. chapter 7.

Even the qualification about "low-conflict marriages" is

under them. They experience the separation of their parents as an inexplicable loss. They experience the ongoing complication of living their lives between two households to be a continual reminder of this loss. The children of never married parents often feel the loss of their fathers' daily influence in their lives or, in some cases, never even knowing the identity of their fathers. These children sometimes suffer from the low income of their mothers or the instability of her love life. I know they feel this way because they come to me after my talks with tears in their eyes. They tell me I'm the first adult they've ever heard say that divorce is hard on children. They sense that I'll listen to them.

Others are both victims and perpetrators. They were victims of lousy information. They got divorced or had a child outside of marriage because they believed the widely-promoted Divorce Ideology. In the process, they may have inflicted incalculable harm on the people around them. If they'd known how painful divorce would prove to be for their children, they would've worked harder at their marriages. If they'd known how difficult single parenthood was going to be, they would've tried harder to find a husband before having children. How do I know? Many of them have told me as much. Why have they told me? Because I'm willing to listen.

---

increasingly coming into question. That is, there is now some evidence that children suffer from the dissolution of even "high-conflict" marriage. See the working paper by David Ribar, Seth Sanders, and Claire Thibout, "Dissolution, Conflict and Australian Children's Developmental Outcomes," Melbourne Institute of Applied Economic and Social Research, July 2017.

The Gender Ideology

The third revolutionary idea is that all differences we observe between men and women are socially constructed. Therefore, society can deconstruct these differences without doing anyone any serious harm. In fact, all differences between men and women are evidence of injustice that must be rectified. If a person wants to be something other than the biological sex they were born, the individual can undertake the bodily reconstruction necessary to fit his or her, or ze or zis, self-understanding.

The Gender Ideology goes far beyond the reasonable demand that men and women be treated with dignity and respect. It insists that differences between men and women are evidence of injustice. All such differences are suspect at least and quite possibly worse.

Beyond the legal landscape, the cultural landscape has deteriorated to the point that saying men and women are different is considered a social heresy. It takes genuine courage to say such a thing on most college campuses or professional settings. Men are simply banned outright from saying men and women are different. Women who say such things run the risk of being treated as traitors.

Is there anything worth considering here? Any problems, downsides, or risks? I refer you to the third list in the previous chapter, including Lynnette. All these people have problems that flow directly from the Gender Ideology. And I haven't even begun to talk about the people who experience serious gender dysphoria. Some of them, no doubt, experience it due to the continual cultural hammering that men and women are identical. If they aren't identical, their differences can be easily eradicated, reconstructed, or deconstructed. It's still too soon to tell what kind of damage that ideology will do to innocent children and well-meaning but ultimately gullible parents.

Competing Forms of Assistance

With all the problems I just catalogued, you may be sure that there are many people sincerely trying to help. Lots of people grasp that something is very wrong. They have different theories about what is wrong and what will help. People from all points on the political spectrum, of many religious backgrounds, and all up and down the socio-economic ladder are trying to help. Some of these efforts seem to make sense. But if we shift the perspective just a bit, those same approaches no longer seem so sensible. Sometimes these different groups with different ideas get along well with the other groups. Sometimes they are bitterly at odds with each other.

Before I offer my analysis of the problem, let's catalogue some of the efforts and explanations. Let me warn you about this list. Quite likely each reader will think some of those listed below are exacerbating the problem. But let us assume good will on their part and grant that they are sincere in their efforts.

People Who Are Trying to Help

- Sex educators: providing contraception to protect people from having children they believe they cannot properly care for.
- Resident advisors in college dorms: teaching students about the importance of seeking consent for all sexual encounters.
- Sexual harassment tribunals at colleges and universities: judging cases of alleged sexual harassment or rape.
- Gender studies programs: seeking to show how gender-based power imbalances in relationships create social injustices.
- Sex-positive affirmation: any program or set of ideas that tries to convey that sexual desire is a normal experience in human life and that any sexual activity is a great positive good for women and men alike, so long as it is consensual.
- Risk reduction sex education programs: conveying the message that using condoms during sexual activity can reduce the risk of sexually transmitted infections.
- Risk avoidance sex education programs: conveying the message that abstaining from sexual activity until entering a monogamous union is the most reliable way to avoid pregnancy and sexually transmitted infections.
- Rape crisis centers: conveying to women that rape is not their fault, they can and should seek help, and they should report their attacker to proper authorities.

- Gay and lesbian community centers and student outreach groups: affirming people in their same-sex attraction.
- Chastity support groups for high school and college students, straight or gay: offering group support for a chaste lifestyle.
- Peer education programs: young people teaching and encouraging other young people on the proper use of contraception.
- Natural Family Planning programs, including the couple to couple peer counseling programs and programs staffed by professionals: sharing information about fertility awareness methods of family planning.
- Abortion promotion organizations: providing women with the ability to have an abortion with as little inconvenience and cost as possible.
- Abortion alternatives programs: offering information and support for mothers to give birth to their children.
- Marriage education programs: teaching relationship skills to engaged, married, and cohabiting couples.
- Mentoring couples programs: experienced married couples offering help and encouragement to newly married couples and engaged couples.
- Parent education programs: teaching parenting skills to parents, whether married or not.
- Pregnancy support centers: offering support for expectant mothers who may not have the material or psychological means to be confident as mothers.

- Battered women's shelters: providing a safe place for women and their children in immediate danger of physical or emotional abuse.
- Fathers' rights support groups: providing legal and emotional support for men who are unjustly separated from their children.
- Post-abortion healing programs: helping women and sometimes men who have been negatively impacted by abortion to confront their feelings and heal from their abortions.

Some of these programs are sponsored or supported by religious organizations, either faith-based para-church organizations or individual churches and denominations. Others are government programs. Still others are provided by private organizations but paid for with government funds.

Looking at this list, it should be apparent that some of these groups are working at cross purposes to each other. But they are all trying to help people navigate the treacherous waters of marriage, sex, and family in the twenty-first century. These waters are treacherous because the institutional structures that once provided guidance for decision-making are no longer serving that function.

Competing Narratives

Let's now take a brief look at some of the narratives that have been offered to explain our current situation. They can't all be correct at the same time. Yet you'll recognize each as part of the current cultural soup in which we're all swimming.

The existence of these contradictory ideas is part of what creates the confusion and conflict so many people experience today.

Each of these explanations suffers from one or both of the following problems. First, these story lines don't offer a complete account for how and why we've reached the point of such profound loneliness. Second, these accounts are not entirely coherent within themselves. That is, some of these narratives either omit relevant social facts or contain within themselves significant internal contradictions.

Impersonal Forces: The March of History Narrative

The **March of History Narrative** suggests that the changes in family life and sexual attitudes came about due to impersonal forces, for which no one is responsible. Phrases like these express this view:

- Modern life puts pressure on the family.
- Urbanization and modernization have reduced the economic need for large families.
- Sexual mores have changed.
- We have moved beyond the old ways.
- The pill caused radical changes in sexual attitudes.
- The modern family is different.

Notice that these sentences and phrases use the passive voice or have an impersonal subject. No one caused the breakdown of the family. Social forces. Technological forces. Historical forces. Economic forces.

In fact, in reviewing one short book, I easily found several examples of this use of passive voice. The author referred to a study called "The Decline of Marriage and the Rise of New Families." This language is designed to convey the notion that no one took any actions that caused marriage to "decline" or the "new families" to "rise." These things happened on their own, like so many forces of nature.

The book's authors state: "Some scholars argue that in the past five decades, the basic architecture of these age-old institutions has changed as rapidly as at any time in human history." No one is responsible. The institutions just "changed" all by themselves.[3]

The March of History Narrative is not satisfactory. This language is insidious because it robs us and our forbearers of human agency. Depending on your point of view, we see ourselves as passive victims or the fortunate beneficiaries of History with a capital *H*. Once we use this type of language, we stop looking for a human explanation because no human actor is required. We have the answer to our question of causality: the changes in sexual attitudes and family structures took place through forces beyond anyone's control.

One specific example of this impersonal narrative concerns the pill. We often hear people claim that changes in sexual behavior and attitudes can be attributed to the introduction of oral hormonal contraception. But the pill is just an inert piece of technology. As a society, we had (and still

---

[3]   Jennifer Roback Morse, "Getting Zapped for a Good Cause: A Review of *Home Economics*," *Ethika Politika,* August 16, 2013, https://ethikapolitika.org/2013/08/16/getting-zapped-for-a-good-cause-a-review-of-home-economics-the-consequences-of-changing-family-structure/.

have) decisions to make about what meaning to assign to this technology, what place to assign it in our individual lives, and how the overall social system ought to adapt to it.

The availability of contraceptive technology is not the revolutionary point. Various methods for spacing pregnancies have been known from time immemorial. In fact, in the "First Demographic Transition," birth rates dropped in half. This was discovered in 1929 by looking at patterns over the previous two hundred years. Obviously, this had nothing to do with modern hormonal contraceptive technology. Demographers might say the decline in fertility took place in response to declining death rates and declining infant mortality.[4]

Let me restate this theory in a positive, non-passive, agency-affirming manner. Millions of ordinary people realized that fewer of their children were dying and that they and their children were living longer. They realized that they didn't need to give birth to so many children in order to end up with the family size they ultimately wanted. Noticing all this, husbands and wives worked together to take steps to have fewer children.

So even something as revolutionary as the pill is not a revolution in and of itself. The way we think about sex and childbearing and the decisions we choose to make constitute

---

[4]　　The concept of a demographic transition, in which birth rates decline after declines in death rates and infant mortality rates, was discovered by Warren Thompson in 1929 based on observations from the previous two hundred years. Wikipedia, s.v. "Demographic transition," http://en.wikipedia.org/wiki/Demographic_transition#cite_note-marathon.uwc.edu-6.

the genuine revolution. The pill didn't make us do anything any more than *coitus interruptus* or periodic abstinence made the peasants of France have fewer children. Those methods of regulating births have been known and available for a long, long time. People made different decisions in different times and places about how and when to use them.

Using impersonal, passive language is even more perilous when applied to our personal lives.

- Our marriage fell apart.
- The marriage broke down.
- Our marriage ended.
- Our marriage failed.
- The love died.

When we make statements like these, we treat a marriage as if it were a mechanical object or perhaps a thoughtless organism. These statements hide the fact that every marriage has two human beings in it whose behavior is relevant to its success or failure, its life or death.

Thus, the March of History Narrative isn't satisfactory. It's not a thorough explanation for the changes we observe around us. It robs us (or relieves us if you are happy to lay such a burden down) of responsibility. If we embrace this narrative, we diminish our power to make positive changes, both in public policy and in our personal lives. This story line diverts us from the truths that love is a decision and that marriage is made up of the daily decisions of each person in the marriage.

The March of History Narrative excuses us from even

asking the question of whether these changes have been good or bad. Our opinion of these changes is irrelevant. It would be like asking our opinion about a hurricane. We can't do anything about a force of nature. We can't stop the March of History. We can't put the toothpaste back in the tube or turn back the clock.

Personally, I have never understood what toothpaste or clocks have to do with failed social policies.

The Feminist Narrative

Another explanation for the changes in family structure and sexual attitudes has no doubt at all about their moral status. The **Feminist Narrative** is that these changes have been one long string of victories for the benefit and advancement of women. Equality for women requires that we eliminate all differences between men and women, including those that are biologically based. Justice for women requires that we eliminate all power imbalances between men and women, including those based on economics, politics, or even the human body itself.

Let me first clarify the use of the term *feminist*. In this context, I don't just mean people who champion the rights and dignity of women. Many people of a variety of points of view can say as much. By the term *feminist*, I mean specifically those who believe that a woman's rights and dignity are bound up in the woman's ability to control her reproductive life. I'm not going out on a limb in using the term this way. The people who are socially permitted to claim the feminist label consider reproductive rights to be the defining characteristic of feminism. I'm well aware that many people would dispute the claim that the advocates of reproductive control are the only people who truly represent women or who respect their dignity or protect their rights. For the sake of convenience in this context, however, I'll use the term *feminist* in this customary manner.

This type of feminist wants to create economic equality between men and women. These advocates correctly see that motherhood is the biggest driver of income inequality between men and women. Even women who are not mothers likely behave differently if they aspire to motherhood someday. These women tend to make different choices about career and education, choices which, in turn, may result in lower incomes. When women become mothers, taking time away from their jobs and careers to raise their children can reduce their earnings compared to their male peers or their childless female peers.[5]

Feminists also advocate for leveling the power relationships between men and women. Only women can bear children. This fact, this primal difference between men and women, makes women uniquely vulnerable in relationships. The feminist solution to this problem is to create legal and social structures that allow every woman to have sex without having babies, or at least without having any babies she does not explicitly decide that she wants.

---

[5]   This point has been in the economics literature since the 1970s. See Jacob Mincer and Solomon Polachek, "Family Investments in Human Capital: Earnings of Women," *Journal of Political Economy* 82(2), Part II, April 1974, http://www.nber.org/chapters/c3685.pdf.

We should note in passing the relationship between contraception and abortion in the Feminist Narrative. If the demand were simply to reduce the probability of pregnancy, abortion might not seem so necessary. But the ideological demand is for much more than reducing the probability of pregnancy from any individual sexual act. The tacit demand is that the connection between sex and babies be completely severed. Since contraception sometimes fails, unlimited abortion is absolutely necessary to shore up the claim that sex doesn't make babies.

The United States Supreme Court said as much in its decision in *Planned Parenthood v. Casey* back in 1992. Writing the majority opinion, Justice Anthony Kennedy stated, "For two decades of economic and social developments, people have organized their intimate relationships and made choices that define their views of themselves and their places in society, in reliance on the availability of abortion in the event that contraception should fail. The ability of women to participate equally in the economic and social life of the Nation has been facilitated by their ability to control their reproductive lives." [6]

The Feminist Narrative also approves of many of the changes that result in relationship instability such as the idea that one can leave a relationship at any time for any reason. Their narrative usually includes an allusion to domestic violence. Women are better off being able to leave an abusive marriage without having to give any reasons or evidence. Whether most divorcing couples are abusive, how divorce

---

[6]   Planned Parenthood v. Casey, 505 U.S. 833, 856 (1992).

law actually functioned prior to no-fault divorce, and what secondary problems the no-fault policy might cause are all questions the Feminist Narrative doesn't address.

Like the March of History Narrative, the Feminist Narrative isn't satisfactory as either an account of the changes we see around us or an analysis of whether these changes are beneficial. It doesn't answer the question of how so much social change took place so rapidly and why. If you pressed them, its adherents might say that feminist social change has taken place because of the success of feminist organizing and political power.

However, this undermines the claim that women have been completely powerless and dominated by the patriarchy throughout all of recorded history. If that domination has been so thorough and so complete, how can it be that so much of it was overturned so quickly? Could it be that other non-feminist forces contributed to the rapid pace of social change? Could it be that some of the people and groups who contributed to these changes hold views wildly at odds with feminism as it is usually understood?

Similarly, the Feminist Narrative can't explain why so many women disassociate themselves from the term *feminism*. The pro-life movement is dominated by women. Evidently, these women don't feel empowered by the current state of marriage and family. They want their babies more than they want the objectives of the feminist movement. That many women want nothing to do with the feminist platform, including its most basic plank of abortion on demand, does not jibe with the Feminist Narrative, which claims that feminism speaks for all women.

The Liberationist Narrative

The **Liberationist Narrative** argues that all these changes in our social order have been beneficial because they allow people more freedom of action. No one has to get married in order to have socially acceptable sex. No one is required to care for a child they don't want. As long as one kills the baby before birth, a person can walk away from all the obligations a civilized society normally places upon parents.

No one is required to remain married a moment longer than they want to. Leaving a spouse for any reason or no reason is perfectly acceptable. As I already noted, feminists and others might say that this policy of unilateral divorce is necessary to protect women from abusive marriages, but the true liberationist doesn't generally resort to this argument. He or she doesn't feel a need to justify divorce. The fact that one person is unhappy or unsatisfied is reason enough to end the marriage.

According to the Liberationist Narrative, men and women alike benefit from being able to have sex without commitments. The increase in freedom benefits anyone and everyone with the courage to embrace it. For example, people who are now called "sexual minorities" are those who wish to have sex that is not strictly "heteronormative." They prefer that society place no constraints before, during, or after sexual activity. According to the Liberationist Narrative, consent is the only constraint that matters.

The view of sex behind the Liberationist Narrative can be traced back to a German psychiatrist named Wilhelm Reich. He authored a book entitled *The Sexual Revolution* in 1929, which was reprinted in 1936, 1945, and 1949. He coined many of the terms in use today, including "sex-positive" and the term "sexual revolution" itself. The concern which opens his book is the need for children to have the sex they desire to have. He builds everything else around this supposed entitlement, including keeping information from their parents, providing reliable contraception to the young, and providing young people with their own private places where they can have sex.[7] The movement to normalize and legitimize various forms of sexual activity is an outgrowth of this basic Liberationist Narrative which has morphed into several different sub-narratives.

The Consumerist Sub-Narrative

The Consumerist Narrative believes in giving people what they want at the least cost of time, money, and inconvenience—sort of the Walmart theory of sex. People get to have large quantities of consumer goods at low cost without ever considering any secondary costs or consequences. This variant of the Liberationist Narrative mainstreams the concept, moving it from the realm of radicalism and sexual minorities and making it more attractive to the bourgeois tastes of ordinary people, perhaps especially ordinary American people.

---

[7] Wilhelm Reich, *The Sexual Revolution: Toward a Self-Regulating Character Structure*, electronic version includes prefaces to the 2nd (1936), 3rd (1945), and 4th Editions (1949).

The Orientation Sub-Narrative

The Orientation Narrative states that people are born with sexual orientations over which they have no control. The pattern of attraction a person experiences is fixed, given at birth, and an essential part of the individual's identity. One denies this identity at their psychological, emotional, and possibly physical peril. Individuals, whether straight or gay, have no control over this part of their personality. If a person experiences attraction to people of their same biological sex, they should not take steps to alter this pattern of attraction. To do so would be a kind of betrayal of their genuine identity given to them through the biological circumstances of their birth.

We're seeing the introduction of a variant of this narrative for what is called "intergenerational sex." What was once called "pedophilia" and treated as pathological, some people would like to redefine as an orientation all its own, an inborn desire for sex with a younger person. This line of thought minimizes any possible harm to the younger person. It also minimizes the possible harm inherent in relationships with large age differences: power imbalances between the younger and the older, or a tendency toward immaturity on the part of the older person seeking a relationship with a younger person.

The Gender Identity Sub-Narrative

The newest version of the Liberationist Narrative is that an individual may discover his or her true sexual identity regardless of what gender has been "assigned" to them at birth. If the individual isn't comfortable with this gender, he or she may, indeed should, take steps to alter the body so as to live in accordance with his or her true sexual identity. They shouldn't take steps to become more comfortable with their biological sex. This would be a betrayal of their true identity.

This combination of beliefs may seem peculiar. On one hand, the *Orientation Narrative* claims that a person's sexual orientation is fixed and can't be changed. A person is "born that way" and must learn to live with their same sex attraction no matter what other beliefs, experiences, or desires they may have. On the other hand, the *Gender Identity Narrative* claims that a person is definitely *not* "born that way" when the subject is the physical body itself. A person who experiences gender dysphoria must take steps to change their bodies to match the pattern of desires and beliefs they hold in their minds.

These seemingly contradictory views do have one thing in common. They both hold that human beings exist independently of their bodies and that the true self is lived outside the body. The Orientation Narrative asserts that feelings of attraction are more significant than the body itself, while the Gender Identity Narrative asserts that the psychological sense of male or female is more significant than the body itself.

The Liberationist Narrative in any of its forms is not an entirely satisfactory account of our situation. It holds that we have been imprisoned by unreasonable social shackles and oppressive cultural constraints since the dawn of time. We moderns, and we alone, have been wise enough, advanced enough, and generous enough to throw off millennia of unnecessary constraints.

The Liberationist Narrative cannot answer one basic question: if the constraints were powerful enough to last for thousands of years, how is it possible that a single generation could throw them off without consequence? How is it possible that the forces of bland bourgeois conformism, like the forces of patriarchy which were powerful enough to oppress the entire human race, have suddenly been overthrown overnight by the oppressed masses? There's no satisfactory answer to that question because it has not been done without consequences. Sexual liberation has cost many; it has cost much.

The Liberationist Narrative is unsatisfactory for another reason. It overlooks the ways in which people have become less free, in fact actually oppressed, by the very forces that are supposedly liberating us. The breaking of family bonds has increased the size and scope of the State, including the intrusion of the State into the everyday lives of ordinary people.

College students are free to have sex in their dorm rooms, but colleges now have tribunals to judge allegations of date rape and sexual harassment, institutions which in the supposedly benighted past were not necessary. Family courts determine how much time parents are permitted to spend with their children or how much money a "non-custodial" parent is required to send the "custodial" parent. Family courts routinely rule on disputes over what schools and churches children attend and whether attending a public event like a baseball game counts toward the non-custodial parent's allotted time. This level of involvement of an agency of the state was unheard of prior to the era of rapid family breakdown.

Fiscal freedom has been reduced as well, as taxes have increased. Fewer constraints on sexual behavior mean more children without permanent relationships with both parents. These children are disadvantaged in many ways that have consequences for the tax burden on the public. Increases in the likelihood of poverty, physical illness, mental illness, poor school performance, and crime have all been associated with being separated from a parent. The ordinary tax-paying citizen faces a greater tax burden than otherwise would be the case as a direct result of what, by the Liberationist Narrative, is an increase in sexual freedom.

It is not just the State that has benefited from the increased sexual freedom and the negative social consequences thereof. As government has expanded, so has the power of big business, bureaucracy, media, and mass entertainment. We're being manipulated by media, advertising, and entertainment to buy certain things, believe certain things, and want certain things. Is there any doubt that this kind of non-governmental manipulation is on the increase? Unfortunately, we are more vulnerable than ever to such efforts due to increased loneliness, our need for belonging, and our craving for sexual stimulation.

In other words, the Liberationist apologia for the changes in sexual mores and family life claims that all these changes have made us freer than ever. This narrative ignores the fact that these same changes have created avenues for government, bureaucratic, and corporate intrusions into our lives that would have been unthinkable in former times.

The Over-Population Narrative

Another narrative used to justify the change in social mores around marriage, family, and sexuality is the **Over-Population Narrative**. This story line asserts that too many people create ecological disaster and economic backwardness. The only practical solution to this problem is to provide and promote birth control, backed up by abortion. These hard-core population controllers believe the earth has too many people, usually too many of certain kinds of people: namely, poor people, people of the wrong color, or people with the wrong belief system. The population controllers are not particularly interested in the secondary consequences, such as gender equality or liberation. The true believer in the Over-Population Narrative advocates the separation of sex from childbearing, whether or not this results in equality, women's empowerment, fun, or freedom.

Some population controllers have no qualms about recommending and implementing coercive measures. The "one-child" policy in China is the most notorious example. Although China has relaxed the one-child policy to permit selected couples to have two children, this doesn't alter the principle behind the program. The government still gives itself permission to issue birth permits and regulate the number of children people can have. This policy is backed up by forced abortion, the destruction of people's homes, and the denial of jobs and education for the parents and the illegal child alike.[8] The Chinese Birth Control Police employs over

---

[8]   Women's Rights Without Frontiers has produced a graphic video illustrating the barbarous practices used to enforce the one-child policy. https://www.youtube.com/watch?v=JjtuBcJUsjY.

a million people, making it arguably the largest law enforcement agency in the world.[9]

The Over-Population Narrative isn't a compelling account. Its advocates haven't been able to adapt the narrative to the changing circumstances of population decline, which the Over-Population Narrative itself helped to bring about. In many countries today, population decline is a more serious economic problem than population growth. Prosperous countries will be unable to meet their obligations to the growing number of elderly people in their midst. Poorer countries will grow old before they grow rich, creating a vice-grip of misery for young and old alike.[10] Yet the person truly committed to the Over-population Narrative is not dissuaded from his or her belief.

The existence and success of this narrative, whether empirically supported by the facts or not, has played a significant

---

[9] "The bureaucracy that oversees family planning in China is enormous. There are over 500,000 administrative staff and technical service providers from the central government down to the township level devoted to both policy enforcement and family planning generally. In addition, more than 1.2 million cadres assist in birth planning at the village level. Many more millions of members of the local Family Planning Association provide information and services related to family planning, childbearing, maternal and child health and adolescent sexual health." Stanley Lubman, ""After the One-Child Policy: What Happens to China's Family-Planning Bureaucracy?" The Wall Street Journal, Nov. 12, 2015, http://blogs.wsj.com/chinarealtime/2015/11/12/after-the-one-child-policy-what-happens-to-chinas-family-planning-bureaucracy/.

[10] Nicholas Eberstadt, "Growing Old the Hard Way: Russia, China, India," *Policy Review* (April/May 2006), https://www.hoover.org/research/growing-old-hard-way-china-russia-india.

role in radically altering the social and sexual landscape. The advocates of the Over-Population Narrative have had enormous influence, particularly in poor countries and communities. They've had large budgets to provide and promote both contraception and abortion.

The historical importance of the Over-Population Narrative cannot be overstated. Even for people who aren't particularly concerned with either female empowerment or sexual liberation, the claim that we must "do something" to control population size provides a justification for the promotion of contraception and abortion.

The (Stealth) Capitalist Narrative

Finally, I must mention one last factor in creating and sustaining the changes in family, marriage, and sexuality. Some people favor these changes because they are, quite simply, making money from them, either directly or indirectly. I call this a "stealth" narrative because few people discuss it directly. The people who are making money, and who might generally be considered pro-business or pro-capitalist, don't want to call attention to their activities. They prefer to allow other people to provide the public justifications and rationales while they themselves go quietly about their (profitable) businesses.

On the other hand, the people who are generally suspicious of capitalism, the profit motive and self-interested commerce, happen to be the same people who are, for other reasons, committed to the changes in family life and sexual mores. Most of these people don't make their usual anti-capitalist critiques against these business interests that profit from the changes in sexual norms and behavior.

Here are just a few of the people making money from the new attitudes by providing the services that facilitate them:

- abortionists,
- pharmaceutical companies, which make money from contraceptive drugs and devices,
- the fertility industry, which is estimated to be between $20 and 30 billion in revenues worldwide,[11]
- and pornographers: the pornography industry was estimated to be a $97 billion industry worldwide in 2014.[12]

Whole industries have arisen to help people deal with the fallout and difficulties created by the changes in family life. Here are a few examples.

- Divorce professionals such as financial analysts, who examine the assets of the separating parties to determine how much the court should require in payments, and psychologists and social workers, who examine

---

[11] "Global Fertility Services Market to Exceed USD 21 Billion by 2020, According to Technavio," *Business Wire*, April 20, 2016, https://www.businesswire.com/news/home/20160420005059/en/Global-Fertility-Services-Market-Exceed-USD-21. "Fertility Market Overview," Harris Williams and Company, May 2015, http://www.harriswilliams.com/sites/default/files/content/fertility_industry_overview_-_2015.05.19_v10.pdf.

[12] John Gaudiosi, "Virtual Reality Livestreams Come to the Porn Industry," Fortune, December 16, 2015, http://fortune.com/2015/12/16/vr-livestream-porn/.

the children, and sometimes the adults, to determine
how much parenting time the court should award to
each parent.

- Family court judges and lawyers.
- Branches of medicine devoted to sexually transmitted
  infections and diseases.
- Social workers who deal with the consequences of
  family breakdown.

We could say that these people profit from other people's
misery. That would not be entirely fair. These people are, I
am sure, sincerely trying to help people handle the trauma
caused by family breakdown. Nonetheless, we must take seriously the fact that many of these people take for granted the
system as it is. They may have ideas about how to improve it
and make it operate more humanely. But it may be difficult
for them to picture a radical restructuring of society where
their profession or industry may no longer be needed.

For instance, there are organizations and individuals trying to make the divorce process work better and the ensu-
ing arrangements more equitable. At the same time, these
organizations take for granted the basic structure of divorce
law, that one party may end the marriage unilaterally. Some
groups work for shared parenting as the default in divorce
cases. Other groups help defend fathers in divorce court. Still
others provide pro bono legal help to indigent clients. The
people involved in these organizations are probably doing
something good, on net, but reimagining the social world
without unilateral, no-fault divorce is beyond the scope of

their organizations' missions, and perhaps even beyond their imaginations.

Finally, some of the changes in family life have benefited employers and universities in a general way. Women have entered higher education in such great numbers that they now outnumber men. This obviously benefits the whole higher educational sector.

The careerist strand of modern feminism argued that women should measure their sense of self-worth by their financial independence, income, and career status.[13] Women who adopt these attitudes as their own will be willing to work for a lower wage and under worse conditions than women who don't. Having a job conveys to a woman that she's a modern, fashionable person.

The relative instability of marriage also benefits employers. Women can't count on their husbands to provide for them financially for a lifetime. Women can only be certain of their own work efforts. Under these circumstances, a woman is inclined to be more committed to the labor force. The widespread acceptance of the careerist mentality provides employers with women workers who are more dependent on them than on their husbands. For these reasons, we can conclude that employers will not necessarily resist the ideology of careerist feminism.

It has become apparent that big business is completely at peace with the entire Sexual Revolution. Corporations support Planned Parenthood and sponsor gay pride events.

---

[13]   Linda Hirshman's aggressively titled manifesto, *Get to Work: A Manifesto for Women of the World*, (New York: Viking, 2006), is an example of this genre.

Major corporations have been supportive of policies promoting the most radical forms of the transgender agenda.
By contrast, I'm not aware of significant support from major
corporations for crisis pregnancy centers, marriage education, or chastity promotion programs.

This (stealth) Capitalist Narrative is a bit different from
the other narratives in that very few people use it to defend
the social changes of the past generations. Nonetheless, these
practices and beliefs are entrenched in the economy and
higher education. These generalized benefits to employers
and universities comprise a force that must be reckoned with
in any attempt to address the root causes of loneliness and
family breakdown, and thus to create genuine social change.

The Catholic Narrative

There is one more narrative that I will mention only in passing
at this point. I call it the Catholic Narrative. The unbroken
teaching of the Catholic Church is that the Contraceptive,
Divorce, and Gender Ideologies are all at war with human
nature and divine law. The Catholic Church continues to
teach that deliberate obstruction of the procreative purpose
of the sexual act is morally wrong. The Catholic Church
continues to teach that marriage is indissoluble during the
lifetime of the married couple. And the Catholic Church
maintains that men and women are different and, thus, have
different roles inside and outside the Church without holding to a doctrinaire rigidity on every point about sex differences and sex roles.

Despite widespread dissent inside and dissatisfaction

outside the Church, the official teaching of the Catholic Church continues to be what was once the common teaching of all the Christian churches. Namely, that contraception, abortion, divorce, non-marital sex, cohabitation, pornography, and artificial methods of reproduction are all grave offenses against natural and divine law. The Catholic Church has held this position counter-culturally against enormous odds and at great cost to herself.

The Catholic Church has been the last and, in some instances, the only holdout against the self-styled progress of the Sexual Revolution. Most importantly, the Catholic Church holds that these Ideologies have no chance of making people happy in this life. I shall have more to say about the Catholic Narrative in later chapters.

Apart from the Catholic Narrative, I'm not satisfied with any of the other explanations for the widespread changes in family life. Nor am I convinced by the various justifications for these changes. These narratives don't fully account for the persistence of these changes despite the negative consequences I catalogued in the first chapter.

What, then, accounts for the changes, their harmfulness, and their persistence in the face of the costs?

Chapter 3

The Sexual State: Why the Sexual Revolution Needs the State

All the confusing and complicated issues raised in the first two chapters arise from the same modern construct: the Sexual State. The Sexual Revolution has never been a grassroots movement. It is and always has been a movement of the elites justifying their preferred lifestyles, imposing their new morality, and, in the process, allowing them unprecedented control over others. The Sexual Revolution came about because elites captured the coercive power of the State and used it for their personal and ideological interests. The State, together with elite institutions of society, support the Sexual Revolution with a continual flow of propaganda.

The major planks of the Sexual Revolutionary platform were put in place through governmental action. The changes we now call the Sexual Revolution were initiated by elites, institutionalized through State power, and are sustained by a steady diet of propaganda and misinformation. The State is at the core of the Sexual Revolution, so much so that it's no exaggeration to call it the Sexual State.

Here are a few examples of the Sexual State at work:

- A fourteen-year-old girl gets pregnant. She had sex with a man ten years older than herself. Her parents don't approve of the guy. They think he's a creep taking advantage of their daughter. Her boyfriend wants her to get an abortion. She confides in the public school nurse. The nurse sends her to get an abortion. The State forbids the nurse from telling her parents about the abortion or even about the pregnancy.

- A married couple encounters difficulties in their relationship. The State takes sides with the person who wants the marriage the least. The family never recovers from the divorce. The reluctantly divorced person is heartbroken. The initiating party didn't get the happiness he or she had hoped for. The consequences of the divorce reach into the next generation because the children of divorce often have difficulty trusting others and sustaining relationships throughout their lives.

- A public school holds a father-daughter dance. The school thinks it will help build closeness between fathers and daughters and give fathers a chance to treat their daughters as special and, hence, help the girls to understand how men should treat them. An ideological group objects that such a dance constitutes sex stereotyping. The State takes their side. The school cancels the dance.

Can any honest person believe that any of these things happened because the masses of ordinary people wanted them to happen? Ideological groups supporting certain goals of elite classes in society captured the machinery of government. This one-two punch of already powerful members of society using a seductive ideology and the power of the State is what created the nexus of laws and social practices that rule so many aspects of our lives.

The Sexual State Narrative offers a more accurate account of how we came to be where we are today than any of the narratives I described in the previous chapter. The Sexual State Narrative has one further major advantage: it acknowledges the fact that the Sexual Revolution has a downside. These ideas have harmed people. Yet the freight train of these ideologies keeps hurtling down the track with no apparent stopping point. The Sexual State Narrative can account for both why the Sexual Revolution has been harmful and why it persists despite the harms it has caused.

The Victims of the Sexual Revolution

We continually hear that changes in sexual attitudes are evidence of the march of progress, liberation, and freedom. Opposing the next phase of the glorious revolution, no matter what that next phase might be, is tantamount to opposing civil rights, history, and progress. The proponents of progress never even suggest that we stop, look over our shoulders, and take stock of what the previous steps of the Sexual Revolution have done.

Has it worked out as promised? Have any glitches emerged

along the path toward the glorious day of no restrictions on sexual activity, orientation, or gender expression? What about the problems the Sexual Revolution was supposed to solve? Did it solve them? Could we have solved them some other, less revolutionary way?

It's a simple fact: the Sexual Revolution has harmed millions of people. No one takes responsibility for the evils caused by the implementation of this pernicious creed. Its victims are socially hidden. Concealing the victims is an essential element in continuing the Sexual Revolution. If people began to talk about the wounds they've experienced, if people could connect the dots between the ideology and the pains they've endured, they'd begin to question the Sexual Revolutionary ideology. This is why the control of information in support of the pro-revolutionary narrative is so essential to sustaining that revolution. The victims raising questions and telling the whole truth would bring down the ideology and all the social structures built around it.

For instance, we are socially forbidden to utter the phrase "family breakdown." We're supposed to substitute less judgmental, more neutral and accepting phrases. Things like "alternative family forms" for instance or "modern family" or "new family structures" are considered more suitable.

These terms are euphemisms. These sanitized phrases hide the fact that some people really do regard their families as broken. Children of divorce often do feel their family has broken when their parents get divorced and remarry, and divorce and remarry again. Abandoned spouses sometimes feel their family broke down when their spouse left them for another partner. Donor conceived people sometimes feel their families and their identities are incomplete because they don't know one of their parents.

Are these people mistaken to feel their families are broken? No. Their feelings are understandable and deserve to be affirmed and validated. Yet such people are socially invisible in today's culture.

When we avoid the term "family breakdown," we're protecting the feelings of people who may have guilty consciences about the ruptures they've caused. We don't seem to realize that people left behind in these break ups, breakdowns, splits, and reconfigurations have feelings too. They feel something has been lost or taken from them. Avoiding the term "family breakdown" doesn't protect them. It victimizes them even further.

Our Cultural Blindness to the Victims

The ideology of the Sexual Revolution has become so all-encompassing that we barely recognize how bizarre it truly is. Sometimes we can't see patterns that are staring us in the face. The evidence of a major cultural contradiction may be right in front of us, but we don't allow ourselves to see it.

Consider these items:

- Young healthy women die from blood clots and strokes: a ballerina in the UK,[1] a journalism student

---

[1] Mark Hodges, "17-year-old ballerina's death caused by birth control pills, doctors believe," *LifeSiteNews*, April 27, 2016, https://www.lifesitenews.com/news/17-year-old-ballerinas-death-caused-by-birth-control-pill-doctors-believe.

from the University of Pittsburgh,[2] and a teenager in Calgary.[3] The cause? Hormonal contraception. *Why do these stories receive so little media attention? Why does the scant media attention include a disclaimer that contraception is usually safe and that the risks are "acceptable?"*

- A female college student does a study[4] showing that neither men nor women really like casual sex and instead long for more intimacy and relationship. Her solution: more "pleasure-centric" sex education, "beginning in middle school and high school and all the way through college." The hook-up culture might collapse, she notes, because men and women alike would have a more realistic understanding that their pleasure depends on the quality of their relationship. They would realize that casual sex is not as fun as they have been led to believe. *Why didn't it occur to her to advocate for education for marriage and education that teaches that sex inside marriage can actually be the most pleasurable?*

- Powerful Hollywood and media men such as Harvey Weinstein and Matt Lauer engage in a long-term systematic pattern of sexual harassment and abuse while

---

2   Alexandra Rowan Foundation, http://www.alexrowanfoundation. org/ and http://www.alexrowanfoundation.org/mpe-research/.

3   Kirsten Andersen, "27 Dutch women's deaths linked to controversial birth control pill," *LifeSiteNews*, October 28, 2013, https://www.lifesitenews.com/news/27-dutch-womens-deaths-linked-to-controversial-birth-control-pill.

4   Leah Fessler, "A lot of women don't enjoy the hook-up culture— so why do we force ourselves to participate? *Quartz*, May 17, 2016, https://qz.com/685852/hookup-culture/.

being lauded in the same media-entertainment complex for being pro-choice, pro-woman, and just plain
progressive. *Where did these men get the idea that sex is
an entitlement and that the women over whom they hold
power exist for their pleasure?*

Why the Sexual Revolution Needs the State

The Sexual Revolution needs the State for one major reason: the premises of the Sexual Revolution are false. Sex does
make babies. Children do need their parents, and therefore marriage is the proper and just context for both sex
and childrearing. Men and women are different. The true
sexual revolutionaries resent these facts. They resent that
human beings live in gendered bodies. The sexual revolutionaries have created a fantasy around their ideology and
have attempted to accumulate sufficient power to reconstruct society around these ideas. But overriding nature on
this scale is no small task. The revolutionaries need a lot of
help for such an ambitious project since their ideas do not
accord with reality. Breaking the connection between sex
and babies in people's minds requires government coercion,
media propaganda, economic restructuring, and educational
indoctrination (not to mention the pills, medical devices,
sterilization surgeries, and abortions.)

Children are helpless and dependent. Their parents are
attached to them and enjoy being attached to them. Convincing the great masses of ordinary people that biological
connections are superfluous requires a lot of effort. People
do not ordinarily believe that any pair of hands that cares for

children is just as good as any other. Convincing women that working in an office is just as worthy an occupation as taking loving care of their own children takes a lot of propaganda as well as restructuring social and economic incentives.

Detaching men from their children does not take quite as much effort. As a matter of fact, most societies spend an enormous effort to do precisely the opposite: attaching fathers to their children. Even so, it requires a lot of effort to make up for the losses men experience due to being separated from their children. Men need to feel needed by their children and their children's mother. Many men in our society are lost and adrift without the sense of purpose that married, committed fatherhood so often brings.

Men and women are different. It requires government coercion, media propaganda, economic restructuring, and educational indoctrination to cancel out the impact of sex differences. If you can make people believe Bruce Jenner, the 1976 male Olympic decathlon winner, is a woman, you can make them believe 2 + 2 = 5. If you can make people afraid to say, "Bruce Jenner is a man," you can make them afraid to say anything.

True believers in the Sexual Revolution regard doing the impossible as a high moral duty. They believe themselves entitled to use all available social and political power to achieve their impossible goals. They believe working toward these lofty moral ends will give meaning to their lives and make them happy. Since their premises are false and their goals are impossible, they'll never be satisfied no matter how much social change they generate. Every mistaken step compounds the previous mistaken steps. The true believer becomes less happy with every step of the "March of Progress."

Some of this dissatisfaction is masked by legitimate goals they sometimes have wrapped inside their ideology. For example, many people agree that increasing women's participation in higher education and the professions is a good thing. Few stop to consider that there were, and still are, many possible ways to bring this about. The sexual revolutionaries claim credit for every woman who has graduated from college since 1965. But they never stop to assess the collateral damage their methods may have generated. They also don't ask whether these legitimate objectives (behind which they hide their revolutionary agenda) could have been achieved in some other way.

The Sexual Revolution needs the State because it needs enormous amounts of power to accomplish its impossible objectives. This one insight unlocks the key to the whole course of the Sexual Revolution. We're now in a position to see why the Sexual Revolution has morphed into a power grab, why it seems so overwhelming, why it is so seductive, why its propaganda seems so relentless, and why the downhill slide seems to be accelerating.

The sexual revolutionary ideology has certain things in common with the other toxic ideologies of the twentieth century. Marxists believed that abolishing private property and creating economic equality with prosperity for all was a moral imperative. But it's not possible to create a prosperous society without private property rights. Nor is it possible to create perfect economic equality across an entire society and still have either freedom or prosperity. Attempting the impossible required a lot of force. The Communists never succeeded in their stated objectives. Their attempts moved them further away from their goals. The leaders were so enamored by their fantasy ideology that they were blinded to the moral and physical nightmare they were creating.

The Nazis believed they could create a society of unity and brotherhood. They believed they could produce an orderly, planned society in which everyone worked together for the benefit of the whole. If they could just rid themselves of the outsiders, the problem people, who kept holding everyone back, they could achieve this utopian goal. If they could move out or enslave or murder all the non-Aryans, the society of people who really matter would develop in an orderly and prosperous fashion. If they could eliminate all those "lives unworthy of life:" the mentally ill, the mentally challenged, and the physically disabled, then at last they could have a perfect society. If they could neutralize the resisters, the people who were not willing to sacrifice themselves and their beliefs and values for the supposed sake of the whole, then at last they could achieve their ideal.

It's not possible, however, to create a society of brotherhood while marginalizing and murdering millions of people. Nor is it possible to plan society down to the last man and still have it be a humane and decent place where people would want to live.

Please do not misunderstand me. I am not saying that the sexual revolutionaries are Nazis or Communists. I am saying something which is, in its own way, even more devastating. I am saying that the Sexual Revolution is an ideology standing all on its own, quite apart from Left or Right.

However, it is exactly like both Nazism and Communism in this respect: the Sexual Revolution is a totalitarian ideology with a blind commitment to the implementation of its tenets, regardless of the human costs. The fantasy ideology of the Sexual Revolution appeals to people on both the Left and Right for somewhat different reasons. This fact is one of the things that blinds people to its power and danger. Let me demonstrate.

Resenting the Body, Left and Right

I often debate on college campuses. On one occasion, I made what I thought was an innocent comment: Sex makes babies. I was surprised that my opponent disagreed.

"Sex doesn't make babies."

"Oh," I said, "what do you mean?"

"Unprotected sex makes babies."

I see. In another debate, I made another comment that I thought was obvious and uncontroversial: every child has a mother and a father. This brought another argument.

"No, they don't."

"Oh," I said, "what do you mean?"

"Every child has a sperm and an egg. The concepts of 'mother' and 'father' are social constructs."

I see.

I recount these debate experiences not because I think my opponents are far-fetched outliers. On the contrary, the people who argued with me are drawing on some of the deepest intellectual currents of modern Western thought. Left and Right alike, we're having trouble processing one of the most basic facts of the human experience: we are bodily creatures and those bodies are gendered.

It takes the genetic material of a man and a woman to make a baby. Men and women are different with respect to this most basic of human activities: bearing, begetting, and raising children. Men and women cannot be made to be equal in this respect. This is what makes the Leftist egalitarian so vulnerable to the sexual revolutionary ideology. They come to see sex differences as a cosmic injustice that society should do something to correct. They come to resent that most basic of human facts: the limitations of the human body, particularly those caused by sexual differences.

We normally think of individualism as the province of the political Right, but I've noticed that many on the Right are vulnerable to a similar temptation. Having a baby is something one literally cannot do alone. A person who wishes to become a parent must secure the cooperation of another person, specifically a person of the opposite sex. This fact can be viewed as a cosmic injustice or, at least, an inconvenience to his or her individualistic ideological structure. Society can and should do something to remove the sting of this affront.

Thus the radical individualist can be seduced by the Sexual Revolution just as completely as the radical egalitarian. Some individualists see nothing problematic with purchasing sperm or eggs, or even the finished product: babies themselves. Some free market individualists see nothing wrong with purchasing the services of a surrogate, either a "gestational surrogate" who gestates the egg of another woman or a "traditional surrogate" who gestates her own egg and then sells the finished product—that is, her own baby—to the "intended parents," sometimes also called "commissioning parents." The radical individualist is driven to the position that purchasing sperm or eggs, or surrogacy services or a baby, from a stranger is morally equivalent to having a lifelong loving relationship with the child's other parent. This kind of individualist averts his eyes from the most basic affront to human freedom: the concept that a human person, even a very small person, shouldn't be bought or sold. These individualists also come to resent the limitations of the human body caused by the fact that reproduction requires a male and a female.

If we only look through political lenses, we might refer to these groups as Left and Right. But from a deeper perspective, both the egalitarian and the individualist are not in opposition to each other. They're on the same side of the line dividing modern from pre-modern.

Our modern era is historically unique in its emphasis on these concepts of equality and freedom. The ancients and the medievals had no problem with people being both interdependent and different. It's not that they had no concept of either liberty or equality, it's that it wouldn't have occurred to them to attach these concepts to the issue of parenthood and, hence, to the human body itself.

One political philosopher who plainly understands this point is Alastair McIntyre. His work spells out some of the implications of our dependency. However, Dr. McIntyre is the exception that proves the rule: he's an unapologetic advocate of pre-modern philosophy, including Aristotle and Thomas Aquinas.[5]

It's true that the ancients and the medievals had more rigid ideas about sexual roles than we do. But we can embrace some fluidity in social roles and still see that we moderns have painted ourselves into a corner. In the interests of gender equality, we've forced ourselves to deny that men and women have *any* significant differences. In the interests of personal liberty, we've forced ourselves to deny that we need *anyone* for *anything*, including the most basic human business of bringing a new human life into the world.

So it is that the gendered nature of the body is under attack, from the Left and Right, as is the connection between sex and babies. Left and Right alike resent the limitations of the human body. There's just one small problem: sex does make babies and men and women are different. An ideology that cannot make room for the basic facts of human reproduction and sex differences is an ideology that will end up at war with the human body, with nature itself, and ultimately with the entire human race. In that war, it will go looking for allies where it can find them. It finds its most powerful, its indispensable, ally in the State.

The Sexual State

The ideas of the Sexual Revolution have been adopted by so many from both Left and Right that we can now speak of the Sexual State as our governing ideology. The government

---

[5]   Alastair McIntyre, *Dependent Rational Animals: Why Human Beings Need the Virtues* (Chicago: Open Court, 1999).

has been commandeered for revolutionary purposes. The policies implementing the Sexual Revolution now have the priority that peace and prosperity used to occupy in political loyalties and discourse. The revolutionary ideology now holds the place of esteem once held by the Judeo-Christian religions.

One way to see this it to examine what "separation of Church and State" is coming to mean. When I was in dialogue with a caller on the *Catholic Answers Live* radio program, he opined that the State should get out of marriage and leave it all to the Church.

"So you think the Church should be allowed to decide which weddings they will solemnize?" I asked.

"That's right."

"And the Church should be allowed to decide which of its members can get divorced?"

"Yes."

"And the Church should be allowed to decide whether divorced people can receive Communion."

"Sure."

"What about property settlement after a divorce: should the Church be allowed to have jurisdiction over the division of property?"

"Uhhhh . . ."

"How about child custody? Should the Church be allowed to decide child custody after divorce?"

"No."

"Why not?"

Long pause. No answer.

Then, I said, "Sir, even if you thought the Church *should*

be allowed to settle property and child custody, do you seriously believe the State would *allow* the Church to have authority over that?"

Only after the program was over did the pattern become fully clear to me: the caller (and the State) will allow the Church to be independent of the State *but only for things they think don't matter.* It's as if the State has said to the Church: "We, the State, allow you, the Church, to be in charge of who gets to have membership in your church, receive Communion, and receive Christian burial. That's because we consider those things unimportant. But we, the State, intend to have full authority over everything we consider important, like property settlements and child custody. As a matter of fact, if there is anything else we come to believe is important, we'll take jurisdiction over that too."

The Supreme Court ruling on the *Hobby Lobby* case illustrates this point. This case considered the federal mandate that all employers include contraception, abortion-inducing drugs, and sterilization in their health insurance plans. The Supreme Court restrained the federal government from imposing upon the Mennonite Hahn family, owners of Conestoga Wood, or the Evangelical Green family, owners of Hobby Lobby, in as onerous and catastrophic a fashion as it otherwise might have. But the State didn't give up its authority over religious institutions and religious people when they deem the subject matter sufficiently important.

Justice Samuel Alito's argument *protecting* the Green and Hahn families turns on the idea that the "compelling interest" of the government that led to the mandate in the first place can be met through some "less restrictive means." The

Hobby Lobby ruling doesn't challenge the government's claim to be in the business of providing, mandating, and promoting contraception. The government still believes making sure women have all the FDA-approved contraceptive drugs and devices they want, at no cost, is a "compelling interest."[6]

The Trump administration issued an executive order in the spring of 2017 providing regulatory relief against enforcement of the Obama administration's rules on contraceptive coverage.[7] While this order provides relief for the Little Sisters of the Poor, it is not a wholesale reversal of sexual revolutionary policies. An executive order can be reversed by legislation or by a subsequent executive order. In fact, as of this writing, two states were already in court challenging the order.[8] The Sexual State has not surrendered its claim to regulate employers into submission with its demands.

In other words, the position of the committed sexual revolutionaries is still: "If we think a subject is important, we intend to be in charge of it."

The State is daily expanding its concept of what is important. The State has decided that the operation of adoption agencies is important to them. They have shut down quite a few under the legal principle that every adoption agency

---

[6]   Burwell v. Hobby Lobby, 573 U.S. (2014), 40.

[7]   Jonathan M. Pitts, "Little Sisters of the Poor approve Trump order on religion," *Baltimore Sun*, May 4, 2017, http://www. baltimoresun.com/news/maryland/politics/bs-md-little-sisters-trump-exec-order-20170504-story.html.

[8]   Brian Fraga, "Blue States Target Little Sisters of the Poor," *National Catholic Register*, November 29, 2017, http://www. ncregister.com/daily-news/blue-states-target-little-sisters-of-the-poor.

must allow same-sex couples to adopt or foster children.[9] The State has already decided that the leadership of college campus clubs is important to them in the *Christian Legal Society v. Martinez* case. All clubs must open their leadership positions to any student regardless of the student's beliefs about the issues the club was founded to promote. Non-Christian or even atheist students could, under this principle, become officers in the Christian Legal Society and completely change the direction of the club.[10]

Please note what all these cases have in common: sex. The beliefs in question aren't beliefs about the Trinity, the resurrection of Jesus, or the Real Presence of Christ in the Eucharist. The issues that fueled the Reformation, the proper understandings of justification, grace, works, the authority of Scripture, and the like: none of these are anywhere in sight. In all these contemporary cases, the government impinges on the freedom of religious people to live in accordance with their *beliefs about sex* and to create and sustain institutions built upon those beliefs. These are beliefs that all the Christian churches held in common throughout the Reformation and early modern period.

---

[9]   Joseph R. LaPlante, "Tough times for Catholic adoption agencies," *Our Sunday Visitor*, May 7, 2014, https://www.osv.com/ OSVNewsweekly/ByIssue/Article/TabId/735/ArtMID/13636/ ArticleID/14666/Tough-times-for-Catholic-adoption-agencies. aspx. A similar situation exists in the United Kingdom. See Martin Beckford, "Last Catholic adoption agency faces closure after Charity Commission ruling," August 19, 2010, http://www. telegraph.co.uk/news/religion/7952526/Last-Catholic-adoption-agency-faces-closure-after-Charity-Commission-ruling.html.

[10]   *Christian Legal Society v. Martinez* 561 US 661 (June 28, 2010).

The government wishes to enact policies that further the Sexual Revolution. The State is using its power to enforce an ideology that is hostile to the gendered nature of the human body. The State declares that they, the elites, have secret knowledge that allows them to see through appearances and know that men and women are the same after all and that sex mustn't be allowed to make babies unless people want it to do so.

The Church declines to participate in this ideological project. Most Americans of faith thought that separation of Church and State meant that the State had to leave faithful people alone. They've come to find out it means that the Church must leave the State alone. The State permits us to have control over unimportant things while it gets to control important things. To add insult to injury, the *State gets to decide what is important and unimportant.*

What, then, is the purpose of the Sexual State? Perhaps you supposed that the purpose of the government was to protect people from force or fraud or to insure domestic tranquility, provide for the common defense, or promote the general welfare. That is all so five minutes ago. The real purpose of government today is to give people the sex lives they want with a minimum of inconvenience. You want to have sex without having a baby? No problem; we'll give you contraception at no cost to you. You wanted to have sex, you got pregnant, and you don't want the baby? That's inconvenient. We'll allow you to have an abortion and even help you pay for it. You want to have sex with someone you aren't married to? That's OK. We'll give you a no-fault divorce so you won't be inconvenienced by your obligations to your spouse and children.

You want to have sex with a person of your sex *and* you want to have a baby. That is *really* inconvenient. We'll restructure the legal system and subsidize the technology that will make it possible for you to obtain all the babies you want without the inconvenience of having to deal with the child's other parent.

Harsh? Maybe. Inaccurate? I don't think so. It's time we face the reality of the government under which we now live: we live in the Sexual State.

On Class Warfare

In the coming chapters, I'll dissect each of the three major premises of the Sexual Revolution: the Contraceptive Ideology, the Divorce Ideology, and the Gender Ideology. I'll show how, in each case, capturing the power of the State was an essential step in implementing these ideologies. The elites, not the people, drove this process of State capture. Elite institutions, not grassroots movements, sustain and maintain these ideologies through disinformation, incomplete information, and outright propaganda.

But before I do, I feel compelled to say something about class warfare. I don't care for its rhetoric for two reasons. First, I don't believe in determinism in any of its variations. An individual's life is not determined by his or her personal circumstances. A society's future is not determined by abstract "social forces" or anything else. And for sure, an individual's economic class does not predetermine his or her beliefs or behavior. I simply do not believe that the people are necessarily destined to be locked in warfare and struggle simply become of their economic situation or class. These modern theories of historical or economic determinism are a secular version of Calvinist predestination without the grace. Calvinism without grace is really scary, even for, maybe especially for, a Calvinist.

As a Catholic, I can't hold with any theory of predestination, secular or theological. Every person has genuine choices about how to behave and what to think. No one's final destination in life is predetermined. Every person has the power to make morally meaningful decisions from the time they reach the age of reason until they draw their last breath.

Second, I am a lifelong free-market advocate. I've had affiliations with all three of the major schools of free market economics. I went to school at the University of Rochester and did a post-doctorate at the University of Chicago, which, at that time, was the mother ship of the Chicago School of Economics. I taught at George Mason University, which is the home of the Virginia School of political economy and houses a center for Austrian Economics. I've always been deeply attached to free market ways of thinking.

Marxists honed the class warfare concept to a fine art, setting groups of people against one another. According to them, capitalists necessarily crush the poor. The working class necessarily resents and struggles against their employers. The true believer in Marxist class struggle will do everything possible to convince ordinary working people that this is how the world really is. Working people *ought* to view themselves and their place in the world in terms of their identity as "proletarians" or "workers."

By contrast, free market advocates generally take a more positive view of differences among people. Where Marxists see inevitable class warfare, free market advocates see possibilities for both groups being better off from interacting peacefully. Where Marxists see dog-eat-dog competition, free market advocates see potential gains from trade and collaboration.

Since I have always been firmly in the free market camp, the idea of class warfare or even class analysis doesn't come naturally to me. All that said, I do think that a class analysis that is not overly deterministic can illuminate our current controversies around the family.

A Non-Deterministic Class Analysis

My thesis is that the members of the managerial class have significant incentives to support the Sexual Revolution and that they generally do so. For a definition of the managerial class, I turn to a distinguished historian, the late Eugene Genovese:

> Who belongs to the managerial elite that increasingly dominates every aspect of our lives? Begin with the executives and bureaucrats of private corporations and add their sometimes rivals and sometimes allies, the executives, and bureaucrats of the federal, state, and local governments. Add the administrators of school systems, universities, large churches, and other institutions. Add the professionals of various kinds, most notably the lawyers, teachers, and doctors, who

command powerful lobbies. Add the media personnel who shape as well as serve the larger elite. And do not fail to include the university intellectuals . . . who now significantly influence policy-making.[1]

For the record, Genovese was a Marxist historian who grew up in a working class Catholic immigrant family. He learned to hate capitalism in that environment. But in his later years, he returned to the practice of the Catholic faith. What he loved became more important than what he hated. This description of the managerial class was written in 1997, during his time of transition from Left to Right.

I recognize that the members of the managerial class are not a monolithic group of people. Plenty of individuals who meet the description of the managerial class are dead set against the tenets of the Sexual Revolution. Some oppose it because they have compelling religious or philosophical commitments that override the class interests I am about to describe. Others are refugees from the Sexual Revolution. They've tried to live by its tenets and have found, for a variety of reasons, that it doesn't work. Some of those people have adopted religious commitments precisely for this reason. (I place myself in this category.) They've discovered alternative philosophies of life that make more sense, provide more guidance, and just all around make life better.

I'm aware that the analysis I am about to offer must be treated carefully. Not every member of each group I'm about

---

[1]   "Secularism in the General Crisis of Capitalism," 42 American Journal of Jurisprudence (1) 195-210 (1997), at 203, cited in Dellapenna, pg. 601.

to discuss will fit into the patterns I describe. Nonetheless, it's helpful to see the structural features of our society that currently reward, and thereby encourage, certain beliefs and behaviors. It's worthwhile to realize the price people must pay to step outside of the sexual revolutionary regime and strike out on the path of independent thought. It's helpful, most of all, because the non-deterministic class analysis helps us understand why the Sexual Revolution has been so persistent and pervasive despite its obvious flaws. This, in turn, will help us make a plan to change course.

A Concrete Example

A friend of mine, Katie, is a brilliant attorney who works part-time for a non-profit public interest legal organization. She lives in the country of coastal California and has nine children whom she homeschools. By any reasonable reckoning, Katie is "having it all:" big family, country living in one of the most beautiful places on earth, and meaningful, intellectually challenging work for a pro-life pro-bono public interest law firm.

Holding a seat on the US Supreme Court represents the pinnacle of achievement in the legal profession. It's safe to say that Katie is unlikely to be appointed to the Supreme Court. She doesn't have the single-minded focus on her career that would allow her to be a serious contender. She has other perfectly legitimate concerns.

Currently three women sit on the US Supreme Court. One of them, Justice Ruth Bader Ginsburg, had two children, born when she was twenty-two and thirty-two. Justice

Ginsberg came of age in the short window of time when women could still get married, have kids, go to law school, and have a career after child-bearing. Thanks to the ideology we now universally call feminism, highly educated women have a much more difficult time doing these things. They can go to law school and have a career all right, but getting married and having children sometime before menopause? Not so much.

Justice Ginsburg had the lifelong support of her husband in her career aspirations. Thanks to no-fault divorce, women today can't count on a lifetime of mutual support from their husbands. Justice Ginsburg has been safely insulated from the negative fallout of the Sexual Revolution which she and her radical feminist colleagues did so much to champion.

The other two women on the Supreme Court, Justices Kagan and Sotomayor, are childless. It's unlikely the two of them understand the lives and aspirations of women like my friend Katie. At the other end of the socio-economic spectrum, less educated women have jobs, not careers. For them, family is everything and "career" is a job to put food on the table. The elite women of the managerial class know nothing of everywoman, the people who have endured the Sexual Revolution and don't have high status, well-paid jobs as compensation.

Women like Katie and I are willing to let ourselves see the harm that the Sexual Revolution has done to the less educated and the lower income. Long ago, women like Katie and me gave up on contraception and abortion as the keys to our happiness and freedom. By contrast, for many women in the managerial class, the Sexual Revolution has made possible their lives as they know them. They cannot imagine what their lives would be like without contraception and abortion.

This is why we have newscasters and jurists and college professors who almost uniformly act as cheerleaders for the Sexual Revolution. They believe their lives depend upon it. Men and women alike have made serious educational and financial commitments to become part of the managerial class. To put it bluntly, delayed child bearing is the price of entering the professional and managerial classes.

Employers, especially employers of the managerial class, benefit from the Sexual Revolution by having a steady supply of highly educated, highly motivated workers of both sexes. These workers are deeply invested in a career path that takes for granted the postponement of parenthood. A large percentage of the people in these positions will be unwilling to challenge the status quo. They have too much at stake. They'll use their influence to maintain the regime as it is, even if it's irrational and impossible and is making them unhappy.

By contrast, the kind of person who valued her family life enough to make career sacrifices for it is less likely to occupy the highest positions of power, authority, influence, and wealth. Katie and I will never hold the seats of power available to childless women. We have good lives with no regrets, but there's no getting around it: childless women have an advantage over mothers in the competition for power and influence in the workplace. Elite woman tends to prevail over everywoman, who wants her children and family more than she wants status, money, or career.

Contesting Feminism

Women who are wedded to the ideology of the Sexual Revolution are sometimes called feminists. Feminism routinely takes credit for the career accomplishments of educated, managerial class women. However, in principle, feminism could mean any set of ideas and policies that promote the betterment and interests of women. Such a broad understanding of feminism could include men or women who promote natural childbirth and nursing, who support women's participation in higher education, who work to prevent or alleviate health hazards that are unique to women, who want to help women find husbands and remain happily married, and many other groups of people. But, as we know, most of these people aren't considered feminists nor are these policies and activities generally considered feminist. This interesting situation cries out for an explanation.

Some Catholic women express their concern for women through a joyful following of *Humanae Vitae*[2] and *Mulieris Dignitatem*.[3] They consider themselves "Catholic feminists" or "John Paul II feminists." They believe they are advocates for womanhood. Their kind of advocacy requires cooperation and collaboration between husband and wife to use periodic abstinence to space pregnancies. Their approach to

---

[2]   Pope Paul VI, Encyclical *Humanae Vitae* (July 25, 1968), http://www.vatican.va/holy_father/paul_vi/encyclicals/documents/hf_p-vi_enc_25071968_humanae-vitae_en.html.

[3]   Pope John Paul II, Apostolic Letter *Mulieris Dignitatem* (August 15, 1988), http://www.vatican.va/holy_father/john_paul_ii/apost_letters/documents/hf_jp-ii_apl_15081988_mulieris-dignitatem_en.html.

bettering the lives of women insists that men respect women in general, especially their wives, and not use women as sexual objects. Their kind of feminism asks the economy to adapt to the woman and the family and their needs rather than demanding that women and the family adapt themselves and their bodies to the economy. What could be more feminist than that? Yet they and their views are not on the public radar in any way. They're certainly not given public recognition as spokeswomen for feminism. Why?

The peculiarity of the situation goes even further. Even among women who can call themselves feminist without contradiction, some receive far more public attention and accolades than others. If we look through the lens of American political categories, we might think the answer has something to do with being on the Left or the Right. But even this is not entirely correct.

For instance, Betsy Hartmann can call herself a feminist without contradiction. She's made important intellectual contributions to the advocacy for women. She's a proponent of both contraception and abortion. These positions secure her feminist and left-wing credentials. She's also the author of a book entitled *Reproductive Rights and Wrongs*, which is critical of the population control movement. She writes against the widespread and indiscriminate promotion of hormonal contraception.[4] She takes these positions because she believes the population controllers don't seek to empower women. Her book spells out in detail the ways in

---

4   Betsy Hartmann, *Reproductive Rights and Wrongs: The Global Politics of Population Control*, Revised ed. (Boston, MA: South End Press, 1995).

which women are manipulated and even coerced by population control programs.

She's skeptical of hormonal contraception because she's aware of its health risks. She's particularly appalled that poor women in the United States and abroad are used as guinea pigs for untested pharmaceuticals and test subjects in an elaborate social engineering project. She advocates for women to have access to more contraceptive options and better information about those options. She views traditional methods of contraception as legitimate options to be discussed and promoted. These traditional methods of spacing births could certainly include what *Humanae Vitae* Catholics call natural family planning: periodic abstinence and extended lactation.

Holly Grigg-Spall is another critic of the widespread and indiscriminate prescription of birth control pills. She has complained about many of the same risks from hormonal contraception that have troubled women from the beginning: mood swings, weight gain, loss of libido, and health risks.

By contrast, Sandra Fluke became a household name during the 2012 election cycle. She was a student at Georgetown Law School who publicly complained about the hardship she would endure from having a co-payment for her birth control pills. Why do you suppose the public heard so much about Sandra Fluke but have never heard of either Betsy Hartmann or Holly Grigg-Spall?

Neither Hartmann nor Grigg-Spall could be described as a raving right-winger. Betsy Hartmann writes for the *Nation* and other Progressive publications. Holly Grigg-Spall has written for such publications as *Ms.*, *the F-bomb,* and *Bitch* magazine.[5] To the best of my knowledge, neither of them are religious or pro-life. But they believe American women are being manipulated into using hormonal contraceptives far more than is necessary.

These women are far enough along the leftward end of the spectrum that they get to call themselves feminists. Yet no one asks them to speak at congressional committees or political conventions. No one supports their efforts to run for public office. I've never seen a puff piece in the elite media written about these women. They don't get large foundation grants. Their ideas are not implemented into public policy through favorable regulations from the State or favorable court rulings from the judiciary.

My explanation for this seemingly odd situation? The elites of this society like the Sexual Revolution. Feminism that supports the Sexual Revolution unambiguously is useful. Anything that calls attention to the inconsistencies inherent in the Sexual Revolution is most assuredly not useful. In fact, it needs to be ignored and perhaps, if necessary, actively suppressed.

The movement that is permitted to call itself feminism is not so much a pro-woman movement as it is a pro-managerial class movement. The forms of feminism that have survived and thrived have been the ideas and policies that favor the interests of the managerial class. The kind of feminism that empowered careerism became dominant over

---

5   Holly Grigg-Spall, *Sweetening the Pill: or How we Got Hooked on Hormonal Birth Control* (Winchester, UK: Zero Books, 2013).

other forms of pro-woman thought, whether from the Left or the Right.

The economic interests of some employers have joined with the ideological interests of some feminists. This created a formidable combination that is difficult for other ideas to penetrate, no matter how pro-woman they may be. The same forces create pressure for individuals to conform to the system, regardless of their personal beliefs or preferences.

Whether poor women have health problems due to their contraception or whether their autonomy in choosing their family size is compromised doesn't concern the managerial class of educated first-world women. Dr. Hartmann can complain all day long about state-sponsored coercion against third-world women. Ms. Grigg-Spall can protest the unhealthy consequences of hormonal contraception. *Humanae Vitae* Catholics can join them in shouting about health risks and the reproductive imperialism of the rich countries against poor countries. The managerial class isn't interested. The people in power favor ideas that support their commitments to their careers and the institutions in which they work. Ideas like these other forms of feminism are less likely to be heard.

So why is Sandra Fluke a household name and . . . wait, what were those other ladies' names?

Let me spell it out for you. You have never heard of Dr. Betsy Hartmann or Holly Grigg-Spall because their critiques of hormonal contraception makes them anathema to the interests of the managerial class. Sandra Fluke, on the other hand, holds beliefs that are useful to the managerial class. This makes her a useful apologist mouth-piece for that class and its interests.

I can't believe I just typed those words. But there it is.

PART TWO

The Contraceptive Ideology

CHAPTER 4

Creating the Contraceptive Ideology: *Griswold v. Connecticut* and Beyond

Contraception is a fact of life in modern America. Everyone takes artificial birth control for granted, with abortion as the backup plan. It may be odd to think that the State, in fact, created the contraceptive culture, yet this is precisely what I aim to show. Of course, the government decides what is legal and what is not. However, I hold that the State is accountable for much more than passively writing into law something that was demanded by the wider society and had become an established fact in our culture. I make the stronger claim that the State bears the greatest responsibility for the toxic sexual culture in which we live. Responsibility for the millions of wounded souls like those introduced in previous chapters can be laid at the feet of the State, which institutionalized and promoted the Contraceptive Ideology.

The Argument

The typical American might reason this way:

Point 1: "Many contraceptive methods are available: natural, artificial, chemical, and mechanical. Individuals and couples should be allowed to use whatever they want. The government's role should be strictly limited to making sure that only safe contraceptive methods are legally available and that these methods are accurately labeled and advertised. The government should not be trying to legislate morality."

This hypothetical ordinary pragmatic American might continue:

Point 2: "The government should not be promoting or subsidizing one particular contraceptive method over others. The government certainly should not be promoting the generalized use of contraception. If people want to use it, they should be allowed. Period. End of government involvement. Whether Mr. and Mrs. Morse have two children, ten children, or no children is not any of the government's business."

Wait, you say. You're no longer sure you agree. You agree with the no legal limits on availability part, but you aren't so sure people's fertility choices are none of the government's business. Maybe you think the government should promote contraception for environmental reasons. Maybe you think the government has a right and perhaps a responsibility to limit the procreation decisions of people who are, or are likely to become, drains on the taxpayer.

Let me point out one thing: if you believe the government *does* have a legitimate role in people's fertility decisions, you've just given up the legal rationale behind all the

Supreme Court's rulings on abortion and contraception. You will recall, that rationale has always been *privacy*.

This chapter will show that the government's role has never been the relatively uncontroversial point 1. The State has been promoting and subsidizing contraception in America almost since the day the Supreme Court removed the ability of states to regulate contraception in any way. In fact, over the past half century, the US government has arguably been the largest single promoter and subsidizer of contraceptives and the Contraceptive Ideology in the world.

The availability of contraceptive technology is not the revolutionary point. Different contraceptive methods of varying degrees of reliability have been known for a long time. Yet no one thought it was desirable or even possible to build a society around the concept that sex is a sterile activity. It's the government's *propagation of the Contraceptive Ideology* that is truly revolutionary.

The Contraceptive Ideology is built upon the idea that we are entitled to act as if the sexual act has been safely sterilized. A good and decent society ought to separate sex and childbearing from each other in the name of freedom and gender justice. Unwanted children are oppressive to women. Unlimited sexual activity without a live baby is an entitlement. We can act as if we have perfectly functioning contraception. A just society must work to bring this about.

The claim that contraception can render sex a sterile activity is not a scientifically accurate claim. Nor is the idea that everyone old enough to give consent is entitled to unlimited sexual activity without a live baby. The technological, scientific fact is that contraception simply reduces the probability that an individual sexual act will result in pregnancy. No contraception reduces the probability all the way to zero.

The average contraception failure rate hovers around 10 percent and is noticeably worse for some demographic groups. For instance, cohabiting poor teenagers were once estimated to have a failure rate of 48 percent for the pill and 72 percent for condom use.[1] No one seems to have reproduced this particularly complete breakdown of failure rates by detailed demographic groups. However, every study I have seen (including one from March 2017) that breaks down contraceptive failure by age, race, poverty status, and marital status comes to similar conclusions. Contraception is most likely to fail for the young, the poor, the unmarried, and racial minorities. Yet these are the groups to whom contraception is most heavily promoted and marketed.[2]

---

[1] This is not a typo. Check out table 2 in Haishan Fu, Jacqueline E. Darroch, Taylor Haas, and Nalini Ranjit, "Contraceptive Failure Rates in the US: New Estimates from the 1995 National Survey of Family Growth," *Family Planning Perspectives* 31, no. 2, 1999, https://www.guttmacher.org/about/journals/psrh/1999/03/contraceptive-failure-rates-new-estimates-1995-national-survey-family.

[2] Aparna Sundaram et al.,"Contraceptive Failure in the United States: Estimates from the 2006–2010 National Survey of Family Growth," *Perspectives on Sexual and Reproductive Health* 49, no. 1 (March 2017): 7–16, http://onlinelibrary.wiley.com/doi/10.1363/psrh.12017/epdf. Kathryn Kost et al., "Estimates of contraceptive failure from the 2002 National Survey of Family Growth," *Contraception* 2008 January; 77(1): 10–21, https://www.ncbi.nlm.nih.gov/pmc/articles/PMC2811396/pdf/nihms164460.pdf. Nalini Ranjit et al., "Contraceptive Failure in the First Two Years of Use: Differences Across Socioeconomic Subgroups," *Family Planning Perspectives*, 2001, 33(1):19–27, https://www.guttmacher.org/sites/default/files/

In addition to the problem of contraceptive failure, the overall ideological framing of the issue is woefully incomplete. Sexual activity has other consequences besides pregnancy. These include the possibility of sexually transmitted diseases and side effects from the contraceptive methods themselves. Sexual activity also carries in its wake a whole train of psychological and social consequences. Attachment to one's sex partner, sexual jealousy, hurt feelings in the event of rejection, and growing so jaded that one no longer expects anything but hurt feelings are all too common consequences of casual sex. Focusing exclusively on avoiding pregnancy or sexually transmitted diseases ignores all these other negative consequences.

Finally, any claims about *entitlements* to sexual activity are obviously not scientific claims. These are necessarily philosophical and moral claims. People who believe these claims should admit that fact and defend their ideas. And we in the general, non-ideological public should stop accepting at face value their proclamations of being "value neutral" and "scientific."

Looking back at history, we will see that the State did much more than simply remove legal barriers to contraception. I will show that in Connecticut, where the landmark case *Griswold v. Connecticut* was decided, contraception had been widely available well before that decision in 1965.

---

article_files/3301901.pdf. James Trussell and Barbara Vaughan, "Contraceptive Failure, Method-Related Discontinuation and Resumption of Use: Results from the 1995 National Survey of Family Growth," *Family Planning Perspectives*, 1999, 31(2):64–72, 93.

Given that, why did a small group of people go on a thirty-year legislative crusade, supplemented by multiple court cases, to overturn the supposed legal "ban" on contraception? Part of the answer is that the State itself wanted to actively promote and subsidize contraception, especially to low-income women.

The birth control advocates in Connecticut brought up their legislation every session beginning in 1935. They never succeeded in getting the duly elected representatives of the people to overturn the restriction on contraception. As that legislative strategy failed year after year, the advocates turned to the courts. Finally, after multiple attempts, the US Supreme Court overturned Connecticut's birth control regulations, along with those for all forty-nine other states.[3]

We will also see that the legal and rhetorical strategy used in *Griswold* set the pattern for future stages of the Sexual Revolution. Advocates claimed to be only interested in a modest, unobjectionable policy change. But once they established the legal principle, they applied that principle far more widely than the public or the courts would have accepted. This shows the pattern of duplicity and outright perjury that advocates of the Contraceptive Ideology employed to obtain the legal rulings and State support they so desperately wanted.

---

[3]   This is the story told in David J. Garrow, *Liberty and Sexuality: The Right to Privacy and the Making of Roe v Wade,* (NY: Macmillan Publishing, 1994).

Contraception Widely Available in Connecticut

The Supreme Court case *Griswold v. Connecticut* prohibited all states from enacting legislation limiting the availability of contraception to married couples. The Connecticut litigation was specifically aimed at overturning the late-nineteenth-century "Comstock law" which prohibited the sale and promotion of contraception as part of a general ban on pornography.[4] Despite what one might imagine from the existence of the Comstock law, various forms of birth control were widely available in the state of Connecticut well before the *Griswold* decision in 1965.

In the fall of 1945, a Planned Parenthood League of Connecticut (PPLC) leader warned her colleagues against a "certain defeatism" that was openly emerging. The widespread apathy, she said at PPLC's annual meeting, no doubt was "due in part to the fact that many doctors continue to give, and private patients receive, contraceptive service," and the resulting "general impression that everyone has access to birth control information." In other words, so many people believed that the old 1879 statute had no actual effect on anyone that the efforts of the Planned Parenthood League were unnecessary.[5]

In the summer of 1954, an incident took place that suggests wide availability of diaphragms. Doctors were fitting

---

4   Allan Carlson, *Godly Seed: American Evangelicals confront Birth Control, 1873-1973* (New Brunswick NJ, Transaction Publishers, 2012.) See esp. ch. 1. Carlson observes in passing that "Comstock's values and initiatives were wholly in line with the right-thinking and progressive currents of his age" (p. 35).

5   Garrow, *Liberty and Sexuality*, p. 112.

women with diaphragms and dispensing them in their offices. Pharmacists were annoyed that the doctors had been cutting them out of the business. The medical professionals were evidently quarreling amongst themselves over it. Connecticut's commissioner of food and drugs, who had regulatory authority over pharmacists, issued a ruling: pharmacists were henceforth only permitted to dispense diaphragms to women with a written prescription from a doctor. We can infer that both doctors and druggists alike were dispensing diaphragms without fear of prosecution.[6]

Condoms were also widely available before *Griswold*. In 1953, a Yale Law School professor and a United Press International correspondent visited a drug store where they easily purchased a box of condoms for three dollars. When they went to the police station and asked to press charges against the drug store, they were told that the articles they had purchased were legal.[7] Thus, the modern "libertarian" aim of people being able to obtain what they wanted was already in place *de facto* if not *de jure:* in fact, if not in the letter of the law.

Even during deliberations before the US Supreme Court, the point arose that the law was seldom enforced. In oral arguments for *Poe v. Ullman*, the last case in which the court upheld the Connecticut statute, Justice Stewart asked about this point. Plaintiffs' attorney Fowler Harper responded somewhat lamely, "I'm ignorant of the extent to which the law is enforced. . . . So far as I know it has never been

---

[6]   Ibid., p. 136.
[7]   Ibid., p. 128. This particular incident took place in 1953.

enforced against a person who used a contraceptive. . . .
Police do not peek into people's bedrooms to see whether
they're using contraceptives. . . . I know of no prosecution of
an individual for use."

Attorney Harper realized the significance of this admission and recovered his bearings. He then pointed out how,
since an earlier decision upholding the Connecticut law, "no
public or private clinic for the purpose of advising on contraception" had operated in the state. "The people in CT who
need contraceptive advice from doctors most—the people in
the lower income brackets and lower educational brackets—
the people who need it most, do not get it, because there are
no clinics available."[8]

While the court was deliberating privately, Harper tried
to get evidence that the law was not in fact a dead letter. He
went so far as to try to persuade the attorney general of the
state to enforce the statute.[9]

Motives for Overturning the Comstock Law

We can infer three motives for the concerted effort to overturn this nearly dead-letter law. First, overturning the old law
allowed freestanding birth control clinics to promote contraception to the lower classes. Second, overturning the ban on
contraception allowed the government itself to begin to get
into the birth control business, both providing and promoting contraception. Finally, some people evidently wanted
birth control more widely available because they wanted to

---

[8]   Ibid., p. 178.
[9]   Ibid., pp. 186–88.

have casual sex. Removing the ban on contraception would create a sexual environment with lower costs, including less shame around non-marital sex.

Of course, this last motive was precisely what the ordinary person feared. They believed removing the legal barriers to contraception, no matter how imperfectly enforced, would undermine standards of sexual behavior. Evidently, a great many people in the mid-twentieth century felt more supported than oppressed by the upholding of public morality that defined marriage as the socially appropriate context for sexual activity.

Establishing Birth Control Clinics

The Connecticut Birth Control League and its successor organization, the Planned Parenthood League of Connecticut, claimed they were working to make contraception available to poor women. "It all adds up to the rich getting contraceptives and the poor getting children," one advocate argued in 1961.[10] So, the argument went, we members of the social elite are looking after the interests of our unfortunate lower-class sisters.

The US Supreme Court had no doubt that the establishment of clinics was the issue. In the oral arguments for *Poe v. Ullman*, Justice Frankfurter asked whether contraceptives were widely available in the state. Justice Brennan asked, "Isn't the operation of the clinics what's at stake here really?

---

[10]   Ibid., p. 197.

. . . I take it the (fictitiously named plaintiffs) Poes and Does can get what they need, almost any place in Connecticut."[11]

During the justices' private conference on this early case, Chief Justice Earl Warren opined that the plaintiffs had made the justices "guinea pigs for an abstract principle." Warren was reluctant for the court to decide "contrived litigation" when contraceptives could be purchased in any Connecticut drugstore and where there was no indication that the 1879 statute had ever or would ever be enforced.[12] Justice Frankfurter said that he could not imagine any doctor failing to give contraceptive advice for fear of going to jail; what the plaintiffs clearly wanted was authorization to open clinics.[13]

Allowing Governmental Promotion of Contraception

For insight into the second motivation for thirty years of litigation and agitation at the state legislature, I turn to attorney Leo Pfeffer and his description of the *Griswold* case. In his 1975 book *God, Caesar, and the Constitution: The Court as Referee of Church-state Confrontation*, he argues the government itself wished to actively promote contraception. He wrote:

> Paradoxically, the anti-contraception laws had to be removed from the books because their presence made it impossible for the state to encourage contraception, something it now *(i.e. in 1975)* increasingly deems necessary to do. . . . The middle income and the affluent,

---

[11]   Ibid., pp. 177–80.
[12]   Ibid., p. 181.
[13]   Ibid., p. 183.

> married, and unmarried, use contraceptives; the poor
> have babies. When the poor, often racial minorities,
> are on the welfare rolls, taxpaying Americans rebel and
> expect the state to do something about it. . . . The real-
> ity of the situation is that welfare recipients are going
> to sleep together no less than the affluent taxpayers,
> and the only practical way to keep welfare costs down
> is to encourage them to practice birth control.[14]

Mr. Pfeffer was fully on board with the *Griswold* case, including these motivations that we might now consider disreputable. To put his comments in perspective, he was the lead counsel on the 1961 case *Torcaso v. Watkins,*[15] a case holding that Maryland's requirement that notaries public state a belief in God violated the constitutional ban on religious tests for office. The American Humanist Association named Mr. Pfeffer the "Humanist of the Year" in 1988.[16] In short, Mr. Pfeffer can hardly be considered a religious zealot attempting to discredit the efforts to repeal state regulation of contraception.

In a peculiar twist of historical fate, social conservative historian Alan Carlson agrees with Pfeffer's analysis. Carlson, who has authored important books on the Swedish welfare state, argues, "As all architects of modern welfare systems discover, birth control becomes essential. Whether in

---

14   Leo Pfeffer, *God, Caesar and the Constitution: The Court as Referee of Church-state Confrontation* (Boston: Beacon Press, 1975) p. 96.
15   Torcaso v. Watkins, 367 U.S. 488 (1961).
16   Wikipedia, s.v. "American Humanist Association," last referenced September 26, 2013, http://en.wikipedia.org/wiki/American_ Humanist_Association.

wealthy Sweden or in urban American ghettoes, government programs of family assistance by their very nature generate an 'illegitimacy problem.'"[17]

When did the government start promoting contraception?

The United States government was already promoting birth control outside its boundaries before *Griswold* was decided. The idea that family planning should be a systematic foreign policy tool was introduced after WWII in 1959. General William H. Draper, a Wall Street financier, had been involved in the US occupation of Japan. As under secretary of the Army, Draper worried that the "rapidly growing population in the next few years would bring Japan back to the level of semi starvation." Population control, he argued, meant "decreasing opportunities for communist political and economic domination" in developing nations. The Draper report called for family planning assistance to supplement military aid programs.[18]

---

[17]   Allan C. Carlson, "The Bipartisan blunder of Title X," *Family Policy*, September-October 2000. Carlson agrees with Pfeffer's analysis but disagrees with his assessment. Carlson regards the government provision and promotion of birth control as a "bipartisan blunder."

[18]   Donald T. Critchlow, *Intended Consequences: Birth Control, Abortion and the Federal Government in Modern America* (New York: Oxford University Press, 1999), pp. 42–43. Perhaps ironically, Japan certainly does not have an over-population problem today (2016). Their total fertility rate is 1.4 babies per woman, well below the replacement rate of 2.1. Japan's average age is 47 years old, making them the second oldest country in the world (CIA World Factbook, accessed December 13, 2016, https://www.cia.gov/library/publications/the-world-factbook/rankorder/2127rank.html#ja).

In December 1974, Henry Kissinger directed the National Security Council to examine the implications of worldwide population growth for US security and overseas interests. The National Security Council's secret National Security Memorandum 200 found that rapid population growth fostered political instability, and it identified thirteen countries of "special U.S. political and strategic interest" where "population stabilization" policies should be pursued.[19] The memorandum recommended discretion to minimize the charges of US cultural imperialism. Where diplomatic relations were strained, the memorandum suggested providing aid through "other donors and/or from private and international organizations" (many of which received contributions from US Aid to International Development.)[20]

In fact, one analyst, writing in 1994, declared: "To understand the changes in the international environment on the abortion issue over the past two decades, analysis must begin with the single most influential actor—the government of the United States." She goes on to describe how the US Agency for International Development (USAID) believed that "access to methods for terminating early pregnancies was an essential element of effective family planning programs" in the 1960s and 1970s.[21] In other words, the federal

---

19 Barbara Crane, "The Transnational Politics of Abortion," in *Population and Development Review* 20, Supplement, *The New Politics of Population: Conflict and Consensus in Family Planning* (1994), pp. 241–62.

20 Dennis Hodgson and Susan Cotts Watkins, "Feminists and Neo-Malthusians: Past and Present Alliances," in *Population and Development Review* 23, no. 3 (September 1997), p. 486.

21 Crane, "The Transnational Politics of Abortion," pp. 241–62.

government was already deeply involved in promoting "family planning," including abortion, before *Roe v. Wade* and even before *Griswold*.

In domestic policy, well before the *Griswold* case, some of the states had already become concerned about too many people. Or, perhaps I should say, too many of the wrong sort of people. As early as 1907, Indiana passed a forcible sterilization statute, followed by Connecticut, Oregon, and California, as a eugenic measure; that is to say, a measure designed to "improve" the quality of the human gene pool.[22] Other states made physical exams a prerequisite for marriage, also as a eugenic measure.[23] In this early period, artificial birth control was considered radical, while eugenics, including forcible sterilization, was considered mainstream and progressive.[24]

Wealthy private individuals made it their business to establish birth control clinics prior to *Griswold*. One expert opined, "These efforts in the South established this region as a leader in the state birth control movement. By 1944 Gunnar Myrdal, in his mammoth study of race relations in the United States, was able to declare, 'The South now leads other sections of the country in accepting birth control. . . . It is reasonable to assume that the large number of undesired

---

22   Christine Rosen, *Preaching Eugenics: Religious Leaders and the American Eugenics Movement* (Oxford: Oxford University Press, 2004), pp. 47–48.

23   Rosen, *Preaching Eugenics*, pp. 68–69 cites Wisconsin, Vermont, and Pennsylvania as states with "health certificate" legislation and Patterson, New Jersey, and Chicago as municipalities with similar practices.

24   Ibid., pp. 153–54.

Negroes in the rural districts also has something to do with the lack of opposition on the part of the white South.'"[25]

Lyndon Baines Johnson launched the Great Society to eliminate poverty in the United States. Family planning became integral to his war on poverty. Because Johnson feared a political backlash from Roman Catholics and African-Americans, his administration quietly pursued a policy of funding family-planning programs through existing federal agencies.[26] In 1966, the Office of Economic Opportunity issued guidelines that allowed federal funding for family planning on the community level to married women with children. Family planning was made available for families of military service personnel, Native Americans, and other groups under federal jurisdiction.[27]

This was not lost on Fowler Harper, the attorney who filed the *Griswold* appeal. He pointed out the social policy benefits of birth control. He observed, regarding the new federal "war on poverty," that "to fight poverty without birth control is to fight with one hand tied behind the back."[28]

Taking all this information together, attorney Leo Pfeffer's assessment is credible. The US government had already incorporated birth control into its foreign policy and its policy in Puerto Rico. Through the war on poverty, the federal government gave itself the responsibility to provide for the needs of the domestic poor. Taking on this federal goal of

---

25　　Critchlow, *Intended Consequences*, pp. 35–36.

26　　Ibid., p. 50.

27　　Ibid., p. 55.

28　　Garrow, *Liberty and Sexuality*, p. 225.

combating poverty created a need for the government to "do something" about the poor having too many children.

If we ask how much time transpired between the Supreme Court removing all legal restrictions on contraception and when the government began actively promoting its use, the answer is: about five minutes. Removing all state level restrictions on contraception simply removed the final hurdles standing in the way of governmental promotion of contraception.

Is the government still promoting contraception?

Of course, the government is still promoting contraception down to this very day. The most notorious current example is the controversial mandate by the Department of Health and Human Services for implementing the Affordable Care Act. Treating pregnancy prevention as "preventive care," and therefore available without a co-pay, amounts to treating pregnancy as a disease or illness rather than as the normal functioning of a healthy woman's body. The revolutionaries promote these concepts in the name of women's empowerment, freedom, and of course "women's right to choose."

This Obama-era policy shows that "choice" was never the issue for the true sexual revolutionary. The Little Sisters of the Poor are an order of nuns devoted to the care of the indigent elderly. They protested that this health insurance regulation amounted to an unlawful infringement on their freedom to practice their religion. The Little Sisters are all women, last time I checked. These women are certainly not "empowered" by the federal government's plan to levy punitive fines on them for non-compliance. The Catholic Church in America runs the largest non-governmental social services network in the world. Yet, under this policy, many of their operations would have been either shut down or taken over by the government.

This policy remains controversial and is being revisited by the Trump administration. But the very fact that something so tangentially related to health care was so important to such a significant portion of the elite class shows that "choice" is a smokescreen for the real issue. The real issue has even gone beyond the promotion of the Contraceptive Ideology. The real issue now, over fifty years after the *Griswold* case, is crushing dissent from the Contraceptive Ideology.

But the Affordable Care Act controversies were not the beginning of the federal government's foray into legislating sexual revolutionary morality. Despite Americans' resistance to the idea of imposing morality on their neighbors, the federal government has been implicitly imposing an anti-natal, anti-fertility morality of its own for quite a while. To see this, let's look at Medicaid, the federal program that provides health care to the poor.

In 2006, Medicaid was responsible for more than 70 percent of public birth-control expenditures, or $1.3 billion.[29] Contraception is a mandatory part of state Medicaid programs and is reimbursed at the most highly favored rate. Contraception must be made available to minors over the

---

[29]   A. Sonfield, C. Alrich, and R. B. Gold, "Public Funding for Family Planning, Sterilization, and Abortion Services, FY 1980–2006," Occasional Report No. 38 (New York: Guttmacher Institute, 2008).

age of puberty, even without the consent of their parents. Under Medicaid rules, contraception must be free to welfare recipients, without even a nominal co-pay. And state governments have an incentive to actively promote family-planning services, especially to minors, since their outreach, advertising, and sex-education expenses are reimbursed at the most favorable rate of 90 percent.[30]

Any state that doesn't want to offer family-planning services will face a penalty and lose other Medicaid funds. When dealing with most other services, including life-saving services such as chemotherapy, the states have a choice about whether to offer them. The unmistakable message is that preventing births is more important than preserving life. This extraordinarily favorable coverage of birth-control costs is not a morally neutral posture.

Embedded within the government's pro-contraception policies is the highly dubious claim that making artificial birth control available promotes health and prevents unwed pregnancy more effectively than alternative policies. Such policies might include promoting the confinement of sexual activity to marriage, currently maligned as non-evidence based "abstinence only" education. Maybe teaching fertility awareness natural methods of family planning would reduce teen sexual activity and pregnancy. Whatever one thinks about the effectiveness of these methods, no one can deny that they are medically safe and that understanding one's

---

[30]   Daniel Patrick Moloney, "Forcing the Poor to Stop Having Children," *The Public Discourse: Ethics, Law and the Common Good,* The Witherspoon Institute (May 1, 2009), accessed December 1, 2012, http://www.thepublicdiscourse.com/2009/05/23.

own body could be empowering to young women and girls. Maybe providing teens with non-sexual activities to fill their time would be a better use of federal money. With the partial exception of abstinence education, none of these ideas are even under serious consideration.

The existing Medicaid rules have one feature that evidently appeals to the sexual revolutionaries. Parents are prohibited from knowing whether their dependent children receive birth control. The rules extend to children the same right to doctor-patient confidentiality that adults have. In effect, the federal government requires the states to undermine parental supervision and authority over their children.

Thus, it is not now, and never has been, the government's policy to simply make contraception legally available and accurately labeled and then leaving families to use as they wish. The federal government has been and continues to be an active promoter of contraception. We do not have a "libertarian" policy in this area. Allowing people to make their own decisions about contraception has never been enough for the true revolutionary.

One more motive for Griswold

Finally, we cannot ignore the most obvious motive for removing legal restrictions on contraception: creating the social space for casual sex. Margaret Sanger herself had lovers to whom she was not married.[31] So did others in the birth

---

[31]   Jonathan Eig, *The Birth of the Pill: How Four Crusaders Reinvented Sex and Launched a Revolution* (New York: Norton, 2014).

control movement.[32] So did some of the important funders of various parts of the Sexual Revolution. For instance, Hugh Hefner, founder of Playboy, contributed to some of the challenges to abortion laws as well as to other legal aspects of the Sexual Revolution.[33]

An indirect way we can discern the presence of this motive is to analyze closely another bit of long-standing pro-birth control rhetoric. Margaret Sanger frequently pointed to her own mother, who had twelve children, as the example of the type of person she was trying to help. Sanger was also instrumental in promoting the development of the pill. Jonathan Eig, author of *The Birth of the Pill: How Four Crusaders Reinvented Sex and Launched a Revolution*, is generally favorable toward the development of the pill and its "crusaders." But he inadvertently gives away the game when he quips, "A contraceptive with an 85% success rate was no good to anyone."[34]

This is obviously untrue. If the people Margaret Sanger

---

[32]   For instance, attorney Mel Wulf described himself as "sexually active, if not promiscuous," and hence, had a personal commitment to birth control and abortion. Garrow, *Liberty and Sexuality*, p. 172.

[33]   For instance, the Playboy Foundation supported an Illinois activist group that called for abortion repeal in the state legislature Garrow, *Liberty and Sexuality*, p. 360. On the occasion of Hefner's death, Richard Green published a grateful retrospective of Hefner's contribution to the founding of the journal *Archives of Sexual Behavior* as well as funding landmark lesbian custody cases. Richard Green, "Hugh Hefner, the International Academy of Sex Research, and Its Founding President," *Arch Sex Behav* (2017) 46:2211–12, https://doi.org/10.1007/s10508-017-1098-y.

[34]   Eig, *The Birth of the Pill*, p. 134.

wished to help were married women such as her own mother, 85 percent effectiveness is actually quite helpful. Instead of having a baby every year or eighteen months, she might have a baby every three or four years. A happily married couple can afford occasional contraceptive failures. Such couples even have endearing names for the children so conceived: "our itty-bitty boo-boo" or "our little surprise" or "our little caboose." These terms describe the darling baby at the end of a family everyone thought was completed and whom the entire family now dotes upon.

But if the object of your concern is the woman having sex with someone to whom she is not married, the calculation is quite different. A pregnancy with someone married to someone else, a pregnancy with someone who would be a completely unsuitable father, a pregnancy when you yourself would not be a well-prepared mother, these pregnancies are far more than an inconvenience. These are the situations in which women sometimes feel they need an abortion. These situations cry out for 100 percent reliable contraception.

According to the Centers for Disease Control's downloadable chart, the average effectiveness of the pill was 91 percent in 2016, not so very much better than the 85 percent that was regarded as obviously inadequate.[35] And, as already noted, the failure rates for the poor, the unmarried, racial minorities, and the young are even worse. Yet these failures do not stop the federal government from promoting the use

---

[35]   Centers for Disease Control, "Effectiveness of Family Planning Methods," page updated June 21, 2016, http://www.cdc.gov/reproductivehealth/contraception/unintendedpregnancy/pdf/contraceptive_methods_508.pdf.

of these contraceptive methods. In fact, the government most actively markets and subsidizes contraception to these very groups through the Medicaid rules mentioned already.

These failures, however, don't stop the spread of the ideology that we are entitled to act as if we have perfectly functioning contraception. On the contrary, the failures of contraception simply lead to more aggressive demands for "education" about their proper use, along with demands for ever cheaper and more thoroughly subsidized abortions in case of contraceptive failure.

Finally, if I may be so bold as to point this out: the benefit of contraception for the man involved in these scenarios is all too obvious. He can have the sex he wants without fear of any legally recognized paternal responsibility. The heart of the Contraceptive Ideology is to make these kinds of sexual encounters seem both harmless and consequence-free. The perpetrators in the Hollywood and Washington sexual harassment scandals of 2017–2018 were men who were highly supportive of abortion rights. This should not surprise us, despite these men's claims to be "pro-woman."[36] They are in favor of a very particular kind of "women's rights," rights that just happen to coincide with their own desires for uncommitted sex.

---

[36]   I made this point about Hollywood mogul Harvey Weinstein in "The Toxic Ideas that Enabled Weinstein and Others," *Crisis*, October 26, 2017, http://www.crisismagazine.com/2017/toxic-ideas-enabled-harvey-weinstein-enablers, and about Senator Al Franken in "Here's What's Fishy about Al Franken's Resignation and Selective Outrage," *Clash Daily*, December 13, 2017, https://clashdaily.com/2017/12/heres-whats-fishy-al-frankens-resignation-selective-outrage/.

The Legal and Rhetorical Strategy: "All We Want to Do"

Finally, the rhetorical and political strategy of the birth control advocates set the mold for future rounds of the Sexual Revolution. The advocates focused on the narrowest possible grounds for invalidating the Connecticut statute. Their initial, very limited goal was to fight for the right of a married woman to use birth control for serious medical reasons.

Their restrained advocacy sounds quaint to us today. In the fight over the 1925 bill, Margaret Sanger testified that birth control information should be available only to married women. She said, "Married women are entitled to the information because they have moral obligations, which unmarried women haven't."[37] In 1938, the lawyer for the Connecticut Birth Control League contended: "It is admitted that, for instance, the indiscriminate dissemination of contraceptive information to high school girls could be prohibited. This would be a justified exercise of the police power, because if contraceptive information was widely available to high school students, the restraints upon immoral practices inherent in the fear of pregnancy would be removed."[38]

One wonders what the citizens of Connecticut in 1938 would think of government schools routinely giving condoms to fourth graders.

When people objected that this modest objective was likely to lead to other, more objectionable practices, the activists insisted that they intended nothing of the sort. In a 1951 legislative hearing, Bridgeport representative Wilton

---

[37]   Garrow, *Liberty and Sexuality*, pp. 18–19.
[38]   Ibid., p. 69.

Reinhardt insisted, "I think these bills can well be a step toward legalizing abortion." New Haven's Reverend C. Lawson Willard replied that the bills were designed "entirely to protect the health and lives of mothers" rather than to facilitate "the limitation of the number of children."[39]

Here is one last, very revealing instance. In 1961, the Planned Parenthood group staged a test case. Yale graduate student Rosemary Stevens knowingly violated the law and later told detectives her interest in the issue.

> She explained that she wanted to delay any pregnancy until she had completed her graduate education, and added more generally that "This opportunity should be made available to all women in this state." (Detective) Blazi interrupted his typing to ask, "Don't you mean *married* women, Mrs. Stevens?" With considerable hesitance, and only because Blazi had been so friendly and helpful, Rosemary Stevens reluctantly agreed to Blazi's adding "married" to her statement before she signed it. "I still feel badly about that," she explained over thirty years later.[40]

She wanted contraception to be available to all women, married or not, without qualification. But under oath, she claimed she believed the principle applied only to married women. In other words, she perjured herself.

Planned Parenthood and their allies at Yale Law School looked for a test case in which "a married woman would be

---

[39]   Ibid., p. 122.
[40]   Ibid., p. 206.

very likely to lose her life."[41] In fact, privately, one of their attorneys criticized their choice of plaintiffs, saying that her condition was so serious that sterilization (which was certainly legal), not contraception, was the appropriate medical solution.[42] Justice Frankfurter raised this very point in oral arguments. He wondered aloud whether Dr. Buxton should have sterilized "Jane Doe" and "Pauline Poe" rather than prescribing contraception.[43]

These qualifiers were swept away after the case was decided and the legal principle established. On the day *Griswold* was announced, one of the attorneys told a supporter on the phone that the next step would be to use the right of privacy to find a constitutional right to abortion.[44] In December of 1965, a mere six months after *Griswold* was handed down, one of the attorneys on the case published a law review article which stated, "It is conceivable that sometime in the future, as mores change . . . all sexual activities of two consenting adults will be brought within the right of privacy. . . . The way would be open for an attack upon significant aspects of the abortion laws."[45]

These people knew perfectly well that they were misleading the court and the public when they claimed to have limited objectives of legalizing contraception for married

---

[41]   Ibid., p. 92.

[42]   Ibid., p. 156. The counsel was Morris Ernst; he was complaining about their choice of plaintiff in the *Doe v. Ullman* case in 1958.

[43]   Ibid., p. 178.

[44]   Ibid., pp. 258–59.

[45]   Thomas Emerson, "Nine Justices in search of a doctrine," *Michigan Law Review* 64 (December 1965), in Garrow, *Liberty and Sexualiy*, p. 260.

women with serious health problems. From the beginning, they intended to expand the principle far beyond those original modest goals. But they knew their long-term goals would have appalled the public.

All We Want to Do . . .

We can look to *Griswold* for the rhetorical formula and winning strategy for subsequent battles in the Sexual Revolution. The *Griswold* activists said:

- "All we want to do is allow married couples to use contraception for serious health reasons."
- "All we want to do is allow poor women the same contraceptive options as rich women."

Later activists adapted that formula:

- "All we want to do is lower the cost of divorce to the handful of people whose marriages have irretrievably broken down, a mere handful of people who will be divorcing in any case."
- "All we want to do is allow abortion for cases of rape and incest."
- "All we want to do is provide sexual education for children whose parents might not be responsible enough to do it themselves."
- "All we want to do is allow underage girls to get abortions and contraception without their parents knowing because some parents might abuse the girl."

The rationale for all these "modest reform" campaigns is the battle cry of freedom. "All we want to do is allow people the opportunity, the freedom, to make their own choices about their lives." Never mentioned in any of these historical episodes is the fact that the purveyors of these lines are simply lying. They want more, much more, than they are admitting. They know that the public would not accept the larger agenda.

Conclusion

The contraceptive revolution was supposed to make "every child a wanted child," but who can take that cliché seriously now? It may very well be that every child born to highly educated members of the leadership class is wanted in the sense of being planned for and prepared for. This is because membership in the educated classes almost demands that a woman abort any unplanned pregnancies, when "unplanned" means "pregnancy that would interfere with educational or career plans."

At the same time, the percentage of children born to unmarried mothers has increased dramatically during the period in which both contraception and abortion were legally available and highly promoted.[46] This increase in non-marital childbearing, including the "multi-partner fertility" endured

---

[46] This was first observed and explained by economists George Akerlof, Janet Yellen, and Michael Katz in "An Analysis of Out-of-Wedlock Childbearing in the United States," *The Quarterly Journal of Economics* 111, no. 2 (May 1996), pp. 277–317. Akerlof went on to win the Nobel Prize in economics, and Yellen has since become chairwoman of the Federal Reserve.

by children like Elise, has been concentrated among the less educated classes.[47] These two disturbing facts found at opposite ends of the socio-economic spectrum tell us something about the Contraceptive Ideology and its adherents' stated desire to make "every child a wanted child." They tell us that, regardless of intent, the results of have been catastrophic for women and children.

We've seen the way in which federal government action overturned state-level restrictions on contraceptives. The way was then clear for the federal and the state governments to actively promote and even subsidize contraception. The next chapter will show how the elites have used the coercive powers of government, principally those of the judicial branch, to establish the promotion of the Contraceptive Ideology as policy. It will become clear why there was no grassroots movement of ordinary people in favor of the Contraceptive Ideology.

---

[47] Kay Hymowitz, Jason Carroll, W. Bradford Wilcox, Kelleen Kay, "The Great Crossover," *The Knot Yet Report*, The National Marriage Project at the University of Virginia, The National Campaign to Prevent Teen and Unplanned Pregnancy, and The Relate Institute, 2013, http://twentysomethingmarriage.org/the-great-crossover/.

CHAPTER 5

The Elites Create the Contraceptive Ideology: Alfred Kinsey, the Rockefellers, and Yale

What was the point of the government getting into the birth control business? One word: eugenics. Behind that one word was a substantial body of progressive opinion dating back to the turn of the twentieth century. Too many of the wrong sorts of people were having children; not enough of the right sorts were having children. The horrors of Nazi application of eugenics discredited the idea after World War II.

But the most ardent believers in eugenics simply repackaged its objectives in more attractive guise with two prominent features: feminism and environmentalism. Feminism, at least a certain sort of feminism, had the advantage of putting the wealthy philanthropists on the side of something positive: women's education and empowerment. Likewise, a certain type of environmentalism made overpopulation appear to be a plague on the natural world. Limiting population growth became something positive: protecting the earth. Both feminism and environmentalism shifted the focus away from "too many of the wrong sort of babies" to other more benign motives.

Of course, the desire to create social space for non-marital sex was also at work. We can see this motive operating in the background of another watershed event: the publication of Alfred Kinsey's books. Kinsey's books purported to show that "everyone was doing it": having far more sex than anyone had previously supposed.

Kinsey, Supported by the Rockefellers

At the same time the birth control battle in Connecticut was unfolding, another cultural time bomb was detonated: the research of Alfred Kinsey at the University of Indiana. The publication of Kinsey's *Sexual Behavior in the Human Male* in 1948, followed by *Sexual Behavior in the Human Female* in 1953,[1] shook the average Americans' ideas about themselves and their sexual behavior. Kinsey reported that Americans were having far more sex in far more situations than anyone had previously thought. The first book and the publicity surrounding it created the impression that "everyone is doing it." American GIs returned from World War II to be told that 50 percent of husbands were adulterers.

---

[1]   Alfred Kinsey, Wardell B. Pomeroy, and Clyde E. Martin, *Sexual Behavior in the Human Male* (Philadelphia: W. B. Saunders, 1948); Alfred Kinsey, Wardell B. Pomeroy, Clyde E. Martin, and Paul H. Gebhard, *Sexual Behavior in the Human Female* (Philadelphia: W. B. Saunders, 1953).

Kinsey claimed that "up to" 67 to 98 percent of American men had premarital sex and that 69 percent of American males had at least one experience with a prostitute.[2]

Serious people criticized Kinsey from the beginning. Famed psychologist Abraham Maslow argued that "volunteer bias" contaminated Kinsey's results. Maslow argued that people who volunteer to participate in a sex survey are unlikely to be representative of the general population.[3] Statisticians also knew that Kinsey's claims that "everyone is doing it" were almost certainly exaggerated. A committee from the American Statistical Association produced a report criticizing him for his non-random sampling procedures. The committee of statisticians also criticized him for drawing conclusions that were far too sweeping for the data he had.[4]

Sexual deviance fascinated Kinsey. He sympathized with sex offenders. He felt they were misunderstood and oppressed. He did numerous interviews with men in prison for sex crimes, including male prostitutes and pedophiles. He cultivated a source known to history as "Mr. X," who reported his sexual "observations" and activities with children, even infants.[5] His studies did show that *someone*

---

[2]   Kinsey, *Sexual Behavior in the Human Male*, pp. 585, 552, 597.

[3]   A. H. Maslow and J. Sakoda, "Volunteer error in the Kinsey study," *Journal of Abnormal Psychology* 47, no. 2 (April 1952):259–62.

[4]   William Gemmell Cochran, W. O. Jenkins, Frederick Mosteller, and John Wilder Tukey, *Statistical problems of the Kinsey Report on Sexual Behavior in the Human Male* (Washington, DC: American Statistical Association, 1954), pp. 2–3.

[5]   James H. Jones, *Alfred C. Kinsey: A Life* (New York: Norton, 1997), pp. 507–12.

somewhere was doing just about anything imaginable, and some things that were frankly unimaginable to the Americans of the 1940s. But his studies did not produce a representative sample to show what *everyone* was doing.

Later, when serious researchers at the University of Chicago conducted population-based analysis of sexual behavior, they stated that Kinsey's pool of study subjects "failed to meet even the most elementary requirements for drawing a truly representative sample of the population at large."[6] Instead of 50 percent of husbands being adulterers in the 1940s as Kinsey had claimed, the Chicago study found that, at most, 23 percent of husbands had had an extramarital sex partner.[7]

---

[6] The definitive study of the topics Kinsey purported to study remains Edward O. Laumann et al., *The Social organization of Sexuality: Sexual Practices in the United States* (Chicago: University of Chicago, 1994). See page 35 for their critique of his sampling methods.

[7] Laumann, *The Social organization of Sexuality*, p. 208, table 5.9 A. See appendix A on the sample design, p. 554. These data were collected in 1992, well after the introduction of the birth control pill and well after the Sexual Revolution was in full swing. It strains the imagination to accept Kinsey's finding that 50 percent of husbands were adulterers in the 1940s. Kinsey's work is also the original source of the claim that 10 percent of the population is "gay." I deliberately put that in quotation marks because the exact meaning of the term *gay* was precisely the issue in contention. Suffice it to say that no serious population-based study has ever come close to replicating Kinsey's 10 percent figure. The studies, going back to the 1990s and across countries, come up with a figure of about 2.5 percent of the male population having sex exclusively with men and 1.5 percent of the female population having sex exclusively with women over the previous five years. Dan Black, Gary Gates, Seth Sanders, and Lowell Taylor,

Despite these well-documented flaws in his research, Kinsey continues to be idolized by many academics. The first time I published a column documenting his skewed sampling techniques and his flawed conclusions,[8] I was astonished by the number of people who defended Kinsey as a great pioneering scientist. And these weren't ordinary people but those with academic credentials.

What exactly was Kinsey's "scientific" approach? He figured out a way to measure sexual behavior. Anything we can quantify must be counted as true, especially back in the immediate post-war period when Science with a capital S was king. Kinsey counted orgasms. He argued that this was a truly scientific procedure since orgasms were easily observed, counted, and reported. However, as any adult with sexual experience should know, the number of orgasms is not the only important feature of human sexual behavior. The quality of the foreplay, the intimacy of the aftermath, the intensity of the friendship outside the bedroom, and of course, the nature of the union itself are just as significant, if not more significant, than the mere orgasm.

None of this interested Kinsey. His skewed pseudo-scientific thinking surely contributed to the dehumanizing sexual culture in which we now live just as much as did his extravagant claims. He contributed to redefining the

---

"Demographics of the Gay and Lesbian Population in the United States: Evidence from Available Systematic Data Sources," *Demography* 37, no. 2 (May 2000), pp. 139–54.

8 Jennifer Roback Morse, "Kinsey is Dead: Long Live Kinsey," *National Catholic Register*, July 15, 2005, http://www.ncregister.com/site/article/kinsey_is_dead_long_live_kinsey/.

meaning of sex from babies and bonding to fun and freedom. Indeed, famed anthropologist Margaret Mead criticized Kinsey for his reductionist approach to the complexities of human sexuality. She said that he took "sexual behavior out of its inter-personal context . . . reducing it to the simple act of elimination." As she put it caustically, "The book suggests no way of choosing between a woman and a sheep."[9]

But the ordinary American was not checking data or pondering metaphysics. What the Greatest Generation heard was Kinsey's passion for a new view of themselves, their sexuality, and the place of sex in society. He called out to the part of their souls that harbored sexual fantasies that society considered shameful and inappropriate. He whispered to them that they need not control these fantasies as they had been doing. These fantasies, if acted upon, would be harmless. In fact, suppressing these desires was perhaps making the ordinary decent American neurotic and sick. Kinsey suggested that they were chumps for restraining themselves. He created a new storyline for the average American. Society's sexual restrictions were repressive. Those who transgressed those restrictions were heroes.

So how did this man Kinsey burst onto the scene and change Americans' perceptions of themselves and their neighbors? How did he change people's views of what counted as normal? The answer is simple: the Rockefeller Foundation. They provided him with grant money. The foundation financed his purchase of video equipment and

---

[9]   She also criticized him for upsetting the balance between ignorance and knowledge upon which social restraint depended; quoted in Jones, *Alfred C. Kinsey*, p. 579.

the hiring of a photographer who filmed people engaged in various sex acts. One of the foundation's officer's, Allan Gregg, wrote the preface to the male volume.[10] The Rockefeller Foundation remains proud of its funding of Kinsey to this day.[11] It's no exaggeration to say that no one would have heard of Alfred Kinsey if it weren't for the Rockefeller Foundation. He would've been an unknown bug doctor with a pathological masturbation and pornography problem. If the Rockefellers don't count as elites, no one does.

Elite Opinion and the *Griswold* Case

Elites also played a pivotal role in the landmark 1965 case *Griswold v. Connecticut.* A subtext running through secondary sources favorable to *Griswold* is that all the best, right-thinking progressive people supported birth control. No modern author comes right out and says so exactly, but once you look for it, the message is unmistakable. Books such as Jonathan Eig's *The Birth of the Pill: How Four Crusaders Reinvented Sex and Launched a Revolution*[12] and David Garrow's *Liberty and Sexuality: The Right to Privacy and the Making of Roe v Wade* take the righteousness of *Griswold* for granted.

---

10   Allan Gregg, preface to *Sexual Behavior in the Human Male* (Philadelphia: W. B. Saunders, 1948), p. v.

11   The Rockefeller Foundation has a whole page on its website devoted to its support of Kinsey's work. "Kinsey Reports," The Rockefeller Foundation, accessed November 12, 2013, http://rockefeller100.org/exhibits/show/health/kinsey-reports, last.

12   Jonathan Eig, *The Birth of the Pill: How Four Crusaders Reinvented Sex and Launched a Revolution* (New York: Norton, 2014).

Garrow recounts the history of attempts to repeal the anti-contraception statute in Connecticut. He begins with legislative battles as early as 1925 and goes through *Griswold* in 1965. Along the way, he illustrates how well-connected the birth control movement was. For instance, in 1952, the Planned Parenthood League of Connecticut received "telephone calls from the campaign manager for Republican Senate contender Prescott Bush. The manager 'asked that the Planned Parenthood court case be postponed for the sake of Mr. Bush's campaign.'"[13] By 1962, when CBS News did a story on the case that became *Griswold*, narrator Eric Sevareid referred to it as "the Yale project,"[14] owing to the heavy involvement of Yale faculty, particularly from the medical and law schools.

Over the years, advocates for repealing the anti-contraception statute included:

- Professor Charles-Edward A. Winslow, who had founded the public health program at Yale,
- Yale medical school faculty member Herbert Thoms,
- Episcopalian clergyman Reverend William T. Hooper,
- Katherine Hepburn (mother of the actress of the same name),
- Lillian Leiterman Joseph (whose husband operated a successful grocery store chain), who financed a birth control clinic in Hartford,

---

[13]   David J. Garrow, *Liberty and Sexuality: The Right to Privacy and the Making of Roe v Wade* (NY: Macmillan Publishing, 1994), p. 124.

[14]   Ibid., p. 214.

- Clarence Gamble, heir to the Procter and Gamble fortune, who was actively subsidizing the establishment of new clinics (Garrow does not mention Gamble's long-standing involvement with the eugenics movement.),
- Anne Chase Hart of the family which founded Chase Brass Company,
- Yale Law School professor Edwin Borchard,
- Yale Law School professor Fowler V. Harper, whose wife, Miriam, held the social work position at Yale's marriage consultation service that was subsidized by Planned Parenthood League of Connecticut,
- St. Louis vaginal foam manufacturer Joseph Sunnen, which provided funding,
- Charles Lee Buxton, chairman of Yale's ob-gyn department, who became the lead plaintiff in an early case in 1957,
- Jean and Marvin Durning, two Yale graduate students, who were plaintiffs in one of the cases,[15]
- and Yale civil liberties law professor Tom Emerson, who was lead counsel on the *Griswold* case.[16]

Who were these "people in the lower income brackets and

---

[15] Ibid., pp. 29, 36, 37, 49, 103, 135, 139–40, 143, 146–47.

[16] We can observe a similar pattern leading up to the *Roe v. Wade* decision. California Committee for Therapeutic Abortion (CCTA) was financed by Joseph Sunnen, the same contraceptive foam manufacturer who helped finance *Griswold*. In 1969, Charles Munger and Warren and Susan Buffett financed the *Belous* case, the California abortion case leading up to *Roe*. Ibid., pp. 306, 365.

lower educational brackets—the people who need it most?" As social historians have long noted, poorer and more marginalized people often don't leave written records of their views. We must resort to indirect evidence from other sources to infer the views of the least educated and lower income brackets.

Garrow reports one telling incident from 1935. Referring to a clinic which gave out birth control, and which was funded by the wife of successful grocery chain owner:

> The Hartford clinic now had over 200 patients, of whom, more than 50% were Catholics. The printing of that statistic energized one Hartford priest, Rev. Andrew J. Kelly of St. Anthony's Roman Catholic Church, who alleged that the Hartford Public Welfare Department and doctors at Hartford Hospital were instructing women clients to go to the Maternal Health Center under the threat of losing their aid if they did not. "Busybody humanitarians from West Hartford," a wealthy suburb, should not "foist their kind of morality" on city residents, Kelly declared. Katharine Hepburn immediately denounced the allegation of coercion, but welfare department officials and hospital doctors offered only vague comments on this issue of referrals, with one physician telling the *Hartford Courant* that, "It is too bad the subject has to be brought up."[17]

---

[17]   Ibid., pp. 37, 40–41.

In other words, the allegations embarrassed the birth control advocates. But they never denied the allegations.

This same Fr. Kelly added that Margaret Sanger had once advocated requiring advance licensing before a woman could have children. When Sanger called the Hartford *Courant* to deny it, Fr. Kelly refused to back down. He cited a 1934 Sanger article, her own words, in print.[18]

Incidentally, these early events in Connecticut took place around the same time, 1936–38, that the federal government was introducing birth control programs in Puerto Rico. These programs were widely criticized, and not only by the Catholic Church. Puerto Rican nationalists denounced the program as imperialist. Suspicions were heightened when "a letter written by Cornelius Rhoads, a physician working in San Juan's Presbyterian Hospital under a Rockefeller foundation grant, became public. . . . Rhoads wrote, 'The Puerto Ricans . . . are beyond doubt the dirtiest, laziest, most degenerate and thievish race of men ever inhabiting this sphere. . . . What the island needs is not public health work but a tidal wave or something to totally exterminate the population.'"[19]

The Catholics in Connecticut were largely recent immigrants of modest means, precisely the economically marginal and less educated part of the population. The "native stock" of New England had a deep-seated and long-standing animus against Catholics going all the way back to the earliest

18 Ibid., p. 94.
19 Donald T. Critchlow, *Intended Consequences: Birth Control, Abortion and the Federal Government in Modern America* (New York: Oxford University Press, 1999), pp. 36–38.

days of the New England settlements. They regarded Catholic immigrants from Ireland, Italy, and Poland as exactly the wrong sort of people to be having lots of children. These poor people, working long and hard just to keep themselves together financially, were not able to defend themselves in the legislatures, in the court of polite public opinion, or, in the end, in the actual court system. Nonetheless, it was not unusual for them to write letters to their elected representatives.

In 1935, the head of the Connecticut Birth Control League complained, "We thought we had a fighting chance but the Senate has had an almost complete reversal. The reason is simply that they have had a FLOOD OF MAIL FROM THEIR CATHOLIC CONSTITUENTS."[20] In 1942, in nearby Massachusetts, the voters overwhelmingly rejected a referendum legalizing contraception for married women for whom a pregnancy would threaten their health.[21] In 1953, Catholics essentially dared the Planned Parenthood League to put a referendum on the ballot knowing that they could soundly defeat it. The Planned Parenthood League of Connecticut remained staunchly opposed to any referendum.[22]

In the main, however, it fell to the representatives of those Catholic immigrant communities to mount a defense of their traditional morals. Clergy such as the previously-mentioned Fr. Kelly regularly presented the Catholic position in the legislature. In 1945, Louise Fisher appeared on behalf of

---

[20] Garrow, *Liberty and Sexuality*, p. 36 (emphasis in original).
[21] Ibid., p. 101.
[22] Ibid., pp. 126–27.

the Diocese of Hartford. She testified that twenty years of Planned Parenthood League of Connecticut publicity "has helped to tear down the moral fiber of our young people," leading to a new wave of "free love and trial marriages."[23]

Catholic publications had their own interpretation of the plight of the poor. They had an answer to some obvious questions: why did upper class ladies believe that access to diaphragm fittings was the highest priority for the lower classes? Why not advocate for better health care for those very same poor women so they could go to a private physician like their upper-class neighbors? Why not advocate for better jobs for the husbands of poor women? The *Catholic Transcript* declared: "The real problem is the rotten, inequitable economic system of which these people are the victims and of which many of the socially prominent birth prevention advocates are the vigilant guardians and fat beneficiaries."[24]

Progressives and State-Sponsored Eugenics

"The religious debate over birth control did not begin with the legalization of contraceptives; it began with eugenics."[25]

---

[23]   Ibid., p. 111.

[24]   Ibid., p. 96. The Catholics of Connecticut continued to oppose the legislative efforts to repeal the Comstock law. In 1963, however, Richard Cardinal Cushing of Boston declared that the Roman Catholic Church no longer advocated anti-contraception statutes such as those in Massachusetts and Connecticut. Without organized Catholic opposition, the cultural tide began to change. Ibid., pp. 217–18. I have yet to find a satisfactory explanation for this change of policy in 1963.

[25]   Kathleen A. Tobin, *The American Religious Debate over Birth Control, 1907 to 1937* (Jefferson, NC: McFarland and Company, 2001), p. 46.

So says an astute student of the religious debate that began in the 1920s and 1930s, obviously well prior to *Griswold*. Opposition to artificial birth control had been common to all Christian denominations and was not just a Catholic position. Mainline Protestants such as Episcopalians, Lutherans, and Presbyterians had shared the ancient Christian teaching opposing contraception going all the way back to Calvin and Luther themselves.[26] The first religious group to seriously challenge this orthodoxy was the Anglican Communion. The Anglicans approved the use of artificial birth control for married couples for serious reasons at its Lambeth Convention in 1930. Margaret Sanger had been in the background of that meeting lobbying for this change.[27]

Once this change took place, the doorway was opened to "race betterment through eugenics." The "old stock" of New England Protestants were concerned about differential fertility between themselves and the "new stock" of immigrants. The mainline proponents of birth control and "race betterment" fully understood that the "lesser stocks" of poor immigrants, whom the "old stock" of Puritan mainline Christians so feared, were largely Catholics. This anxiety of being out-populated was a continual undercurrent in the discussion of birth regulation by the mainline Protestants going all the way back to the post-Civil War period.[28]

---

[26]   Allan Carlson, *Godly Seed: American Evangelicals Confront Birth Control, 1873-1973* (New Brunswick NJ: Transaction Publishers, 2012), pp. 7–10.

[27]   Ibid., pp. 101–3.

[28]   Ibid., pp. 51–75.

In the meantime, Evangelical Christians[29] thoroughly disapproved of contraception. They associated it with the millennialism of the Social Gospel, of which they also disapproved. Evangelicals regarded artificial birth control as a crime against nature comparable to the "sin of Onan," the biblical basis for the prohibition on masturbation. Evangelical outlets such as the Moody Bible Institute, the Bible Institute of Los Angeles, and the *Christian Worker* magazine editorialized against contraception in the 1920s.[30]

Advocates of birth control and eugenics recognized the Catholic Church as their most serious opponent in terms of both numbers of people and the sophistication of the arguments they could mount. Margaret Sanger specifically drove the Evangelical Protestants into the pro-birth control column. She used the ever-reliable anti-Catholic sentiment of this group to overcome their natural aversion to birth control and to the Progressive Social Gospel Mainline.[31] Thanks to Sanger's efforts, by the time of the *Griswold v. Connecticut* decision, the entire country considered opposition to birth control to be a uniquely Catholic position.

Humanist of the Year Leo Pfeffer, whom we met in the previous chapter, cuts through the lofty rhetoric of the birth control advocates and makes explicit the anti-poor bias of this movement. Pfeffer also observes that the controversy

---

[29]   This term refers in a general way to conservative Protestantism. Alan Carlson traces the rise of this term, first as a more attractive alternative to the term *Fundamentalist*, and later as the last bastion of Protestant opposition to artificial contraception. Ibid., pp. 113–18.

[30]   Ibid., pp. 88–91.

[31]   Ibid., pp. 79–108.

over the domestic policy taking place in Connecticut was part of the larger issue of the US government's advocacy of contraception as part of its foreign policy:

> The national government already established this policy as part of its program to aid underdeveloped countries, but the States could hardly follow suit as long as their own laws forbade the practice. After all, how can a city allow or instruct doctors and nurses in municipal hospitals to counsel welfare mothers giving birth in these hospitals regarding birth control or even allow advertisements of Planned Parenthood groups to appear in municipal buses and subways when contraception is a crime against the State?[32]

The grand dame of birth control herself, Margaret Sanger, was a professed and unabashed advocate of eugenics. Her views on undesirable people having too many children are simply too egregious to overlook. Her statements to this effect are too numerous to leave any doubt that she meant it.[33]

"More children from the fit, less from the unfit—that is the chief issue of birth control," proclaimed an editorial quoted in her magazine in 1919.[34] In her 1922 book *The*

---

[32] Leo Pfeffer, *God, Caesar and the Constitution: The Court as Referee of Church-state Confrontation* (Boston: Beacon Press, 1975), p. 96.

[33] Angela Franks, *Margaret Sanger's Eugenic Legacy: The Control of Female Fertility* (Jefferson, NC: McFarland & Co Publishers, 2005).

[34] "Intelligent or Unintelligent Birth Control?" *American Medicine*, in *The Birth Control Review* III, no. 5, accessed September 27, 2013, http://library.lifedynamics.com/Birth%20Control%20 Review/1919-05%20May.pdf.

Pivot of Civilization, she called for the sterilization of genetically inferior races and the insane and feeble-minded. The board of her American Birth Control League included a worldwide collection of racist ideologues.[35]

Old Wine in New Wineskins: Rockefellers, Eugenics, and the Population Council

In the meantime, the Rockefeller Foundation, under the direction of John D. Rockefeller, Jr., supported various eugenics causes in the 1930s.[36] John D. Rockefeller, Jr.'s son, John D. Rockefeller III, believed passionately that no serious world problem could be solved without controlling population growth.[37] He was convinced that contraception and abortion were the only practical ways to control population growth. His money and influence were crucial in creating the Contraceptive Ideology.

Rockefeller III was involved in a variety of private sector initiatives, all with the long-term goal of reducing population and, most importantly, getting the US government to commit itself to population control as a matter of public

---

[35]   Robert Zubrin, *Merchants of Despair: Radical Environmentalists, Criminal Pseudo-Scientists, and the Fatal Cult of Antihumanism* (New York: Encounter Books, 2012), p. 88.

[36]   Wikipedia, s.v. "Rockefeller Foundation," https://en.wikipedia. org/wiki/Rockefeller_Foundation. The most notorious of these eugenics causes included the laboratory of Otmar Freiherr von Verschuer, for whom Josef Mengele worked before he went to Auschwitz.

[37]   "John D. Rockefeller became increasingly alarmed by the crowded conditions he saw during his travels in Asia and Africa following World War II." Critchlow, *Intended Consequences*, p. 20.

policy. He was unable to persuade his father's Rockefeller Foundation to take up the population control cause. So Rockefeller III organized the Population Council in 1952 as an independent entity with exactly that purpose.[38] He used the Population Council as a vehicle for bringing together like-minded people of means and influence to shape public policy and private practice. The council financed a series of meetings at Notre Dame University with Catholic scholars thought to be persuadable on the birth control issue.[39] Rockefeller III met with Pope Paul VI in the months before the pontiff released the long-awaited "birth control encyclical," *Humanae Vitae*. There is even some evidence to suggest that Rockefeller offered to write the encyclical for him.[40]

The Population Council sponsored contraception promotion and distribution projects overseas. It worked with governments such as South Korea, Pakistan, Malaysia, Ceylon, Barbados, Hong Kong, Taiwan, Tunisia, Thailand, and the United Arab Republic. By 1968, the council had field officers stationed in approximately fifty nations, a staff of over ninety professionals, and a budget of over $11 million.[41] Rockefeller felt the US government should be contributing to these efforts by supporting family planning through its foreign assistance aid program. Beginning in the late 1950s,

---

[38] Ibid., p. 21.

[39] Ibid., pp. 62–64.

[40] E. Michael Jones, *Libido Dominandi: Sexual Liberation and Political Control* (South Bend IN: St. Augustine's Press, 2000), p. 435.

[41] Critchlow, *Intended Consequences*, pp. 27–28.

Rockefeller increasingly lobbied American policymakers to pursue more activist public policies.[42]

But the population control cause encountered resistance and not only from Catholics. Black nationalists saw birth control as a means of race control and even genocide. Just as Puerto Rican nationalists had resisted the birth control programs on the island in the '30s, so some Hispanic leaders resisted on the mainland in the '70s. When Rockefeller formed the Commission on Population Growth and the American Future, he, to his credit, included on the commission some members who were closer to the lower income communities likely to be the targets of population planning.

To his discredit, however, he did not take their advice seriously. Paul Bertau Cornely was a professor at the historically black Howard University. Grace Olivares was a Hispanic lawyer from Phoenix and the first Hispanic woman to graduate from the Notre Dame Law School. Cornely and Olivares pushed the commission to take up problems related to unemployment, poverty, and income distribution.[43] These lone ethnic minorities on the commission opposed the majority recommendation to provide contraceptive information and services to minors, including voluntary sterilization. When society accepts giving contraceptive advice and services to minors, they argued, "then we are striking at the foundation and the roots of family life, which are already weakened by the misuse of affluence and technology." Without addressing society's other responsibilities to the poor,

---

[42]   Ibid., p. 41.
[43]   Ibid., p. 162.

the "contraceptive approach to minors is the cheapest and most irresponsible way for our society to solve the problem of teenage pregnancy."

This argument drew little support from the commission. The majority concluded that access to contraceptive services for minors would not necessarily lead to sexual irresponsibility. The recommendation on abortion and contraceptive services to minors easily won a twelve to two vote with Cornely and Olivares dissenting.[44] Thus, ethnic minorities were not all on board with the Contraceptive Ideology as promoted by Rockefeller's Population Council in 1970. To this day, some African Americans continue to resist the pro-abortion, pro-contraception ideology on the same grounds as their predecessors. They believe it is a form of soft genocide and that black participation amounts to race suicide.[45]

Long-term, however, the idea of separating sex from reproduction needed a more appealing rationale, something more than population control for the poor and casual sex for the rich. "Feminism" provided what was lacking. John D. Rockefeller III worked out a new formula. He figured that pushing feminism to the foreground, and population control to the background, would improve the prospects of both causes. And so it did. And so it has been doing ever since.

Rockefeller's speech at the Third World Population

---

[44]   Ibid., pp. 165–66.

[45]   See, for example, this news release from July 25, 2016, on the drop in black fertility: Walter B. Hoye, "In 163 Years the Total Black Fertility Rate Dropped 77%—God Help Us!" *Christian Newswire*, July 25, 2016, http://christiannewswire.com/news/5004578195.html.

Conference in Bucharest in 1974 was the turning point. Rockefeller advanced the idea that promoting women's rights was a key to reducing world population, both directly and indirectly. Directly, people had known for some time that women's education reduced fertility. Eugenicists were less than enthused about making this particular point. After all, they wanted to see the most educated classes reproducing the most. Promoting female education as a brake on fertility was counter-productive for their overall eugenic goal.[46]

But the indirect impact of promoting women's development overcame this classic eugenic concern. By framing his arguments in terms of women's education and empowerment, Rockefeller distanced himself from the old-style population control agenda. He garnered the support of many female delegates from around the world who were deeply suspicious of population control and did not want "reproductive imperialism" or "reproductive colonialism."

Rockefeller's speech at Bucharest was an initial step away from the old rhetoric of population control hysteria. It embraced the language of empowerment and female betterment. It was much more attractive than his previous persona. The very same policies that had been staples of "reproductive colonialism" became repackaged as policies of female empowerment.

---

[46]   Matthew Connelly, *Fatal Misconceptions: The Struggle to Control World Population* (Cambridge: Harvard University Press, 2008), p. 332. Rockefeller's speech was reprinted in the journal of the Population Council, John D Rockefeller, III "Population Growth, the Role of the Developed World," *Population and Development Review* 4(3) (1978) pp. 509–16.

It's true that many feminists spoke out against the coercive aspects of many of these policies.[47] This criticism forced the population controllers to change their rhetoric, if not their policies. Sadly, it's also true that coercive "family planning" policies continued in the immediate aftermath of the Bucharest conference right down to this very day.

In India, for instance, the Emergency Period from 1975–77 included a mass sterilization program, complete with humanitarian rhetoric.[48] "Foreign donors closely watched these developments. They responded by increasing their support."[49] In a table entitled "Reproductive rights and wrongs," anthropologist and human rights activist Steven Mosher reports on systematic abuses around the world dating from the 1970s to the present day. These abuses include sterilization without informed consent, human experiments with unproven contraceptives without informed consent, quotas, bribes, sanctions, and sterilization campaigns targeting minority populations.[50] If one includes the many policies which utilize the "soft coercion" of government-sponsored educational propaganda and incentive programs, we can see

---

[47]   Dr. Betsy Hartmann, for instance, whom we met in a previous chapter.

[48]   Steven W. Mosher, *Population Control: Real Costs, Illusory Benefit* (New Brunswick, NJ: Transaction Publishers, 2009) p. 142. Betsy Hartmann, *Reproductive Rights and Wrongs: The Global Politics of Population Control* (New York, NY: Harper and Row, 1995), pp. 251–54. Connelly, *Fatal Misconceptions*, pp. 320–24.

[49]   Connelly, *Fatal Misconceptions*, p. 321.

[50]   Mosher, *Population Control*, pp. 128–29, table. See pp. 121–54 for explanatory text.

that the impulse for the elites controlling the fertility of the poor is widespread indeed.

Conclusion: The Beat Goes On

Rockefeller was the first, but certainly not the last, of the very rich who believe that we must do something about too many poor people. In 2014 alone, George Soros contributed a cool $1 million to the Center for Reproductive Rights and another $1.65 million to Planned Parenthood.[51] Warren Buffett has spent over $1 billion supporting abortion, Planned Parenthood, and related organizations in the United States over the past decade.[52] In 2014 alone, the Susan Thompson Buffet Foundation, with assets of over $2 billion, gave $58 million to various Planned Parenthood affiliates in the United States, another $9.6 million to the International Planned Parenthood Federation, and $28 million to Marie Stopes International, USA, and contributed to organizations too numerous to list, including NARAL Pro-Choice America, National Institute for Reproductive Health, National Latina Institute for Reproductive Health, National Network of Abortion Funds, National Women's Law Center, and so on.[53]

---

51   See the Form 990 for the Open Society Institute for 2014, Part XV, Line 3, http://www.guidestar.org/FinDocuments/2014/137/029/2014-137029285-0c25cf2f-F.pdf.

52   Katie Yoder, "Warren Buffett: The Billion Dollar King of Abortion," Media Research Center, http://www.mrc.org/articles/warren-buffett-billion-dollar-king-abortion.

53   Form 990 for Susan Thompson Buffett Foundation (with assets of over $2 billion,), accessed August 20, 2016, Part XV, Line 3,http://www.guidestar.org/FinDocuments/2014/476/032/2014-476032365-0b9faf84-F.pdf.

Some of these organizations provide contraception and abortion. Others are dedicated to changing public opinion or public policy. One reporter calculated that the top twenty donors to Hillary Clinton's 2016 campaign for president could fund Planned Parenthood's entire operations at its current levels for the next fifty years. These same donors could replace all the taxpayer money going to Planned Parenthood for over a century.[54] But that's not how these wealthy individuals choose to spend their money. Instead they try to elect the next president of the United States. They're investing in what the government will do. They're using their wealth to manipulate people's opinions and to control the outcome of the political process.

No one elected George Soros or Warren Buffett to anything. No one grants them the authority to shape political institutions so they can use the government to recreate the world in their own image and likeness. I don't begrudge these people their wealth. An extravagant lifestyle doesn't bother me. In fact, I would prefer they spend their money on self-indulgence rather than doing what they're doing. They aren't just spending money on themselves; they're trying to shape the world in which the rest of us must live.

I very much begrudge them that.

---

[54]   Chuck Ross, "Clinton's Billionaire Donors Could Fund Planned Parenthood For the Next 120 Years," The Daily Caller, August 2, 2016, http://dailycaller.com/2016/08/02/clintons-billionaire-donors-could-fund-planned-parenthood-for-the-next-120-years/.

CHAPTER 6

Propaganda for the Contraceptive Ideology

Many of us want desperately to believe that we can have unlimited, problem-free sex, but this is wishful thinking. One might even call it a superstition: a belief we hold despite the evidence because we like the way the belief makes us feel.

People commonly think of superstition as the exclusive provenance of the illiterate masses, the inevitable result of their ignorance and fear. But this superstition did not take root in society because of uneducated poor people. On the contrary, the well-educated, wealthy elites of society created this idea out of their imaginations. They've been working diligently to make it real throughout society. Since their idea is untrue, it cannot sustain itself.

The idea that sex makes babies can sustain itself without either force or propaganda. People receive direct evidence on a regular basis that sex makes babies. Convincing people that it's both possible and desirable to act as if sex does NOT make babies, now that's a real trick. This is a complex claim consisting of scientific, empirical claims and moral, philosophical propositions. Like a house of cards, if any one of them is disproven, the whole structure could be threatened. Hence, the sexual revolutionaries invest an enormous amount of time, energy, and money in their propaganda efforts.

Let's look at what one must believe to embrace the Contraceptive Ideology.

1. Contraception works perfectly.
2. The use of contraception entails no negative health, psychological, or social consequences.
3. There are no realistic alternatives to artificial contraception.
4. Abortion is available as a backup in case of contraceptive failure.
5. Abortion has no negative health, psychological, or social consequences.
6. There are no realistic alternatives to abortion for women with unplanned or ill-timed pregnancies.
7. And, most important of all, sexual activity is necessary for a happy, healthy, and fulfilled life.

Any evidence that contradicts these points must be suppressed. Otherwise, people will begin to question the whole Contraceptive Ideology and its empty promises. Yet these points are obviously debatable. In fact, some are self-contradictory. For instance, if contraception works perfectly, why do we even need to consider abortion as a backup plan? Let's examine these claims one by one.

Contraception Works Perfectly (False)

Contraception Sometimes Fails

As noted earlier, the average failure rate of contraception in general is around 9 or 10 percent. As also noted, the failure rates vary by demographic group. This is most likely due to a combination of factors. Young people do not always fully grasp and act upon the possibility that contraception might sometimes fail. (Though it may surprise some people, immaturity is rampant among the young.) The young and the poor may be using their contraceptive methods inconsistently or incorrectly. Younger women are, in general, more fertile than older women. So even without contraception, the probability of pregnancy is lower for older women.

The professionals understand this, of course. Princeton population studies professor James Trussell once stated, "The Pill is an outdated method because it does not work well enough. It is very difficult for ordinary women to take a pill every single day. The beauty of the implant or the IUD is that you can forget about them." Even emergency contraception "is not a magic bullet. If you want to seriously reduce unintended pregnancies, . . . you can only do it with implants and IUDs."[1]

Unfortunately for women, these long-acting reversible contraceptive methods are among the most dangerous to their health. This brings us to our next point.

---

[1]   Rebecca Smith, "'Contraceptive Pill is outdated and does not work well', expert warns," *The Telegraph*, June 25, 2008, http://www.telegraph.co.uk/news/uknews/2193112/Contraceptive-Pill-is-outdated-and-does-not-work-well-expert-warns.html.

Contraception Entails No Negative Health, Psychological, or Social Consequences (False)

Combined Oral Contraceptives Increase the Risk of Strokes and Heart Attacks

Contraception has numerous costs associated with it. Consider these women:

- Nancy Berry died from a heart attack when she was sixteen years old. [2]
- Charlotte Porter died from a blood clot when she was seventeen from a medication she was taking to control her acne.[3]
- Trudi Banning, a twenty-two-year-old "super-fit" female soldier, was stricken with a stroke that created gangrene in her digestive system and ultimately left her infertile.[4]
- Maria Santa, a healthy and gifted 17-year-old ballerina, died from a blood clot.[5]

---

[2]   Claire Hu, "Nancy took the Pill at 16 . . . and Died," *Evening Standard*, March 4, 2002, https://www.standard.co.uk/news/nancy-took-the-pill-at-16-and-died-6311225.html.

[3]   Angella Johnson, "My beautiful cheerleader daughter died in agony all because she took this acne drug: Heartbroken mother fights to ban dangerous pill," *Daily Mail*, June 8, 2013, http://www.dailymail.co.uk/news/article-2338072/Dianette-My-beautiful-cheerleader-daughter-died-agony-took-acne-drug.html.

[4]   Lois Rogers, "Have 800 women been killed by the Pill?" *Mail Online*, February 12, 2014, http://www.dailymail.co.uk/femail/article-2558029/Have-800-women-killed-Pill-The-alarming-dangers-called-generation-contraceptives.html.

[5]   Mark Hodges, "17-year-old ballerina's death caused by birth control pill, doctors believe," *LifeSiteNews*, April 27, 2016, https://

What do all these women have in common? They were taking the so-called "third generation" of birth control pills, such as Femodene and Dianette. Each one of these stories lists other women who have been harmed by hormonal contraception.

Hormonal contraception has been implicated as a risk factor for heart attacks and strokes, cancer, and even glaucoma.[6] These studies are well-known within the medical

www.lifesitenews.com/news/17-year-old-ballerinas-death-caused-by-birth-control-pill-doctors-believe.

6   Øjvind Lidegaard et al., "Thrombotic Stroke and Myocardial Infarction with Hormonal Contraception," New England Journal of Medicine, June 14, 2012 366(24):2257, http://www.nejm.org/doi/full/10.1056/NEJMoa1111840. This study of 1.6 million Danish women showed that women who used oral contraceptives at an intermediate dosage had a risk of strokes that was 1.3 to 2.3 times as high as the risk among non-users of contraceptives and risks for heart attacks that were 1.3 to 2.1 times as high as non-users.

J.M. Kemmerman et al., "Risk of Arterial Thrombosis in Relation to Oral Contraceptives (RATIO) Study: Oral Contraceptives and the Risk of Ischemic Stroke," Stroke, May 2002; 33:1202-1208, http://stroke.ahajournals.org/content/33/5/1202. This study of Dutch women found that women using any type of oral contraceptives had a risk of stroke that was 2.3 times higher than women using no oral contraceptives.

Another study performed a "meta-analysis" of the relationship between contraception and strokes and heart attacks from fourteen independent studies. The conclusion: "current use of low-dose Oral Contraceptives significantly increases the risk of both cardiac and vascular arterial events, including a significant risk of vascular arterial complications with third generation Oral Contraceptives." The risk of strokes and heart attacks was roughly twice as high for current users of oral contraceptives (OCs) compared with non-users. And incidentally, this study did not find that more recent, "third generation" of new types of pills community but media and medical professionals routinely minimize these risks. For instance, a European review prompted the UK's Medicines and Healthcare Products Regulatory Agency (MHRA) to write to the nation's 60,000 general practitioners warning them to be alert to the risk of life-threatening clots in patients using Femodene, Marvilon, or Mercilon. However, at the same time, Dr. Sarah Branch of the MHRA's Vigilance and Risk Management of Medicines Division asserted that contraceptive pills are safe and highly effective: "The benefits associated with their use far outweigh their risks. These have been recently reviewed at a European level and no important new evidence has emerged. The review simply confirmed what we already know, that the

---

were safer than the earlier generations. The summary risk estimates associated with current use of low-dose OCs were 1.84 for myocardial infarctions and 2.12 for ischemic strokes. The overall summary odds ratio for both outcomes was 2.01. Second generation OCs were associated with a significant increased risk of both myocardial infarction and ischemic stroke events (1.85 and 2.54 respectively); and third-generation OCs, for ischemic stroke outcome only 2.03. Jean-Patrice Baillargeon et al., "Association between the Current Use of Low-Dose Oral Contraceptives and Cardiovascular Arterial Disease: A Meta-Analysis," The Journal of Clinical Endocrinology & Metabolism 90, no. 7 (July 1, 2005), http://dx.doi.org/10.1210/jc.2004-1958.

"Combined Estrogen-Progestogen Contraceptives and Combined Estrogen-Progestogen Menopausal Therapy," IARC Monographs on the Evaluation of Carcinogenic Risks to Humans 91 (2007), p. 175.

Yes, glaucoma. American Academy of Ophthalmology, "Long-Term Oral Contraceptive Users Are Twice As Likely To Have Serious Eye Disease," Ophthalmology Web, November 19, 2013, http://www.ophthalmologyweb.com/1315-News/150975-Long-Term-Oral-Contraceptive-Users-Are-Twice-As-Likely-To-Have-Serious-Eye-Disease/.

risk associated with all combined hormonal contraceptives is small."[7] If the risks are so small, why did this agent of the State write to all the general practice physicians in the UK warning them of "small" risks?

This pattern of minimizing the risk showed up in the media reporting around a major Danish study of 1.6 million women implicating hormonal contraception in both strokes and heart attacks. WebMD published a piece entitled "Heart, Stroke Risk Low with Birth Control Pills: No-Estrogen and Lowest-Estrogen Contraceptives Safest, Study Finds." "Risk today is significantly lower than it was decades ago in the era of high-dose pills," says University of Copenhagen professor Ojvind Lidegaard, MD, who led the research. Arizona State University researcher Diana B. Petitti, MD, MPH, writes that the Danish study should reassure women and their doctors about the safety of oral contraceptives."[8]

Tell that to the parents of Nancy Berry, Charlotte Porter, and Maria Santa. They're not interested in whether it is "lower than it was decades ago." They want to know how risky it is now. And they want justice for their daughters and protection for other people's daughters. Some of them are suing the drug manufacturers.

---

[7]   Lois Rogers, "Have 800 women been killed by the Pill?" Mail Online, February 12, 2014, http://www.dailymail.co.uk/femail/ article-2558029/Have-800-women-killed-Pill-The-alarming-dangers-called-generation-contraceptives.html, emphasis added.

[8]   Salynn Boyles, "Heart, Stroke Risk Low With Birth Control Pills: No-Estrogen and Lowest-Estrogen Contraceptives Safest, Study Finds," WebMD, June 13, 2012, http://www.webmd.com/ sex/birth-control/news/20120613/heart-stroke-risk-birth-control-pills?page=2.

The *Boston Globe* published an article on this study entitled "Birth control pills raise risk of heart attacks and strokes, but only slightly." Here's a quote: "I would say in many ways, this is a good news story," said Dr. Isaac Schiff, chief of obstetrics and gynecology at Massachusetts General Hospital. "This is a lengthy, large study that helps to confirm that the birth control pill is relatively safe, recognizing that no drug is 100 percent safe."[9]

The same Danish study of 1.6 million women also looked at the impact of smoking on strokes and heart attacks. They found that smoking is associated with a 1.6 times as high a risk of stroke and a 3.6 times as high a risk of heart attack as not smoking.[10] Looking closely at the chart shows that stroke risk associated with smoking is comparable to the risk associated with the three forms of hormonal contraception *most commonly used* by the women surveyed for the study.[11]

---

[9]   No, I did not make up this headline: Deborah Kotz, "Birth control pills raise risk of heart attacks and strokes, but only slightly," *Boston Globe,* June 13, 2012, http://www.boston.com/dailydose/2012/06/13/birth-control-pills-raise-risk-heart-attacks-and-strokes-but-only-slightly/G3wQiKMFSVbc9W7HKJeWqO/story.html.

[10] Øjvind Lidegaard et al., "Thrombotic Stroke and Myocardial Infarction with Hormonal Contraception," *New England Journal of Medicine,* June 14, 2012 366(24):2257, table 1, http://www.nejm.org/doi/full/10.1056/NEJMoa1111840.

[11] Ibid., table 2. Gestodene at 30-40-microgram dosages had 1.3 million woman years of use, and an increased risk factor of 1.8, and Gestodene at the 20-microgram dosage has over 564,000 woman years of use and a risk factor of 1.7. Desogestrel at the 20-microgram dosage has almost 700,000 woman years of use and a risk factor of 1.5 compared with non-users of hormonal contraception.

Even more disturbing are the results from this same Danish study for long-acting reversible hormonal contraception (LARC). The risk of strokes associated with LARCs is greater than the risk associated with smoking. The risk of stroke for smokers is 1.6 times greater than for non-smokers. Yet users of the contraceptive patch are 3.15 times more likely, and users of the vaginal ring are 2.5 times more likely to have a stroke than non-users of contraception.[12]

Did the *Boston Globe* even mention the comparison between smoking and the "acceptable" risks associated with combined oral contraceptives or LARCs? Crickets. *WebMD*? Nada.

Smoking has been all but banned, tobacco companies have been sued, and smokers have been socially shunned. By contrast, the government actively promotes the use of hormonal contraception while the media downplays the risks, even though "the first report on the occurrence of stroke in women using oral contraceptives was published in 1962, followed by many others."[13] Where is the FDA when you need them? But publicly admitting these risks associated with hormonal contraception would threaten the entire ideological house of cards. One could no longer seriously maintain that society should try to construct itself around the idea that sex is a sterile activity with no negative consequences.

---

[12]   Ibid., table 2, middle columns.

[13]   J.M. Kemmerman et al., "Risk of Arterial Thrombosis in Relation to Oral Contraceptives (RATIO) Study: Oral Contraceptives and the Risk of Ischemic Stroke," *Stroke*, May 2002; 33: 1202-1208, http://stroke.ahajournals.org/content/33/5/1202.

Combined Oral Contraceptives Are Carcinogenic

The World Health Organization has classified oral contraceptives as Group 1 carcinogens since at least 2005. However, they assured the public:

> As stated in IARC's review, the use of COCs (Combined Oral Contraceptives) modifies slightly the risk of cancer, increasing it in some sites (cervix, breast, liver), decreasing it in others (endometrium, ovary). Some of these data refer to older higher-dose COC preparations. Assessments based on risk-benefit calculations are carried out by different teams within WHO. Several WHO committees work on creating evidence-based family planning guidelines and on keeping them up-to-date on a continuous basis. They regularly review the safety of COCs and assess the balance of risks and benefits of COC use, and they have determined that for most healthy women, the health benefits clearly exceed the health risks.[14]

The International Agency for Research on Cancer reports that combined oral contraceptive increase the risk of breast cancer, cervical cancer, and liver cancer. At the same time, COCs have a protective effect against cancer in the endometrium and ovary.[15] This monograph concludes, "Combined

---

[14]   "Carcinogenicity of combined hormonal contraceptives and combined menopausal treatment," Department of Reproductive Health and Research, World Health Organization, September 2005, http://www.who.int/reproductivehealth/topics/ageing/cocs_hrt_statement.pdf.

[15]   "Combined Estrogen-Progestogen Contraceptives and Combined

oral estrogen-progestogen contraceptives are *carcinogenic to humans (Group 1)*. There is also convincing evidence in humans that these agents confer a protective effect against cancer of the endometrium and ovary."[16]

Contrast this guarded conclusion with the much stronger statement made in the same publication regarding menopausal hormone replacement therapy: "Overall evaluation: Combined estrogen–progestogen menopausal therapy is carcinogenic to humans."[17] No fooling around in that evaluation. No balancing of costs and benefits. No reassurance that experts are monitoring these medications for new evidence

---

Estrogen-Progestogen Menopausal Therapy," *IARC Monographs on the Evaluation of Carcinogenic Risks to Humans* 91 (2007), p. 175. A 164-page extract from this full 500-page report can be found at this web address: http://monographs.iarc.fr/ENG/ Monographs/vol91/mono91-6E.pdf. (IARC stands for International Agency for Research on Cancer. The agency is part of the World Health Organization. Further evidence on the association of COCs with cervical cancer can be found in Jennifer S. Smith, et al., "Cervical cancer and use of hormonal contraceptives: a systematic review," Lancet 2003; 361: 1159–67, April 5, 2003. Twenty-eight eligible studies were identified, together including 12,531 women with cervical cancer. Compared with non-users of oral contraceptives, the relative risks of cervical cancer increased with increasing duration of use: for durations of approximately less than 5 years, 5–9 years, and 10 or more years, respectively, the summary relative risks were 1·1 (95% CI 1·1–1·2), 1·6 (1·4–1·7), and 2·2 (1·9–2·4) for all women; and 0·9 (0·7–1·2), 1·3 (1·0–1·9), and 2·5 (1·6–3·9) for HPV positive women.

[16]   "Combined Estrogen-Progestogen Contraceptives and Combined Estrogen-Progestogen Menopausal Therapy," *IARC Monographs on the Evaluation of Carcinogenic Risks to Humans* 91 (2007). See pp. 3–5 for a complete list of participants in the conference which produced this volume.

[17]   Ibid.

and that women should feel fine about accepting the risks associated with hormone replacement therapy. After all, getting a good night's sleep is beneficial to your health, and embarrassment over continually dripping with sweat could be stressful for some women. Some women might be willing to accept the cancer risks for the lifestyle benefits of these medications. Most menopausal women are, after all, mature women capable of making decisions for themselves. But no word from our experts on that possibility. Why the double standard?

Combined Oral Contraceptives
Double the Risk of Glaucoma

"Research presented today, at the 117th Annual Meeting of the American Academy of Ophthalmology in New Orleans, has found that *women who have taken oral contraceptives for three or more years are twice as likely to suffer from glaucoma.*" In this same press release, the American Academy of Ophthalmology offered this advice: "The researchers caution gynecologists and ophthalmologists to be aware of the fact that oral contraceptives might play a role in glaucomatous diseases, and *inform patients to have their eyes screened* for glaucoma if they also have other risk factors."[18]

"Inform patients to have their eyes screened." They don't

---

[18]   "Long-Term Oral Contraceptive Users Are Twice As Likely To Have Serious Eye Disease," American Academy of Ophthalmology, November 19, 2013, http://www.ophthalmologyweb. com/1315-News/150975-Long-Term-Oral-Contraceptive-Users-Are-Twice-As-Likely-To-Have-Serious-Eye-Disease/, emphasis added.

caution women to reconsider their decision to take oral contraception. Maybe that's because the researchers realize that for the many women in their forties whom they area screening for glaucoma, the horse has already left the barn. But what about younger women who are still making crucial life choices? What about their mothers and doctors who are assisting and advising them? Shouldn't they consider the possibility of not taking hormonal contraception?

Non-Fatal Side Effects

Barbara Seamans alerted the public to the dangers of contraceptive pill use in her book *The Doctors' Case Against the Pill*.[19] Many of the problems she identified in 1969 are still with us. Young women continue to complain about weight gain,[20] moodiness, and irritability. They dislike being told by their doctors that the problems are all in their heads or to just switch to another brand of pills. Some feminists are still suspicious that the pharmaceutical industry is covering its tracks with the help of apologists with feminist credentials.[21]

A comprehensive review of the psychobehavioral effects

---

[19]   Barbara Seamans, *The Doctors' Case Against the Pill: 25th Anniversary Edition* (Atlanta: Hunter House Publishers, 1995).

[20]   Mags E. Beksinkska, et al., "Prospective Study of weight change in new adolescent users of DMPA, NET-EN, COC's, non-users and discontinuers of hormonal contraception," *Contraception*, 2010 January 8(1):30-34, http://www.ncbi.nlm.nih.gov/pmc/articles/PMC3764463/. Women using DMPA or NET-EN gained an average of 6.2 kg compared to average increases of 2.3 kg in the COC group, 2.8 kg in non-users and 2.8 kg among discontinuers.

[21]   Holly Grigg-Spall, *Sweetening the Pill, or How We Got Hooked on Hormonal Birth Control* (Alresford Hants, United Kingdom: John Hunt Publishing, 2013).

of hormonal contraceptive use found that women who use hormonal contraception report higher rates of depression, reduced sexual functioning, and higher interest in short-term sexual relationships compared to their naturally-cycling counterparts. Women using hormonal contraceptives exhibited more symptoms of borderline personality disorder (BPD), a disorder characterized by a pervasive pattern of instability in affect regulation, impulse control, interpersonal relationships, and self-image. Importantly, women with high pre-existing levels of BPD symptoms became significantly worse after starting hormonal contraceptive use.[22]

A recent study confirms women's complaints that the pill decreases libido and causes other sexual dysfunctions.

> Dr. Claudia Panzer, an endocrinologist in Denver, CO, and lead author of the study, noted that "it is important for *physicians prescribing oral contraceptives to point out to their patients, potential sexual side effects,* such as decreased desire, arousal, decreased lubrication and increased sexual pain. Also, if women present with these complaints, *it is crucial to recognize the link between sexual dysfunction and the oral contraceptive and not to attribute these complaints solely to psychological causes.*
>
> "There are approximately 100 million women worldwide who currently use oral contraceptives, so it is obvious that more extensive research investigations

---

[22]   Lisa L. M. Welling, "Psychobehavioral Effects of Hormonal Contraceptive Use," *Evolutionary Psychology*, 2013, 11(3): 718-742, http://evp.sagepub.com/content/11/3/147470491301100315. full.pdf.

are needed. The oral contraceptive has been around for over 40 years, but *no one had previously looked at the long-term effects of SHBG*[23] *in these women.* The larger problem is that there have been limited research efforts in women's sexual health problems in contrast to investigatory efforts in other areas of women's health or even in male sexual dysfunction."[24]

Let that sink in: the oral contraceptive has been around for over forty years, but no one had previously looked at the long-term effects in these women. The idea that taking powerful hormones every day might do something to women's sexual desire should not be such a stretch that it took the medical community forty years to think of it. This oversight is a testimony to the power of the Contraceptive Ideology, or maybe I should just call it the Contraceptive Superstition, which could be stated as follows: *contraception is always and everywhere a great boon to women and to the entire human race, now and forever. Amen.*

I give great credit to these researchers who had the courage to take on this question.[25]

---

[23]   Sex hormone binding globulin (SHBG) is the protein that binds testosterone, rendering it unavailable for a woman's physiologic needs. Either too much or too little SHBG can cause problems. See https://www.urmc.rochester.edu/encyclopedia/content.aspx?-ContentTypeID=167&ContentID=shbg_blood.

[24]   B. Coleman, "Birth Control Pill Could Cause Long-Term Problems with Testosterone." *Medical News Today,* January 4, 2006, http://www.medicalnewstoday.com/releases/35663, emphasis added.

[25]   Their names are: Dr. Claudia Panzer, MD, Sarah Wise, MS, Gemma Fantini, MD, Dongwoo Kang, MD, Ricardo Munarriz,

On a more colloquial note, feminist Holly Griggs-Spall quotes one disgruntled pill-taker: "I started to think hormonal birth control was a patriarchal plot to keep women down by rendering us completely loony. The question, 'How can we ever break the glass ceiling if we can't stop crying?' actually came out of my mouth."[26]

So much for the pill being "sex positive."

The Sexual Revolution depends upon the idea that sex and babies can be safely and consistently separated from each other. Perfectly functioning, perfectly safe contraception is an ideological prerequisite for maintaining this belief system. The sexual revolutionary paradigm of the Good Life for Women would not be reasonable unless contraception is risk-free, foolproof, and costless. Therefore, evidence that contraception does not work perfectly or that it poses significant problems of its own must be suppressed. At this point in history, it would require almost superhuman insight and fortitude to step outside the reigning paradigm of the Sexual State and just evaluate the evidence on its own terms.

MD, Andre Guay, MD, FACP, FACE, and Irwin Goldstein, MD.

[26] Griggs-Spall, *Sweetening the Pill, or How We Got Hooked on Hormonal Birth Control*, p. 108.

There Are No Alternative Means of
Spacing Pregnancies (False)

There Are, in Fact, Excellent Alternative
Means of Spacing Pregnancies

This is a logically necessary accessory to the Contraceptive Ideology. Natural methods of spacing pregnancy actually work reasonably well. Fertility awareness methods, as well as extended breastfeeding after giving birth, can help women space their pregnancies. These methods are seldom discussed in a serious manner in sexual education classes or at birth control clinics. In fact, a woman is likely to be ridiculed if she inquires about them. As the old joke goes, "Do you know what we call people who use the rhythm method? Parents."[27]

Notice that these methods are only suitable for women with very close relationships with their sexual partners. Insisting on periodic abstinence is not practical in a casual sexual relationship. A nursing mother is not a terribly attractive prospect on the hook-up scene. The fact that these methods are not discussed points to the fact that the Sexual Revolution is not really about helping married couples with "family planning." The real point of the Sexual State and the Contraceptive Ideology is that everyone able to give meaningful consent is entitled to unlimited sex without a live baby showing up. Which brings us to the next necessary ingredient of the ideological cocktail.

---

[27]   I have my own retort to this. "Do you know what we call people who plan to only have one child? Wimps." But I digress.

Abortion Access in Case of Contraceptive Failure Is a Moral Imperative (Dubious)

First, this is not a scientific claim but a highly dubious moral claim. Second, the insistence on abortion in case of contraceptive failure directly contradicts planks 1 and 2 of the packaged deal that is the Contraceptive Ideology. If contraception were truly always reliable, why do we need abortion as a backup plan? Finally, the insistence on abortion as a backup plan illustrates that the revolutionaries know perfectly well that contraception sometimes fails. In fact, "Some specialists argue that it is unethical to provide contraceptives in national family planning programs without also ensuring that abortion is available when contraceptives fail."[28]

Abortion Has No Negative Health, Psychological, or Social Consequences (False)

Abortion Often Has Profound Negative Health, Psychological or Social Consequences for the Mother, to Say Nothing of What It Does to the Baby

If the backup plan of abortion presents significant downsides, risks, or problems, the claim that casual sex is an entitlement

---

[28]   Barbara Crane, "The Transnational Politics of Abortion," *Population and Development Review* 20, Supplement, *The New Politics of Population: Conflict and Consensus in Family Planning* (1994), pp. 241–62. However, note 25, the reference for the quote in the text, does not give specific names of people with this view. In context, the author gives the impression that this view was so widespread that no specific reference was needed. (The note does cite a study showing contraceptive failure rates ranging from 3 to 23 percent.)

would no longer make sense. Therefore, sexual revolutionaries have tried hard to convince people that abortion is just like any other medical procedure. Removing a baby (oops, not a baby, a fetus) from the womb is no more traumatic or medically risky than removing tonsils or an appendix or pulling a tooth.

Notice how strong this claim really is. It can be refuted with a single counter-example. I don't need to claim that every woman everywhere regrets her abortion or was seriously harmed by it. All I need to show is that some women are harmed in some way. Once the idea of harmless abortion is dislodged from the public mind, then every woman must consider whether she could be one of the women likely to be harmed. Responsible medicine would then require that all health care personnel take these risks seriously and provide full information so women can give properly informed consent. Once the public begins taking that set of questions seriously, the whole ideological structure is threatened. "Maybe I should not sleep with a guy who would be a lousy father. Maybe I should not sleep with anyone at all if I am not ready to be a mother. In fact, if abortion might be painful for me, and contraception might fail, I'd better be careful about my sexual choices."

Medical Risks Associated With Abortion: Immediate and Longer Term

Immediate complications from abortion for the mother can include hemorrhage, infection, uterine perforation, and cervical laceration. Another complication is an unsuccessful (sometimes called a "failed") abortion, in which the fetus survives. This means that some additional procedure must be done to ensure the child is killed, which can be traumatic for the mother. Or if the mother chooses to carry the child to term, the abortion attempt may harm the child.[29] Gianna Jessen was bathed in a saline solution in utero to end her life. She survived and has cerebral palsy.[30]

Women who undergo abortion suffer higher rates of pelvic inflammatory disease (PID) than the general population. The well-documented side effects of PID include chronic pelvic pain, subfertility, infertility, ectopic pregnancy, intraamniotic infection, neonatal sepsis, and stillbirth in subsequent pregnancies. Women are also at higher risk for cervical incompetence, resulting in miscarriage or preterm births in subsequent pregnancies.[31] Placenta previa occurs when the placenta implants in the lower uterine segment near or covering the cervix. Induced abortion increases the probability of placenta previa, and this risk appears to increase with each additional induced abortion a woman undergoes.[32]

---

[29]   Angela Lanfranchi, Ian Gentles, and Elizabeth Ring-Cassidy, *Complications: Abortion's Impact on Women* (Toronto: The deVeber Institute for Bioethics and Social Research, 2013), pp. 96–108.

[30]   See Gianna Jessen's website for her full story: http://giannajessen.com/.

[31]   Lanfranchi, *Complications: Abortion's Impact on Women*, pp. 167–81. Intraamniotic infection (IAI) refers to infection of the amniotic fluid, membranes, placenta, and/or decidua. Neonatal sepsis is a type of neonatal infection and specifically refers to the presence in a newborn baby of a bacterial blood stream infection (BSI) (such as meningitis, pneumonia, pyelonephritis, or gastroenteritis) in the setting of fever.

[32]   Ibid., pp. 190–91.

One of the most serious long-term medical risks associated with abortion is the elevated risk of breast cancer. The link between abortion and breast cancer has been confirmed in numerous studies around the world, including Iran, China, Turkey, Armenia, India, and Bangladesh. In fact, the author of the survey states: "Induced abortion is now a commonly-accepted risk factor for breast cancer—except in North America, where it is denied chiefly for political reasons."[33] The American medical profession is complicit in suppressing the knowledge of this well-documented risk.[34]

In 2003, the National Cancer Institute (NCI) held a "Workshop on Early Reproductive Events and Breast Cancer Risks." The conclusion of this workshop is often cited as the authority for disregarding any link between abortion and breast cancer. Yet researchers with an opposing point of view were not permitted to present papers in this workshop. Nor were their dissents recorded in the proceeding.[35] Yet the event continues to be portrayed as if all one hundred physicians present agreed with its conclusions. The NCI updated its website to allude to the dissent but gave no hint as to its nature.

---

[33]   Ibid., pp. 115–16.

[34]   Academic texts have been subtly altered over the years. In the 1991 and 1998 editions of one important medical text on breast disease, the text states clearly that induced abortion is a risk factor for breast cancer. In later editions, this information was removed. Ibid., pp. 138–39.

[35]   Joel Brind, "Early Reproductive Events and Breast Cancer: A Minority Report," Breast Cancer Prevention Institute, March 10, 2003, http://www.bcpinstitute.org/papers/NCI_minority%20 report-3_2003-brind.pdf.

In fact, the NCI website on breast cancer prevention has one glaring error as of the time I examined it. The website claimed "estrogen levels are lower during pregnancy,"[36]in its third bullet point in a chart called, "Exposure of breast tissue to estrogen made in the body."

Actually, estrogen levels increase dramatically during pregnancy. One can easily confirm this by looking at websites that have nothing to do with cancer or abortion or similar contested topics. Even a site dealing with migraine headaches reports in passing that pregnancy is a high-estrogen event, as a matter of course.[37]

How could the National Institute of Cancer make such a blunder? It is quite true that exposure to estrogen increases a woman's vulnerability to breast cancer. It is also true that having a baby, especially early in life, decreases one's risk of

---

[36]   "Breast Cancer Prevention (PDQ), Patient Version," National Cancer Institute, accessed January 2, 2018, http://www.cancer. gov/types/breast/patient/breast-prevention-pdq#section/_12. I took a screen shot of this to confirm that it really claimed that "estrogen levels are lower during pregnancy."

[37]   For instance, look at this chart showing dramatically increased normal levels of estrogen over the course of a pregnancy. "Reference Values During Pregnancy," perinatology.com, accessed August 27, 2016, http://perinatology.com/Reference/Reference%20 Ranges/Estradiol.htm.
Estradiol is a form of estrogen. Drugs.com, s.v. "Estradiol," accessed January 2, 2018, https://www.drugs.com/estradiol.html. http://www.medicalnewstoday.com/articles/277177.php?page=3; "Estrogen Levels," SheCares, accessed April 24, 2018, https:// www.shecares.com/hormones/estrogen/levels. This is the site dealing with migraine headaches shows a similar chart with estrogen increasing during pregnancy, Jeremy Orozco, "Pregnancy, a Migraine Cure?" Migraine Key, accessed April 24, 2018, http:// www.3dayheadachecure.com/blog/pregnancy/.

breast cancer. And people have observed since the Middle Ages that nuns (who have no children) are more vulnerable to breast cancer than other women. Why does exposure to estrogen generally increase a woman's risk of breast cancer while having babies, which is a high-estrogen event, evidently decreases a woman's risk?

The explanation has to do with the fact that women's breasts change over the course of their lifetimes and some types of breast tissues are more vulnerable than others. Before a woman's first full-term pregnancy (FFTP), her breasts are composed of cancer-vulnerable Type 1 and Type 2 lobules, where ductal and lobular cancers, respectively, start. With increasing levels of the pregnancy hormones estrogen and progesterone, the numbers of these cancer-vulnerable lobules increase, thereby increasing the risk of breast cancer.

By thirty-two weeks of pregnancy, however, early in the third trimester, the pheromones hCG and hPL (human chorionic gonadotropin and human placental lactogen) made by the pregnant woman's body have caused significant maturation of breast tissue. By the end of the third trimester, 85 percent of the breast consists of cancer-resistant Type 4 lobules containing colostrum. When a pregnancy is interrupted before thirty-two-weeks gestation—whether naturally through a live premature birth, a miscarriage, or through abortion—the breast has not significantly matured the increased numbers of cancer-vulnerable Type 1 and Type 2 lobules made during the first and second trimesters. Until maturation is well underway after thirty-two weeks of gestation, the longer a woman is pregnant before premature delivery or induced abortion, the higher her risk of breast cancer because her breasts have greater numbers of lobules where breast cancers start. But if the pregnancy is carried past thirty-two weeks of gestation, her breasts become highly cancer resistant.[38]

It beggars belief that the National Cancer Institute is unaware of these basic facts. Maybe they don't know everything about breast development. But it's difficult to imagine they don't know that estrogen increases during pregnancy.

One simple explanation accounts for this "oversight," including the careful selection of authors to contribute to the report, and the blunder on the website. The National Cancer Institute is circling the wagons around legal abortion. They don't wish to alarm the public about the health risks associated with abortion, even though these risks are easily explained by well-established medical facts.

Let me conclude with one final anecdote. After the National Cancer Institute's workshop in 2003, one of the chief participants made a telling admission.

> Leslie Bernstein, an epidemiologist and workshop leader who was interviewed after the workshop, said that having a child was the surest, most effective way to reduce breast cancer risk. In an interview about the workshop she told a reporter: "The biggest bang for the buck is the first birth, and the younger you are the better off you are," followed by: "I would never be a proponent of going around and telling them that

---

[38] Angela Lanfranchi, "The Federal Government and Academic Texts as Barriers to Informed Consent," *Journal of American Physicians and Surgeons* 13, no. 1 (Spring 2008), pp. 12–15.

having babies is the way to reduce your risk." She also added, "I don't want the issue relating to induced abortion to breast cancer risk to be a part of mix of the discussion of induced abortion, its legality, its continued availability."[39]

Dr. Angela Lanfranchi, who reported this incident, considers it evidence of bias. And so it is, but I'd like to look closely at the nature of the bias.

Why do you suppose Dr. Bernstein doesn't want to tell women they should have a baby, and the younger the better, to reduce breast cancer risk? Let's give her the benefit of the doubt. She knows our society isn't organized around people getting married and starting families in their early twenties, even though they are biologically fully prepared to do so. As a professional woman, an epidemiologist with the credentials to be a workshop leader at the National Cancer Institute, she's certainly aware that delayed childbearing is the price for participating in the higher education system and the professions. Denying women access to abortion under those circumstances reduces their opportunity to participate.

What she probably can't see is that *society doesn't have to be organized in this way.* Twenty-year-olds used to be able to get married, have kids, and make a good living. This is no longer the case. The whole society has restructured itself around contraception and abortion. Two salaries have become the norm for buying houses, paying off student loans, and many other aspects of middle-class life.

We now ask women to adapt their bodies to the needs of

---

[39]   Ibid.

this newly reorganized society. If we want women to be able to participate in the professions and higher education, we could, instead, reorganize higher education and the professions to accommodate women and their bodies. We could enable young people to get married and stay married and work together to meet their educational, career, and child-bearing goals. As a side benefit, a young couple could survive on one salary instead of everyone being economically pressured into the work force. Dr. Bernstein can't see this, captivated as she is by the fantasy ideology of the Sexual Revolution.

If we were not inclined to give her the benefit of the doubt, we might say something like this: she, along with many others, is prepared to obscure or at least minimize well-established medical truths—putting the lives and health of younger, less-educated women at risk—to preserve her position of privilege as one of the educated members of the professional, managerial class.

Psychological Risks Associated With Abortion: Contested Research

Yes, the research on abortion's psychological impact on women is highly contested. It's important to notice the nature of the contest. On one side, we have the full weight of the major professional association the American Psychological Association (APA)—the APA has been on record supporting legal abortion since 1969.[40] On the other side, we have a handful of underfunded but dogged researchers.

---

[40]   Adler et al., "Psychological Factors in Abortion: A Review,"

The APA's 2009 report states: "The relative risk of mental health problems among adult women who have a *single, legal, first-trimester* abortion of an unwanted pregnancy for nontherapeutic reasons is no greater than the risk among women who deliver an unwanted pregnancy." (Emphasis added.) Year in and year out, however, just under half of all American women who procure an abortion have already had one or more abortions. In 2012, the most recent year for which data is available, 45 percent of aborting women had already had an abortion.[41] Thus, the APA's conclusion, guarded as it is, isn't relevant for nearly half the women who've had abortions.

Likewise, the APA's statement obscures the fact that women having second-trimester abortions are more likely to experience negative consequences than those having first-trimester abortions.[42] To be fair, a solid majority of abortions do take place in the first trimester. But this carefully guarded official statement offers no hint that this qualifier may be significant to the decision-making woman.

In this contest, no one denies that *some* women experience abortion as a traumatic event. Even the American Psychological Association admits as much in its comprehensive

American Psychologist 47, no. 10 (October 1992), p 1194.

[41]   Karen Pazol, Andreea A. Creanga, and Denise J. Jamieson, "Abortion Surveillance — United States, 2012, Surveillance Summaries," Centers for Disease Control, November 27, 2015, http://www.cdc.gov/mmwr/preview/mmwrhtml/ss6410a1.htm#tab16, table 17.

[42]   Adler et al., "Psychological Responses after Abortion," *Science*, n.s., 248, no. 4951 (April 6, 1990), p. 42.

report, which otherwise gives abortion a passing grade.[43] The APA simply disputes whether abortion causes the harm. Perhaps there were pre-existing conditions that are the real cause of psychological distress. Perhaps there are conditions in the woman's life that cause the perceived need for an abortion and the psychological distress. The APA task force is trying to be even-handed. I am willing to give them credit for that. But they don't seem to realize what they are, in fact, admitting, even in their attempts to dismiss the research connecting abortion with psychological harms.

Suppose it's true that a woman's prior psychological distress, poor psychological functioning, or depression predicts distress, depression, or poor functioning after an abortion. That doesn't seem implausible. But if so, doesn't the medical community have an obligation to screen women on that trait? If abortion is "just another medical procedure," why not develop a protocol for discovering when abortion is contraindicated by pre-existing conditions that may aggravate the impact of abortion? Why, after forty years of legal abortion, has no one developed such a thing?

No one would ever say that a person's right to access medical care was somehow compromised because a doctor asked if you were allergic to penicillin. If you are allergic, we expect the doctor to say, "This treatment is bad for you. We must consider some other solution to your problem." But no doctor in today's Sexual State would ever say, "I see you have a

---

[43]   Brenda Major et al., "Abortion and Mental Health: Evaluating the Evidence," *American Psychologist* 64, no. 9 (December 2009), 863–890, http://204.14.132.173/pubs/journals/features/amp-64-9-863.pdf.

prior history of depression. Some women become depressed after abortion. Perhaps we should consider another solution to your problem." Why do they never say that? Because it would interrupt the narrative flow that tells us that abortion is safe if it's legal and that sex without a baby is an entitlement.

The earliest research on abortion and psychological distress had a very limited view of what constituted "long-term" reactions to abortion. Researchers in the early 1990s took measures of emotional functioning thrity minutes after the abortion and at the three-week follow-up appointment.[44] When I first read this, I thought it was a joke. A survey published in 2003 examined twenty-four studies deemed to be of high quality. Of these studies, only seven surveyed the women after more than a month.[45] Yet surveys like these have been the basis of the APA's insistence that abortion does not cause women long-term psychological distress.

Clinicians have noticed that the full impact of abortion sometimes doesn't surface for years. Therapist Theresa Burke noticed the connection while leading a counseling group of women with eating disorders. Of the eight women in the group, six had had abortions. When Dr. Burke suggested to

---

[44]   Brenda Major and Catherine Cossarelli, "Psychosocial Predictors of Adjustment to abortion," *Journal of Social Issues* 48, no. 3, pp. 121–42.

[45]   Zoe Bradshaw and Pauline Slade, "The effects of induced abortion on emotional experiences and relationships: A critical review of the literature," *Clinical Psychology Review* 23 (203): 929–58. See appendix A for the list of studies and the length of follow-up.

her supervisor that perhaps the group should discuss abortion, he forbade her to bring it up.[46]

More recent research has taken longer-term looks at objective measures. One large meta-study found that women who have had abortions experience a statistically significant increased likelihood of a variety of psychological harms. These include anxiety disorders, depression, alcohol use and abuse, marijuana use and abuse, and suicidal behaviors.[47] Another study from 2010 found that women who had abortions had an increased likelihood of mood disorders and substance abuse disorders as well as suicidal thoughts and suicide attempts.[48] Even in 1998, researchers reported a significant minority of women experienced relationship difficulties and sexual difficulties that they attributed to their abortions.[49]

The real kicker is, no matter what you may conclude about correlations or causality or significance or anything else, the

---

[46]   Theresa Burke, *Forbidden Grief: The Unspoken Pain of Abortion* (Springfield IL: Acorn Books, 2002), pp. xv–xvii.

[47]   Priscilla K. Coleman, "Abortion and mental health: quantitative synthesis and analysis of research published 1995–2009," *The British Journal of Psychiatry* 199, no. 3 (2011), pp. 180–86, http://bjp.rcpsych.org/content/bjprcpsych/199/3/180.full.pdf.

[48]   Natalie Mota et al., "Associations between Abortion, Mental Disorders, and Suicidal Behavior in a Nationally Representative Sample," *The Canadian Journal of Psychiatry* 55, no. 4 (April 2010), pp. 239–47.

[49]   W. B. Miller, "An empirical study of the psychological antecedents and consequences of induced abortion," *Journal of Social Issues* 48 (1998), pp. 67–93. "Testing the model of the psychological consequences of abortion," in L. J. Beckman and S. M. Harvey, eds., *The new civil war* (Washington, DC: American Psychological Association), pp. 235–67.

research shows that between 10 and 30 percent of women experience various forms of distress from their abortions. This fact has been in the literature in one form or another since 1990.[50] Women have had approximately one million abortions per year, every year since 1973. Even if only 10 percent of them experience serious negative consequences, that's about one hundred thousand women per year. That's a lot of suffering women walking around untreated and even unnoticed. Yet neither the medical community nor the mainstream psychological associations have offered treatment or care for these women.

The sexual revolutionaries act as if they don't exist. Their

---

[50]   The best summary is Zoe Bradshaw and Pauline Slade, "The effects of induced abortion on emotional experiences and relationships: A critical review of the literature," *Clinical Psychology Review* 23 (2003), pp. 929–58. In their review, they refer to papers from the 1990s, such as Brenda Major and Catherine Cossarelli, "Psychosocial Predictors of Adjustment to abortion," *Journal of Social Issues* 48, no. 3 (1992), pp. 121–42; G. Zolese and C. V. R. Blacker, "The psychological complications of therapeutic abortion," *British Journal of Psychiatry* 160 (1992), 742–49; E. J. Posavac and T. Q. Miller, "Some problems caused by not having a conceptual foundation for health research: An illustration from studies of the psychological effects of abortion," *Psychology and Health* 5 (1990), pp. 13–23; R. Henshaw et al., "Psychological responses following medical abortion (using mifepristone and gemeprost) and surgical vacuum aspiration: A patient-centered, partially randomized prospective study," *Acta Obstetrica et Gynecologica Scandinavica* 73 (1994), pp. 812–18; P. Slade et al., "A comparison of medical and surgical methods of termination of pregnancy: Choice, psychological consequences and satisfaction with care," *British Journal of Obstetricsand Gynaecology* 105 (1998), pp. 1288–95; P. Lauzon et al., "Emotional distress among couples involved in first trimester induced abortions," *Canadian Family Physician* 46 (2000), 2033–40.

presence disturbs the narrative. They can't be allowed to exist. Keeping them invisible, diminishing them, marginalizing them is all part of the propaganda effort necessary to keep the fantasy ideology of the Sexual State alive and unquestioned.

There Are No Alternatives to Abortion for Women With Unplanned or Ill-Timed Pregnancies (False)

There Are Alternatives to Abortion for Women With Unplanned or Ill-Timed Pregnancies

Pregnancy care centers accompany the mother throughout her pregnancy. Some centers help mothers find work or housing. Most centers provide mothers with material assistance through the child's first year. Many centers provide classes on childcare and healthy relationships.

One might suppose that all advocates for women would rejoice in the proliferation of these organizations. One would be mistaken, however. The advocates of "women's right to choose" are adamant opponents of the network of pregnancy care centers.

The California legislature passed a bill regulating what pro-life pregnancy care centers can say and how "loudly" or "softly" they can say it. Pregnancy care centers in California are required to announce that abortion is available elsewhere. The State regulates where this signage must be and how large the type face must be. Evidently, the Big Abortion industry feels threatened by these centers.[51] Even very liberal

---

51   Cities in California intend to enforce this law. As of this writing, both Los Angeles and Oakland have sent menacing letters to

California has 167 pregnancy care centers. This is according to the breathless NARAL Pro-choice America "report" modestly entitled "Crisis Pregnancy Centers Lie." Nationwide, according to this same "report," there were 2,460 pregnancy care centers and only 438 abortion clinics.

The Big Abortion industry's claims that "crisis pregnancy centers lie," doesn't hold water. In a section of the "report" purporting to show how much pregnancy care centers "shame and judge" pregnant women, we find these items:

- "69% of CPCs investigated in Montana displayed or presented fetal 'dolls'—models that are often developmentally incorrect, and used to shame and dissuade women from abortion." *What exactly does "often" and "incorrect" mean?*
- "61% of CPCs investigated in North Carolina pressured women not to have abortions by providing baby items." *Those big meanies!*
- "In the New York City investigation, 73% of the CPC staffers referred to the fetus as a "baby" or "unborn child" and to abortion as "killing," and 89% of CPCs did so in their written materials."

Every state in America has regulation against consumer fraud. These "lies" do not come anywhere near meeting the legal standard for "consumer fraud." Sexual revolutionaries

---

the pregnancy care centers under their jurisdiction. Jay Hobbs, "Two of California's most dangerous cities targeting pro-life centers," *LifeSiteNews,* August 5, 2016, https://www.lifesitenews.com/news/two-of-californias-most-dangerous-cities-targeting-pro-life-centers.

have been unable to get their friends in the legislature to redefine *fraud* to mean "failing to use the politically correct euphemisms." So the revolutionaries get their friends to pass legislation specifically targeting the pregnancy care centers.

The idea that pregnancy care centers are "tricking" or "misleading" women into having their babies is preposterous. The decision to carry a child to term must be reaffirmed every day throughout the pregnancy. But the decision to abort can be carried out in a single afternoon. The woman can change her mind about giving birth, walk into the abortion clinic, and her baby will be gone forever. The pregnancy care centers would have to be "tricking" women, and restraining them from entering an abortion clinic, every single day for nine months.

Big Abortion is in the business of maintaining the fantasy ideology of the Sexual Revolution. They try to convince people that everyone has the right to act as if sex were a sterile activity with no moral or social consequences. Since this is patently untrue, the revolutionaries must suppress those who dissent from their orthodoxy. If people are left alone to consider their own experience as well as the available evidence, most people come to realize that sex does in fact make babies. Even contraceptive sex sometimes makes babies.

Pregnancy care centers tell women that contraception sometimes fails. Their clients have probably already guessed as much. Roughly half of women who come for abortions say they were using contraception the month they got pregnant. In one study, it was 54 percent.[52] The pregnancy care

---

[52]   Not a typo. See Rachel K. Jones, Jacqueline E. Darroch, and

center may tell women that abortion sometimes has negative consequences. Most of all, pregnancy care centers tell women that having their babies and being good mothers is a realistic possibility for them.

The true believers in the Sexual Revolution, on the other hand, can't allow heresies like these to go unchallenged. Various jurisdictions have limitations on sidewalk counseling near abortion clinics.[53] These peaceful activities offer alternatives to the clinic. One Oakland, California, pastor was jailed for thirty days due to his activities inside the "bubble" of forbidden speech. This African-American pastor's crime? Approaching women, extending his arm, offering them a pamphlet, and saying, "May I talk with you about alternatives to the clinic?" His baseball cap displaying "Got Jesus?" was considered illegal signage inside the bubble.[54]

One might think that those who want abortion to be "safe, legal, and rare" would welcome health and safety regulations for abortion clinics. One would be mistaken.

Stanley K. Henshaw, "Contraceptive Use Among U.S. Women Having Abortions in 2000-2001," *Perspectives on Reproductive and Sexual Health* 34, no. 6, (November/December 2002), pp. 294–303, table 1, https://www.guttmacher.org/about/journals/psrh/2002/11/contraceptive-use-among-us-women-having-abortions-2000-2001.

[53] Most recently, Australia enacted a clinic bubble law. Tim Minear, "Mother of 13 arrested in East Melbourne clinic protest," *Courier-Mail*, August 4, 2016, http://www.couriermail.com.au/news/mother-of-13-arrested-in-east-melbourne-clinic-protest/news-story/a90d71765491cd1189348579a4f98a0b.

[54] Henry K. Lee, "Pastor jailed for Oakland anti-abortion acts," *SFGate*, March 21, 2009, http://www.sfgate.com/bayarea/article/Pastor-jailed-for-Oakland-anti-abortion-acts-3247604.php.

Abortion advocates fought tooth and nail against the Texas regulations treating abortion clinics like other medical facilities. The revolutionaries took their case all the way to the Supreme Court. They won.[55]

Where did the abortion lobby obtain the resources to finance these court challenges? After the court decision, it was revealed that large foundations had been steadily funneling money into the research that supported these challenges for over a decade. These foundations include the William and Flora Hewlett Foundation, the David and Lucile Packard Foundation, the John Merck Fund, the Educational Foundation of America, and most significantly, the Susan Thompson Buffett Foundation, named for the late wife of one of the richest men in the world. "Buffett's main academic partner (receiving at least $88 million from 2001 to 2014) has been the University of California, San Francisco."[56]

When the people of Texas, acting through their duly elected state legislators, enacted health and safety legislation for abortion clinics, the elites of society knocked it down. With research funded by one of the richest men in the world and the fourth largest family foundation in the United States, combined with the collaboration of academics and attorneys, the elites get what they want.

---

[55]   Whole Women's Health v. Hellerstedt, 579 U.S. __ (2016).
[56]   Nina Martin, "Behind the Supreme Court's Abortion Decision, More Than a Decade of Privately Funded Research," *ProPublica,* July 14, 2016, https://www.propublica.org/article/supreme-court-abortion-decision-more-than-decade-privately-funded-research.

And, Most Important of All, Sexual Activity Is Necessary for a Happy and Fulfilled Life (False)

Sexual Activity Is Not Necessary for a Happy and Fulfilled Life

Without this point, people could just shrug off the whole issue. Don't want a baby? Don't have sex. Don't want sexually transmitted diseases? Don't have sex. Somehow, the full implications of this premise are hardly discussed and defended. Rather, this premise is merely assumed. This is where the work of Alfred Kinsey is so insidious. It was he, financed by the Rockefeller Foundation, who laid the groundwork for people believing that a life without sex is barely worth living.

Besides Kinsey, one other person deserves our attention here: Wilhelm Reich. Reich was a German psychiatrist who authored a book titled *The Sexual Revolution*. His primary concern was the need for children to have the sex they desire to have. He built everything else around this supposed entitlement. Of course, adults are entitled also. He wrote as if a person simply cannot be healthy or happy without having sex. A Wikipedia entry on orgastic impotence informs us about Reich's "discovery:" "For Reich, 'orgastic impotence,' or failure to attain orgastic potency (not to be confused with anorgasmia, the inability to reach orgasm) always resulted in neurosis, because during orgasm that person could not discharge all libido (which Reich regarded as a biological energy). According to Reich, 'not a single neurotic individual possesses orgastic potency.'[57]

To put this man in perspective, he had invented and was marketing a machine that supposedly collected "orgone" from the atmosphere and would help people attain "orgastic potency." The FDA considered this consumer fraud. Reich was sentenced to federal prison in Lewiston, Pennsylvania, where he died in 1957.[58]

Conclusion

There's more I could say about the propaganda needed to prop up the Contraceptive Ideology. We could talk about the "studies" such as "Has Virginity Lost Its Virtue? Relationship Stigma Associated with Being a Sexually Inexperienced Adult."[59] This piece of work was produced by the Kinsey Institute at the University of Indiana (yes, it is still

---

[57]   Wikipedia, s.v. "Orgastic potency," last modified March 11, 2018, 00:43, https://en.wikipedia.org/wiki/Orgastic_potency.

[58]   Both Reich's critics and supporters agree with these basic facts. Paul Kengor, *Takedown: From Communists to Progressives, How the Left has Sabotaged Family and Marriage* (Washington DC: World Net Daily Books, 2015), p. 112, is critical of Reich. However, The Institute for Orgonomic Science, founded to continue promoting Reich's work, concurs that Reich died in prison for consumer fraud. "Wilhelm Reich (1897-1957)," The Institute for Orgonomic Science, http://www.orgonomicscience.org/wilhelm-reich/.

[59]   A. N. Gesselman, G. D. Webster, and J. R. Garcia, "Has Virginity Lost Its Virtue? Relationship Stigma Associated With Being a Sexually Inexperienced Adult," *Journal of Sex Research* (March 16, 2016), pp. 1–12, http://www.ncbi.nlm.nih.gov/pubmed/26983793.

in existence) and partially financed by the manufacturers of K-Y Jelly (no, I'm not kidding.)[60] We could talk about how the media is astonished every time a report comes out showing that kids are not all "doing it." The number of young adults born in the 1990s who report they are not having sex is more than twice as high as it was for the baby boomer generation.[61] The sexual revolutionaries in the media cannot understand this. Every chaste teenager is a rebuke to them.

We could talk about the Obama administration passing a federal law forbidding any state from voting to defund Planned Parenthood and similar organizations. That is a

---

[60]   The principal researcher received a grant from the K-Y Brand Touch Initiative. "Amanda Gessleman, Ph.D.," Kinsey Institue, Indiana University, https://www.kinseyinstitute.org/about/ profiles/agesselman.php. RB, the company that owns the K-Y brand, describes its interest in the project in a press release: "National Survey Uncovers Potential Barrier to Better Intimacy Connections for Couples," K-Y Brand, February 9, 2016, http:// www.multivu.com/players/English/7749151-k-y-the-touch-initiative-survey/. The "study" commissioned by K-Y from the Kinsey Institute is little more than a marketing document for their massage oil. For more, see "Kinsey Institute's Commercial Connections," *Ruth Speaks Out* (blog), July 14, 2016, http:// www.ruthinstitute.org/ruth-speaks-out/kinsey-institutes-commerical-connections.

[61]   J. M. Twenge, R. A. Sherman, and B. E. Wells, "Sexual Inactivity during Young Adulthood Is More Common among U.S. Millennials and iGen: Age, Period, and Cohort Effects on Having No Sexual Partners After Age 18," *Archives of Sexual Behavior* 46, no. 2 (2017), pp.433–40, https://doi.org/10.1007/s10508-016-0798-z. The study found that 15 percent of millenials aged 20–24 said they had not had sex since age 18, more than those born in the late 1960s (6 percent), 1970s (11 percent), or 1980s (12 percent). That is lower than their fellow millenials born in the previous decade.

perfect example of the Sexual State at work, implementing the fantasy ideology of the sexual revolutionaries. They cannot implement that ideology without the help of the State's power to coerce and propagandize.[62]

We could talk about the sexual "education" programs offered in most public schools that use taxpayer dollars to promote a fantasy ideology that sex can be safe if you use a condom every time. The very act of teaching about sex in school is itself an ideological statement. The implicit dogma is that sex can be safely removed from its relational context: kids can and should be taught by non-relatives, outside the home, without parental input. Sex is a scientific discipline, not a subject of deep personal, relational, or spiritual significance. Obviously, every point of this dogma can be, and is, highly contested.

The United States federal government was slated to spend over $200 million in fiscal year 2016 teaching young people about sex, which is none of the government's business.[63] Not

---

[62]   Steven Ertelt, "Obama Proposes Rule Prohibiting States From Defunding Planned Parenthood," *LifeNew.com,* September 6, 2016, http://www.lifenews.com/2016/09/06/admin-proposed-rule-prohibiting-states-from-defunding-planned-parenthood/.

[63]   "Support Federal Adolescent Sexual Health Education & Promotion Programs," The Sexuality Education and Information Council of the United States, accessed April 25, 2018, http://siecus.org/document/docWindow.cfm?fuseaction=document.viewDocument&ID=07E5A0647538BFBAE5887831506AF85D88976995AD3CC0C6D329D0B0ADB5CF140E44FC566087638521D737023E39E8C6. The point of this particular fact sheet was to provide people with the information they would need to lobby the federal government to remove any funding at all for abstinence education.

your local school board, mind you, which is bad enough, but the largest, most powerful government in the world has taken upon itself the right and responsibility to promote a particular view of human sexuality. Some of these programs are of dubious value, even in terms of the goals set by the sexual revolutionaries themselves.[64]

The Personal Responsibility Education Program (PREP) is part of the Affordable Care Act and allocates $75 million per year for sexual education.[65] The Teen Pregnancy Prevention Initiative allocates over $100 million per year.[66] Advocates for Youth, funded by George Soros and Warren Buffett, will helpfully tell you how your state can receive its share of this federal largesse.[67] I could say much more about the role of the State and of wealthy "philanthropists" who insist that, just because they are rich, they have the right to remake society in their own image.

I don't care whether schools are teaching comprehensive sexuality education or abstinence only until marriage. I don't

---

64   K. Buckles and D. M. Hungerman, "The Incidental Fertility Effects of School Condom Distribution Programs," *NBER Working Paper*, no. w22322 (June 2016), http://papers.ssrn.com/sol3/papers.cfm?abstract_id=2794728.

65   "Personal Responsibility Education Program (PREP)," Advocates for Youth, accessed April 25, 2018, http://www.advocatesforyouth.org/publications/1742-personal-responsibility-education-program-prep.

66   "Teen Pregnancy Prevention Program (TPP)," U.S. Department of Health and Human Services, http://www.hhs.gov/ash/oah/oah-initiatives/tpp_program/.

67   "Personal Responsibility Education Program (PREP)," Advocates for Youth, accessed April 25, 2018, http://www.advocatesforyouth.org/publications/1742-personal-responsibility-education-program-prep.

care whether the material they're teaching is age-appropriate or science-based or peer-reviewed or anything else. It is propaganda for the Sexual State: all of it.[68]

---

[68] I suspect that most advocates of abstinence education would agree with me. Their position in the schools is defensive; that is, given that the government is financing and teaching about sex in the schools, these advocates want their point of view represented. But for many of them, the better option would be for parents to teach their children about sex at home and keep it out of the school and the hands of the state altogether. Just guessing.

CHAPTER 7

What the Catholic Church Says About Contraception

There is only one large organization left on the earth that opposes the Contraceptive Ideology. That organization is, famously, the Catholic Church. The unbroken teaching of the Church is that the unitive and procreative aspects of the sexual act must not be separated. Pope Paul VI reaffirmed this ancient teaching and explained it in 1968.

> The Church . . . teaches that each and every marital act must of necessity retain its intrinsic relationship to the procreation of human life.
>
> This particular doctrine . . . is based on the insepa-rable connection, established by God, which man on his own initiative may not break, between the unitive significance and the procreative significance which are both inherent to the marriage act.
>
> The reason is that the fundamental nature of the marriage act, while uniting husband and wife in the

closest intimacy, also renders them capable of generating new life—and this as a result of laws written into the actual nature of man and of woman. And if each of these essential qualities, the unitive and the procreative, is preserved, the use of marriage fully retains its sense of true mutual love and its ordination to the supreme responsibility of parenthood to which man is called.[1]

The Church has upheld this teaching, at great cost to herself, I might add, despite the widespread dissent within and disdain outside.

Notice how the pontiff refers to human reason, and the human good, as part of his analysis. In the years since 1968, American society has become even more untethered to both reason and goodness. We avoid facing reality. Rather than submitting to the "laws written into the actual nature of man and of woman," we are increasingly at war with our own bodies.

But Blessed Paul VI's real tour de force comes in paragraph 17 of *Humanae Vitae,* where he analyzes the likely consequences of the widespread moral acceptance of contraception. Bear in mind that he wrote these words in 1968. "Let them (responsible people) first consider how easily this course of action could open wide the way for marital infidelity and a general lowering of moral standards. Not much experience is needed to be fully aware of human weakness and to understand that human beings—and especially the

---

[1]   Blessed Paul VI, Encyclical *Humanae Vitae* (1968), nos. 11–12.

young, who are so exposed to temptation—need incentives to keep the moral law, and it is an evil thing to make it easy for them to break that law."[2]

No serious person can argue that he was mistaken when he predicted a "general lowering of moral standards."

The pontiff continues with words that could have come from today's headlines: "Another effect that gives cause for alarm is that a man who grows accustomed to the use of contraceptive methods may forget the reverence due to a woman, and, disregarding her physical and emotional equilibrium, reduce her to being a mere instrument for the satisfaction of his own desires, no longer considering her as his partner whom he should surround with care and affection."[3]

Can anyone deny that many men have grown "accustomed to the use of contraceptive methods?" We have raised men who didn't "forget" the reverence due to a woman: they never knew it in the first place. The women that Harvey Weinstein and Al Franken and Matt Lauer abused were not "partners" in any sense, much less partners to be surrounded "with care and affection."

"Finally," says Blessed Paul VI, "careful consideration should be given to the danger of this power passing into the hands of those public authorities who care little for the precepts of the moral law." The horrors of population control around the world testify to his foresight and wisdom.

> Who will blame a government which in its attempt to
> resolve the problems affecting an entire country resorts

---

2   Ibid., no. 17.
3   Ibid.

to the same measures as are regarded as lawful by married people in the solution of a particular family difficulty? . . . Should they regard this as necessary, they may even impose their use on everyone. It could well happen, therefore, that when people, either individually or in family or social life, experience the inherent difficulties of the divine law and are determined to avoid them, they may give into the hands of public authorities the power to intervene in the most personal and intimate responsibility of husband and wife.[4]

As we have already noted, the far-reaching power of the Chinese and other governments over the lives of their citizens shows that this was no idle fear, no scare mongering or hysteria. In short, Blessed Paul VI was prophetic. He was correct.

It is quite true that many Catholics do not embrace this teaching. Many priests and even bishops do not proclaim it. Some theologians have sought ways to minimize the impact of the teaching. It is as if they ask, "What is the minimum we have to do to get by, and be a Catholic in good standing, while still fitting in with the society around us?"

Permit me to say: the Church is correct about contraception. The Church has been correct all along. We should be proud of this teaching and embrace it. The world is literally dying for want of this teaching. We have no right to keep it to ourselves.

Despite the lukewarmness of many Catholics, we nonetheless can be proud of our record. It was Catholics who

---

[4]   Ibid.

had the foresight to fight the Contraceptive Ideology in Connecticut prior to *Griswold*. It was Catholics who formed the pro-life movement and who still provide the bulk of its membership.

Down to this day, it is Catholics who battle population control at the United Nations. Not only has the Holy See consistently opposed the sexual revolutionaries. But initiatives organized, financed, and run by Catholic laymen and laywomen have kept the UN from going completely overboard on population control and other sexual revolutionary measures. I'm thinking of groups like the Population Research Institute, Women's Rights without Frontiers, and C-Fam, the Center for Family and Human Rights. And those are just the American organizations. Around the world, if you look at the organizations opposing the Contraceptive Ideology, you will be sure to find Catholics deeply involved.

The sexual act has the natural potential to create bonds between the man and woman and to create new life. The sexual act is a community-building, family-building act. Under the tutelage of the Contraceptive Ideology, we have turned the sexual act into a consumer good: something we attempt to acquire for ourselves, at the least cost to ourselves, and without regard to the impact on those around us. Instead of seeing others as persons deserving of love, we see others as objects to be used or opponents to be feared.

The Church offers us a more excellent way, the way of love. More about that later. Now, we must turn to the second plank of the Sexual Revolution: the Divorce Ideology.

PART THREE

The Divorce Ideology

On the Essential Public Purpose of Marriage

Children of divorce were the first victims of the Sexual Revolution. Children of unmarried parents followed quickly behind them. Now, children of same-sex couples and children of donor conception are the latest victims. To understand why I call these children victims, let me take a moment to unpack what marriage does for children.

What Marriage Does

The institution of marriage, in every known society, is the socially approved and preferred context for both sexual activity and childbearing.[1] Marriage attaches mothers and fathers to their children and to one another. This is the essential

---

[1]   See Jennifer Roback Morse, "Marriage and the Limits of Contract," *Policy Review*, April 1, 2005, https://www.hoover.org/research/marriage-and-limits-contract. See also David Blankenhorn, *The Future of Marriage* (New York: Encounter Books, 2007).

public purpose of marriage because, without it, we wouldn't need marriage as a social institution at all. If we were different kinds of creatures, if we did not reproduce through the sexual interaction of male and female, if our children were born alive and mature rather than helpless and immature, we wouldn't need marriage. No one would have ever thought of a social convention requiring sexual exclusivity and long-term commitment. As it is, however, every known human society has something like marriage.

This public purpose contrasts with all the private purposes individuals might have for wanting to get married, such as for social approval or to get their parents off their backs. People might want to get married for financial benefits or for the big elaborate party. People can have all kinds of personal reasons for wanting to get married, some better than others, but these reasons don't add up to a public reason to have marriage in the first place. After all, people can have parties, health insurance, and social approval without the institution of marriage.

Opponents of natural marriage sometimes claim that marriage is not fundamentally about children since many married couples don't have children. Of course, it is certainly true that not every married couple has children. However, *every child has parents*. Every child has a legitimate interest in having a relationship with both parents. I'd go so far as to say that children have a *right* to know and be known by both parents in the absence of some unavoidable tragedy. All children, without exception, have a right to know their genetic and social heritage.

Even the United Nations agreed to these truths in its

1959 Declaration of the Rights of the Child. Principle 6 states, "The child, for the full and harmonious development of his personality, needs love and understanding. He shall, wherever possible, grow up in the care and under the responsibility of his parents, and, in any case, in an atmosphere of affection and of moral and material security; a child of tender years shall not, save in exceptional circumstances, be separated from his mother."[2]

My dream is that every child be welcomed into life in a loving home with a married mother and father. This allows every child to have a relationship with his or her own parents unless some unavoidable tragedy prevents it. This also ensures that everyone can know his or her cultural heritage, genetic identity, and medical history. Children need and deserve their own parents. When children are deprived of these rights without a compelling reason, I call this a *structural injustice* to the child.

Children cannot possibly defend these rights and protect themselves against this injustice. Adult society must protect them by preventing harm, not through restitution after the fact. By the time a child is old enough to grasp that something of value has been withheld from him, he has already experienced a loss that cannot be entirely restored. A six-year-old child cannot march into court and say, "See here: I have not seen my father in a year. Someone come over here and do something about it."

---

[2]   In addition, principle 3 states, "The child shall be entitled from his birth to a name and a nationality." "Declaration of the Rights of the Child," United Nations (1959), https://www.unicef.org/malaysia/1959-Declaration-of-the-Rights-of-the-Child.pdf.

Once I had a law professor argue with me on this point.
She observed that children go to court all the time through
the appointment of a guardian *ad litum*. This is perfectly
true. But this fact does not damage my point and, in some
respects, supports it. Some adult somewhere had to see that
the child's interests were being harmed. A series of adults had
to intervene and make the determination that a guardian
was required. The guardian represents the child's interests
precisely because the child cannot represent his or her own
interests without adult assistance. The child didn't *literally*
go to court. The child was represented in court due to the
intervention of a series of actions taken by adults.

I'm not a lawyer. I'm a mother and an adult member of
society. I'm concerned about a deeper, more fundamental
point. While all these legal proceedings are plodding through
the court, the child's developmental clock is ticking. A child
only gets twelve months to be a two-year-old or a six-year-
old. The child has a whole series of developmental tasks that
he or she needs to accomplish during that window of time.
Children need adult assistance, preferably the loving, atten-
tive assistance of their own parents. By the time the adults
pull themselves together to go through the courts and do all
the legal procedures that need to be done, the child's developmental window may be closing.

The concept of a "developmental clock" or "developmental window" is a concept that specifically applies to children,
not to adults. Our modern political philosophies don't recognize the existence of such a thing as a developing human
being. Modern political philosophy has blinded us to the
significance of childhood helplessness. Our family courts

and other social institutions have been functioning on the accumulated social capital of the common law and tradition, which did recognize the unique vulnerability of children. Tragically, our generation is in the process of consuming this precious social capital that protects children and their needs.

Every known society has an institution to protect these universal and legitimate interests of children. That institution is, of course, marriage. Adults make a lifelong commitment to each other and to their children, hopefully, before the union produces any children. Their commitment is much more than a contract, a carefully orchestrated exchange of services rendered. Rather, the marriage vow is "for richer or for poorer, for better or for worse," in other words, an unconditional commitment to the relationship.[3] This solemn vow, as well as the legal and social structure that supports it, provides an institutional basis for protecting the legitimate entitlements of children.

Marriage attaches mothers and especially fathers to their children, and mothers and fathers to one another. This essential purpose is profoundly social. Marriage creates a small society of mother, father, and children. That small social unit contributes to the larger society by creating a functioning future, a next generation. Everyone benefits from having a next generation in place to sustain the society and keep its institutions going. Even if I have no children myself, I will benefit from the fact that younger people are building cars and houses, providing medical and legal care, starting new

---

[3]   Jennifer Roback Morse, "Why Marriage is not a Contract," in
        Love and Economics: It Takes a Family to Raise a Village (San Mar-
        cos, CA: Ruth Institute Books, 2008).

businesses, and running old ones. The benefits of marriage go far beyond the benefits to the individual members of the family; they extend to every member of society.

The objection that some marriages don't have children stands the rationale for marriage on its head. It views marriage from the adult's perspective rather than the child's. The fact that we must even answer this objection tells us how profoundly adult-centered our understanding of marriage has become.

Freedom, Structures, and Behaviors

Marriage as an institution provides boundaries for people's behavior. Have sex with your spouse and no one else. Take care of the children born to you and your spouse. Respect the parenting decisions of other families. Once you get married, stay married, unless someone does something demonstrably awful. These limitations can sometimes chafe. We feel unfree and constrained.

On the other hand, these boundaries create a zone of freedom. As long as a couple behaves within these structural boundaries, they can do pretty much anything they want. No one monitors their household division of labor, their eating habits, their spending habits, or their sex lives. No one tells them how to treat each other or forces them to be polite. No one tells them how many children to have or how to raise those children. Some couples will treat one another with respect and love; others will nag and fuss and complain. Unless they do something egregious, no one bothers them.

This is a perfectly sound, sensible social structure, one

that would be difficult to improve upon. This structure is suitable to the public purpose of marriage. It takes account of the one task every society must accomplish: provide for the needs of children and so ensure that the society has a next generation. In short, the ethic of lifelong married love provides justice to the child and a future for society.

This is why marriage is not simply a special case of the market and family law is not simply a subset of property and contract law. Marriage exists to meet the social necessity of caring for helpless children who are not and cannot be contracting parties. Children are protected parties; marriage should protect the interests of both parents in pursuing their common project of rearing their children.

The genius of marriage as a social institution is this: by providing an extremely minimal legal structure, the State facilitates a huge amount of voluntary cooperation. The State doesn't care about the details of a particular couple's arrangements. As long as they fulfill the basic requirements, the State has no further concern. Marriage is a largely self-regulating, voluntary system of long-term cooperation between parents.

Thus, we should not be surprised to learn that totalitarians of all stripes have sought to control the family. Inside the family, people develop loyalties to real people, not the Dear Leader. They develop habits that may not further the interests of the totalitarian State, with its all-embracing designs on every person. Inside the family, people may commit to ideas other than the state-sanctioned ideology.

We sometimes confuse structures with behaviors, especially when things go wrong. The structures may be perfectly sound, but people may still be behaving badly. We may have the best possible set of legal rules, social norms, and institutional practices, but people can still manage to be selfish, stupid, shortsighted, and just plain mean. We may not need new rules, but better behavior.

This points to another reason that those with totalitarian ambitions cannot abide the family. The true radical wishes to restructure society to obliterate every evil and wipe away every tear. Real people committed to living with other real people recognize this objective as folly. No matter how sound the social structures, some problems will always remain.

The ordinary person intuitively grasps the reality of "original sin" without necessarily calling it by this name. Even non-religious people can acknowledge the fact that the human condition is fundamentally and deeply troubled. Original sin is the true equalizer: no one is exempt from this trouble. No one has an intrinsic right to rule over anyone else. Trying to eliminate all human problems is a fool's errand that can only empower some people at the expense of others.

We are faced with two competing worldviews. The worldview of people of faith is this: Every child (and hence every adult) has identity rights and relational rights with respect to their parents. These rights impose legitimate *obligations on adults to provide these things to children.* We don't like to say this too loudly because people in our time resist hearing that they have obligations to others that they didn't explicitly choose to bear.

The competing worldview is this: Every adult has a right to the sexual activity they want, with a minimum of inconvenience, *and children must accept whatever the adults choose to give them.* We don't just blurt out that last part explicitly because we would be ashamed of ourselves if we heard ourselves say it. But that is approximately the position of most of the people in power in most of the so-called developed countries: they believe it is the job of the government to minimize the inconvenience that adults experience from their sex lives.[4] The Divorce Ideology, created and supported by the Sexual State, is neatly contained in that worldview.

---

[4]   See Jennifer Roback Morse, foreword to *Primal Loss: The Now-Adult Children of Divorce Speak*, ed. Leila Miller (Phoenix, AZ: LCB Publishing, 2017).

CHAPTER 8

How the Divorce Ideology Harms Children (and Sometimes Adults)

The Old Structure Protected the Interests and Needs of Children

To show that the presumption of permanence in marriage had many desirable features, let me tell you a bit about growing up in the 1950s. You have, no doubt, been told that this was an era of the oppression of women in loveless, abusive marriages and the confinement of men in dreary conformist jobs. I don't know exactly what it was like to be an adult in those days, but I can tell you something about what it was like to be a child.

Our mothers and fathers were there. Our fathers went to work every morning, came home every night, and were sober most of the time. Our mothers took care of us without hovering over us. We had safe neighborhoods in which to roam, unsupervised, most of the time. We slept in the same bed every night. We didn't shuttle between two households.

Everything we needed for our homework or school project was right there at our mom's house, which was also our dad's house, which was the only house we had.

We didn't have to worry about how to behave around our mothers' boyfriends or our fathers' girlfriends. Our mothers didn't bring a parade of boyfriends through the house. Our fathers didn't make fools of themselves, remarrying a string of women whom everyone else could see were gold-diggers. It was unthinkable that our parents would present us with new lovers to whom we would have responsibilities, with whom we would have relationships. We sometimes saw our parents quarrel. But we seldom wondered whether these quarrels would mean the end of their marriages and the end of our lives as we had known them.

We had brothers and sisters. When our moms had a new baby, that brother or sister was not a symbol of our mom's new relationship with a new husband, an unmistakable and final sign that our parents would never get back together. Sure, we sometimes felt neglected by our parents' preoccupation with a new baby, but we didn't have to deal with the feeling that many of today's children must face: the feeling that the new baby completes and solidifies the new marriage and that we are unwelcome leftovers from an old relationship, the way Elise feels.

Each new baby became a permanent part of our family. We didn't worry about getting too attached to a new half-sibling or stepsibling who might disappear if an adult relationship broke up. We all grew up with the same set of brothers and sisters for our entire childhood. Our family photos included all our siblings. The photos on the wall included our relatives from both sides of our families. Excluding a child from a family photo because they were "somebody else's child" would have been considered unconscionable.

Most kids I grew up with never had judges deciding where they would go to school or church. We spent Christmas Day and Thanksgiving Day with both parents. Our moms might say, "Don't tell dad," if she had spent too much money. But our moms never asked us to keep signs of wealth hidden from our dads when we went to visit him for fear this would upset their financial arrangements. We weren't asked by one parent to perjure ourselves against the other. I don't know anyone from my childhood who ever went to family court even once.

Those of us who grew up in the 1950s could take for granted things which seem like luxuries to children of today. We had no idea what we were overthrowing when we rebelled against our parents, when we indulged ourselves by taking advantage of the new laws. For the first time, spouses could abandon a blameless spouse for any reason, or no reason, and never be asked to offer any account of themselves. Quite obviously, this system benefits the spouse who wants to renege on their marriage vows at the expense of the faithful spouse. No-fault divorce, which was supposed to lower the costs for the handful of people whose marriages had broken down, in fact, induced a whole range of new bad behaviors that would have been unimaginable in earlier ages. Compared with the problems children face today, we were unbelievably fortunate.

Different Behaviors, Not Different Structures

Sometimes when I speak this way about growing up in the 1950s, people assume that I am indulging in some naïve nostalgic exercise. But I assure you, despite all I have said here, there were problems in the family of the fifties. After all, these were the people who rushed to the new liberation movements of the sixties. What were they running from? Quarrelling, jealousy, anger, selfishness, family secrets, pettiness, shame. What was the solution to these problems? More patience, less self-regard, more telling the truth in love, more generosity, appreciation, and gratitude. The women's liberation movement, in particular, gave us more things to quarrel about, more grievances and grudges, more permission to focus on ourselves, and easier exit options. What we really needed was more love, all of us. More love from parent to child, from child to parent, and above all, between husbands and wives.

We didn't realize that when we rushed for the exits, our own faults came with us and roughly half the problems of the earlier relationship. These problems and faults just played themselves out in different arenas: in the family courts, in the work place, and in the new families that we kept creating and breaking apart. The institutional, social structure of the family was fine. What we lacked wasn't freedom, but love.

The Victims

Secure attachments between a child and each of his or her parents build the foundation for the development of the child's personality. In the child's little world, mother and father are the most powerful and important people. Parents act as "stand-ins" for God himself. From this most basic relationship, the child develops his sense of himself as a social and spiritual being. Is the world a safe place for me? Do I belong here? Am I worthy of love? Do I care about anyone else? Do my actions matter to my life or to anyone else's? [1]

Divorcing parents may say to their child: "We still love you. We just don't love each other anymore." But the child's other parent is half of who he or she is. The child cannot make sense of these contradictory claims. In the child's little heart, he or she knows these things cannot both be true. The parent creating the separation is telling the child, "I want something else more than I want a relationship with your other parent; that is, with half of you."

The child cannot make sense of this impossible situation. He or she is trying to deal with something that is fundamentally unjust, and which everyone around is trying to justify. It's no wonder children of divorce experience a large range of difficulties and pathologies. These negative outcomes are many and well-documented. The authors of one extensive survey summarized their findings this way: "Divorce . . . permanently weakens the family and the relationship between children and parents. It frequently leads

---

[1]   My first book argued that the secure attachments between parents and children are the foundation of the entire social order, including the economy. *Love and Economics: Why the Laissez-Faire Family Doesn't Work* was first published in 2001. Since 2008, it has been available in paperback under the title *Love and Economics: It Takes a Family to Raise a Village* (San Marcos, CA: Ruth Institute Books, 2008).

to destructive conflict management methods, diminished social competence and for children, the early loss of virginity, as well as diminished sense of masculinity or femininity for young adults. It also results in more trouble with dating, more cohabitation, greater likelihood of divorce, higher expectations of divorce later in life, and a decreased desire to have children."[2]

The research summary finds that children of divorce, on average, have poorer relationships with not only mother and father but often grandparents as well. Children of divorce are more likely to have a weakened ability to handle conflict, are more likely to be aggressive, and as adults, tend to be less able to communicate effectively with their own spouses. Children of divorce have more behavior problems in school, more depression and anxiety, diminished learning capacity, and lowered school performance. Child abuse and neglect are more common, especially in stepfamilies. Children of divorce have lifelong increased health burdens, including a risk of premature death. This summary of research goes on in this vein for 48 closely-typed pages and 333 footnotes.

Obviously, not every child of every divorced family experiences every one of these problems. Nevertheless, there is simply too much evidence, compiled over too many years, to leave any doubt. Divorce is a high-risk event for children. The Ruth Institute has a website called Kids Divorce

---

[2]   Patrick Fagan and Aaron Churchill, "The Effects of Divorce on Children," Marriage and Religion Research Institute, January 11, 2012, p. 1, http://marri.us/effects-divorce-children.

Stories,[3] where people write about what it was like for them when their parents divorced.

One woman named Clare wrote that her mother consistently made fun of the statistics showing the harms that children experience as a result of divorce, saying, "you kids turned out fine." But what Clare heard was a blanket prohibition on ever bringing up the subject of how much she missed her father, or how much the divorce had impacted her. There was literally no space in the family system for her to express those feelings. A woman named Jennifer wrote that her stepfather would come home from trips with gifts for her mother and for the daughter that the two of them had together, but no gift for her.

I met a college professor some years ago who told me he was grateful for my writings on the permanence of marriage. He'd been married for thirteen years at that time, and he realized that no one in his family had ever been married that long. He felt like a ship on uncharted waters. I invited him to contribute to our Kids' Divorce Stories project. "I can't. It's still too painful," he replied.

I hear that regularly from people my age and older. I once asked a priest to contribute. "Father, the story of your childhood would bless many people." "It's still too painful." I once had a woman my age leave the room during one of my talks about divorce. She couldn't bear to listen. Her parents' divorce and all that followed upon it were too painful for a woman in her sixties.

---

3   "Kids' Divorce Stories," The Ruth Institute, http://www. marriage-ecosystem.org/divorcestories.html.

The underlying concept of the divorce ideology is that "kids are resilient" and "kids don't really need their own parents." Sometimes we hear that "the kids will be fine as long as their parents are happy." Many parents have dissolved perfectly acceptable marriages because they didn't anticipate the full impact divorce would have on their children. They thought their kids would be fine and would adjust to a new father figure or mother figure. They believed that divorce would end the conflict.

I once made this statement to a roomful of family law attorneys: "People divorce because they believe divorce will end the conflict." Their reaction? They burst out laughing. The main part of their business is managing post-divorce conflict. I think we should name these statements for what they are: lies. Divorce does not always end conflict. More often it simply transfers the conflict to another arena. The culture we live in actively hides this truth from us. The kids don't all get over it. Kids do need their own parents.

Other Victims of the Divorce Ideology

The Divorce Ideology has claimed many other victims besides children of divorce. Other children lose access to both their parents, or perhaps never had access to both their parents. Children of unmarried parents, for instance, or children of cohabiting parents, are likely to lose contact with their fathers. When their mothers acquire new love interests, all the problems of stepfamilies appear in addition to the instability inherent in the non-marital situation.

All too often, their mothers made decisions based on the

lie that children don't need both parents, that single-mother-
hood is a noble badge of honor, and that she would become
a folk-hero of resourcefulness and love. Quite often, women
underestimate the difficulties of raising a child alone: the
exhaustion of caring for infants, the anxiety of wondering
if her childcare provider is reliable, and the lack of respect
from a teenaged son who is bigger and stronger than she is.
And loneliness can sometimes overwhelm a woman's best
judgment when entering a new relationship.

Children whose parents divorce are victims of the Divorce
Ideology because they're deprived of a stable relationship
with both their parents. The parents are victims because the
Divorce Ideology systematically misleads them into making bad decisions. In an even more profound manner, people conceived through anonymous gamete (sperm or egg)
donation are victimized by the Divorce Ideology. They never
know one of their parents, by design. They do know that
their anonymous donor accepted money for his sperm or
her egg; that is, half of the child's genetic material. The child
does know that their donor parent agreed never to have anything to do with them, their own child. Like Genevieve,
whom we met in chapter 1.

Advocates for donor conception try to create the impression that donor-conceived children are so wanted by their
parents that the fact that they were chosen will override all
other considerations. The problems that arise from living
with an unrelated adult,[4] the pain that children feel from

---

4   Jessica Kern was the child of a "traditional surrogacy" arrange-
      ment; namely, her father paid a woman to use his sperm to
      impregnate herself, carry the child, and hand her over to him.

the absence of one of their biological parents, all these risks can be safely disregarded. In fact, many advocates of these practices barely notice that the children have issues later as adults.[5] They rationalize these issues and claim they are not barriers to the adults bringing the child into being.[6]

Children of donor conception have their own perspective. Many of them do long for their missing parent. Some feel shame about being partially purchased. Some have anxieties about inadvertently encountering an unknown half-sibling.[7] I met a young man who has reason to believe he has five hundred half siblings. He left his hometown and moved a

---

Jessica's adoptive mother—that is, her father's wife—abused her. Jessica testified against the "Surrogacy Parenting Act of 2013," the bill that permitted surrogacy for the first time. Jane Ridley, "Child of surrogacy campaigns to outlaw the practice," *New York Post*, June 16, 2014, http://nypost.com/2014/06/16/children-of-surrogacy-campaign-to-outlaw-the-practice/. Her testimony is here: http://www.cbc-network.org/wp-content/uploads/2013/06/Kern_TestimonyDC20-32.pdf. She blogs at "I am a product of surrogacy," www.theothersideofsurrogacy.blogspot.com.

[5] Blogs by law professors Julie Shapiro, www.julieshapiro.wordpress.com/, and Nancy Polikoff, "Beyond (Straight and Gay) Marriage," http://beyondstraightandgaymarriage.blogspot.com/, discuss how to make parental rights of non-genetic parents more secure and how to exclude egg and sperm donors from parental rights. But the impact that donor conception may have on the child are scarcely mentioned.

[6] I. Glen Cohen, "Regulating Reproduction: The Problem with Best Interests," *Minnesota Law Review* 96 (2012), p. 423, https://papers.ssrn.com/sol3/papers.cfm?abstract_id=1955292.

[7] See for instance Alana Newman, ed., *The Anonymous Us Project: A Story-Collective on 3rd Party Reproduction*, 2 vols. (New York: Broadway Publications, 2013–16). Other stories are collected on the Anonymous Us Project's website: www.anonymousus.org.

thousand miles away because he had had too many encounters with people who looked strangely like himself.

Although he has an understandable desire to know his relatives, these chance encounters with strangers who might be relatives proved to be unnerving.[8] Those of us who grew up with our own parents and siblings cannot even imagine how donor conceived persons feel. Where we have solid ground under our feet, they have ever-shifting sands.

Third-party reproduction arrangements are morally problematic for all the same reasons as divorce and unmarried parenthood, only more intensely so. For most of these children, their gamete donor is anonymous and is not part of their family. One of the parents has decided to completely cut the other parent out of their lives. This is a greater injustice than a divorce or separation because it's deliberate from the beginning and permanent.

All these children have at least this one thing in common. The adults' relationship with their sex partners is more important to them than their relationship with the child's other parent. Needless to say, this conflict does not arise in families where the mother and father are continuously and faithfully married to each other.

---

8   Matt Doran started the website DonorChildren to help donor conceived adults locate their genetic relatives and share experiences. He recounts the story of believing he has over 500 half-siblings on the "About Us" page. "Through DNA and two years of research Matt was able to find his biological father and family. He also discovered he is one of suspected 500+ siblings. . . . Matt will continue searching for his half-siblings the rest of his life." "About Us," DonorChildren (blog), http://www. donorchildren.com/about-us.

Adult Victims of Divorce: The
Reluctantly Divorced Person

Another whole class of victims of the Divorce Ideology is almost completely invisible in society: the reluctantly divorced. This is the person who would like to stay married. This person may be a man like Todd, whom we met in the first chapter. In his mind, he still considered himself married. He lived all the practical realities of marriage—caring for his children and remaining faithful to his wife—even though she had abandoned the family. This person may be a woman like Katrina, whose husband left her for another woman, or like Bethany, whose husband left her for a computer screen and eventually another woman.

All these people would have liked to stay married. They were willing to work on improving the relationship. They would have been considered innocent spouses under the old fault-based rules. Their spouses would have been considered offending spouses. And some of their offending spouses would never have even considered doing the things they did if the serious disincentives of a fault-based divorce system had been in place.

The Divorce Ideology conceals all these people and their sufferings. The Divorce Ideology teaches us that divorce should be cheap and easy. After all, we are asked rhetorically: *Why does the State have any interest in keeping lifeless marriages together? Why should the State stand between two people who have decided to call it quits?* The Divorce Ideology cannot admit the possibility that one person wants the divorce, not only more than the other, but against the expressed wishes of the other. Nor can it admit that the State is taking sides in a family dispute, and always for the party who wants the marriage the least. Admitting these facts would certainly tarnish the appeal of the Divorce Ideology.

Until recently, no one really knew how often no-fault divorce meant unilateral divorce. The government has a policy of not asking too many questions about people's motives for divorce, so they don't keep the statistics that would allow us to answer this question. Even now, we have only a small amount of evidence, collected indirectly in the process of studying something else.

The 2014 Relationships in America project is a nationally representative, privately conducted (that is, non-governmentally-conducted) survey of just under fifteen thousand adults aged eighteen to sixty. While asking "who most often wants divorce, women or men?" the researcher gave the 3,900 divorcees the option "we both wanted it to end." Only 27 percent of men and 24 percent of women said, "We both wanted it to end." That means that whether asking men or women, we find that over 70 percent of divorces take place against the wishes of one party.[9]

This fact has profound implications. It means that the archetypical story that the Divorce Ideology presents us

---

[9]   Mark Regnerus, *Cheap Sex: The Transformation of Men, Marriage, and Monogamy* (New York: Oxford University Press, 2017), pp. 160–61, figure 5.2. The description of the Relationships in America survey can be found on pp. 12–14. And the answer to the question, "who most often wants divorce, women or men?" is women, by far. Among women, 55 percent said they wanted the marriage to end more than their spouses did, while only 29 percent of divorcing men said the same.

cannot be the full story. It is not always the case that two sensible adult people agree to amicably split. Quite often, in fact *most* often, one adult is *not* agreeing.

In situations where one party to the divorce does not want it, the Sexual State enforces the divorce. The coercive machinery of the State is wheeled into action to separate the reluctantly divorced party from the joint assets of the marriage, typically the home and the children. Justice for the reluctant party? Justice for the children? These concepts go out the window. The Divorce Ideology presents itself to the public as a great expansion of personal liberty. In reality, no-fault divorce has led to an unprecedented increase in the power of the government over individual private lives.

Family courts tell fathers how much money they must spend on their children, and how much time they get to spend with them. Courts rule on which parent gets to spend Christmas Day with the children, down to and including the precise time of day they must turn the child over to the other parent. Judges rule on whether bilingual parents must speak English to their own children as a condition of visitation.[10] Judges make decisions about the religious practices of estranged parents around their children.[11] I have even heard of family court judges making a decision about a teenage

---

[10]   "Judge: Speaking Spanish at Home is Child Abuse," *New York Daily News*, August 30, 1995, http://www.nydailynews.com/archives/news/judge-speaking-spanish-home-child-abuse-article-1.698045. "Nebraska Judge Tells Man He Must Speak English to Visit His Daughter," *Associated Press*, October 14, 2003.

[11]   Eugene Volokh, "A gag order on parents," *LA Times*, February 6, 2007, http://www.latimes.com/news/la-oe-volokh6feb06-story.html.

girl's prom dress because the estranged parents couldn't work it out.

Involving the family court in the minutiae of family life is hardly the behavior of a minimal government, so beloved by libertarians and many conservatives. America does not permit any other agent of the government to intervene in people's private business so intimately, so frequently, and so routinely. People under the authority of the family courts can have virtually all their private lives subject to its scrutiny.[12]

In fact, some feminists are proud of blurring the boundaries between the public and the private. They say the private sphere of the home allows the oppression of women by men. Therefore, they applaud the state entering the home to protect women from domestic violence. This type of feminist has expanded the definition of domestic violence. Harvard law professor Jeannie Suk laments, "The overwhelming majority of domestic violence arrests are for misdemeanor crimes, which, by definition, do not involve serious injury. . . . The definition of violence itself has expanded to include a lot of conduct that is not physical violence."[13] A man can be permanently removed from his home and barred from contact with his children and his wife, even if she wants contact with him, because of a misdemeanor.

We could compare the fault and no-fault regimes this

---

[12]   Stephen Baskerville, *Taken Into Custody: The War Against Fathers, Marriage and the Family* (Nashville, TN: Cumberland House Publishing, 2007).

[13]   Quoted in Alec Baldwin, *A Promise to Ourselves: A Journey Through Fatherhood and Divorce* (New York: St. Martin's Press, 2008), p. 194. See also Jeannie Suk, "Criminal Law Comes Home," *Yale Law Journal* 116, no. 2 (2006).

way. Under a no-fault legal regime, we are freer on the front
end: we can leave a marriage without cause or accountability.
But we are less free on the back end, as the State steps in to
manage the consequences of the breakup of the little society
of the family.

At the same time, the breakup of families, or the failure
to form families, leads to an expansion of State expendi-
ture. As we've already noted, children from disrupted families do worse than children of intact married households
in virtually every way.[14] Children are more likely to have
physical and mental health problems. Even accounting for
income, fatherless boys are more likely to be aggressive[15] and
to ultimately become incarcerated.[16] A British study offers
tantalizing hints about the possibility that the children of

---

[14]   The Fagan and Churchill study cited earlier looks exclusively
at the impact of divorce on children. Other forms of family
breakdown are analyzed in useful summaries, such as Maggie
Gallagher and Joshua Baker, "Do Moms and Dads Matter? Evi-
dence from the Social Sciences on Family Structure and the Best
Interests of the Child," *Margins* 4 (2004), pp. 161–80; Kristen
Anderson Moore, Susan M. Jekielek, and Carol Emig, "Marriage
from a Child's Perspective: How Does Family Structure Affect
Children and What Can We Do About It?" *Child Trends Research
Brief* (June 2002); Jennifer Roback Morse, *Smart Sex: Finding
Life-long Love in a Hook-up World* (Dallas, TX: Spence Publish-
ing, 2005).

[15]   Nancy Vaden-Kiernan et al., "Household Family Structure and
Children's Aggressive Behavior: A Longitudinal Study of Urban
Elementary School Children," *Journal of Abnormal Child Psychol-
ogy* 23, no. 5 (1995), pp. 553–68.

[16]   Cynthia C. Harper and Sara S. McLanahan, "Father Absence and
Youth Incarceration," *Journal of Research on Adolescence* 14, no. 3
(2004), pp. 369–97.

single mothers are more likely to become schizophrenic.[17] An extensive study of family structure in Sweden took account of the mental illness history of the parents as well as socio-economic status. Yet even in the most generous welfare state in the world, with very accepting attitudes toward unmarried parenthood, the children of single parents faced double the risk of psychiatric disease, suicide attempts, and substance abuse.[18] All these issues are expensive to the taxpayer through health care, special education services, mental health services, substance abuse recovery, or the criminal justice system.

Studies have calculated the taxpayer costs of family breakdown. One study, prepared by the National Fatherhood Institute, announces its conclusion in its title: "The One Hundred Billion Dollar Man." This figure is their estimate of the taxpayer costs of fatherlessness nationwide.[19] Another study, using slightly different methodology, concludes that the total annual cost of fatherlessness to federal, state, and local taxpayers amounted to $112 billion.[20]

---

[17] Sarah Hall, "Schizophrenia much more likely in children of single parents," *UK Guardian*, November 2, 2006.

[18] Gunilla Ringback Weitoft et al., "Mortality, severe morbidity and injury in children living with single parents in Sweden: a population-based study," *The Lancet* 361, no. 9354 (January 25, 2003).

[19] Steven L. Nock and Christopher J. Einolf, "*The One Hundred Billion Dollar Man: the annual public cost of father absence*," The National Fatherhood Initiative, June 30, 2008, http://portal.hud.gov/hudportal/documents/huddoc?id=100_billion_dollar_man.pdf.

[20] Benjamin Scafidi, *The Taxpayer Costs of Divorce and Unwed Child-bearing: First Ever Estimates for the US and all 50 States* (New York: Institute for American Values, 2008), http://americanvalues.org/catalog/pdfs/COFF.pdf.

In other words, we are spending the equivalent of the GDP of New Zealand to deal with the costs of family breakdown. Speaking of New Zealand, researchers there also did a study calculating the taxpayer costs of family breakdown. Likewise, similar calculations have been performed for the United Kingdom and Canada.[21] Around the world, family breakdown costs taxpayers enormous sums of money. This, of course, doesn't include the personal costs—financial, emotional, and spiritual—to individual men, women, and children.

Thus, the social experiment of no-fault divorce, which was accepted as an expansion of personal liberty, has resulted in an unprecedented intrusion of the State into the private lives of ordinary, law-abiding citizens. The social pathologies that result from family dissolution, and the consequent failures of some families to form, are expensive to the taxpayer. Civil libertarians, fiscal conservatives, and open-minded liberals

---

[21]   Patrick Nolan, *The Value of Family: Fiscal Benefits of Marriage and Reducing Family Breakdown in New Zealand* (Wellington, New Zealand: Family First New Zealand, October 2008), https://irp-cdn.multiscreensite.com/64484987/files/uploaded/NewZealand Report.pdf. In the United Kingdom, the Relationships Foundation has published a "Cost of Family Breakdown Index" annually since 2009. The most recent report is for 2016, "Counting the Cost of Family Failure: Update 2016," http://knowledgebank. oneplusone.org.uk/wp-content/uploads/2016/03/Counting-the-Cost-of-Family-Failure-2016-Update.pdf. Rebecca Walberg and Andrea Mrozek, *Private Choices, Public Costs: How failing families cost us all* (Ottawa, Canada: Institute for Marriage and Family, Canada, 2009), https://irp-cdn.multiscreensite.com/64484987/files/uploaded/CanadaPrivateChoicesPublicCostsFinal.pdf. (All sites in this note last accessed November 7, 2016.)

should all be troubled by the actual results as opposed to the supposed benefits of this "freedom."

So where did the Divorce Ideology come from? Whose bright idea was this, anyway?

CHAPTER 9

The Elite Origins of the Divorce Ideology

The Legal Establishment and No-Fault Divorce

In 1968, California removed fault from divorce law. At that time, the divorce rate per one thousand married women was just under 10 percent. Removing fault from divorce was supposed to reduce the costs: financial, emotional, and social. However, the advocates of this change evidently did not anticipate that this seemingly modest modification in the law changed the incentives for everyone, not just for the relatively few people who would have gotten divorced in any case. Millions of people changed their behavior. The divorce rate had doubled by the 1980s.[1]

Removing the fault basis for divorce redefined marriage in two ways. Obviously, no-fault divorce removed the

---

[1]   "Social Indicators of Marital Health and Well-Being: Trends of the Past Five Decades," The State of Our Unions, table 5, http://www.stateofourunions.org/2012/social_indicators.php#divorce.

presumption of permanence from the marriage bond. At the same time, no-fault removes the presumption that marriage is a sexually exclusive union: adultery had been considered a marital fault. One party was the offending party; the other was the innocent party. This was precisely the language that the advocates of no-fault wished to eliminate. Under this new legal regime, the presumption that marriage is a lifelong sexually exclusive union came to an end.

Given the enormity of this change, we might be curious as to its origin. Contrary to popular perception, feminism had little to do with the enactment of no-fault divorce legislation during the late 1960s and early 1970s. "Rather, the shift from fault (adultery, desertion, abuse, etc.) to no-fault (unilateral assertion of irreconcilable difference) resulted from predominantly male lawyers and lawmakers seeking to reduce fraud, lessen husbands' alimony burdens, and streamline the divorce process into a less controversial, more perfunctory proceeding."[2]

Once no-fault was in place, feminists mobilized to improve women's post-divorce lot, but the legislative change itself came about with little ideological agitation or discussion outside the legal profession.

Inside the legal profession, the push for no-fault divorce had been brewing for some time through the American Law Institute (ALI). Founded in 1923 with support from the Carnegie Foundation, the ALI attempted to nationalize law by creating model codes and restatements. These

---

2   Ryan C. MacPherson, "From No-Fault Divorce to Same-Sex Marriage: The American Law Institute's Role in Deconstructing the Family," *The Family in America* 25, no. 2 (Spring 2011), p. 131.

publications were the result of the work of numerous experts summarizing case law pertinent to specific subjects. History professor Ryan MacPherson explains: "The self-defining professional class of legal experts who established the ALI—predominately Ivy League law professors—pioneered a juristic methodology that would not merely recognize the changing needs of contemporary society, but also 'restate' the law in such a way as to accommodate those social realities."[3]

Beginning well before the change in divorce laws, the institute's model penal code promoted the concept that private sexual acts between consenting adults should be decriminalized. This notion, now widely accepted but at the time rather revolutionary, drove a wedge between private acts and public morality, indeed, it undermined the very idea of public morality.[4] In fact, it is safe to say that this "private sexual acts between consenting adults" image is probably the predominant template most people have in mind when they consider what the government's role should be.

The idea of decriminalizing "private acts between consenting adults" was instrumental in cases concerning the states' ability to regulate obscene materials (1957) and in the contraception cases (1965). Illinois even passed a generalized

---

3   Ibid., p. 126.

4   Ibid., p. 129. Professor Lynn Wardle argues that this unwillingness to see any public meaning to marriage continues in the more recent (2002) work of the ALI, *Principles of the Law of Family Dissolution.* Lynn D. Wardle, "Beyond Fault and No-Fault in the Reform of Marital Dissolution Law," in *Reconceiving the Family: Critique on the American Law Institute's Principles of the Law of Family Dissolution*, ed. Robin Fretwell Wilson, (New York: Cambridge University Press, 2006), pp. 9–27.

statute decriminalizing all private sexual acts between consenting adults in 1962.[5]

With the private/public dichotomy in place, state legislators failed to realize the full implications of eliminating the presumptions of permanence and exclusivity from marriage. The behavior of married couples toward one another is not entirely private, because their behavior affects their children and may affect their parents, siblings, and other family members. Nor is the behavior of married couples toward one another entirely public, in the sense that it is a fit subject for detailed government regulation.

A better way to understand the significance of married couples' behavior toward one another is to see it as "social": a concept that acknowledges the interpersonal nature of their actions without giving the government free reign to regulate it. But this is precisely the point that is obscured by a sharp private/public dichotomy[6] promoted by the American Law Institute.

By 1974, all but five states had adopted some form of no-fault divorce. In 1974, the National Conference of Commissioners of Uniform State Laws, with funding from the Ford Foundation, led an effort toward nationwide simplification of family law. The 1974 promulgation of the Uniform Marriage and Divorce Act, with the endorsement of

---

[5]   MacPherson, "From No-Fault Divorce to Same-Sex Marriage," p. 129.
[6]   I make this distinction between private, public, and social in "Why Consumer Sex is Anti-social," in *Smart Sex: Finding Lifelong Love in a Hook-up World* (San Marcos CA: Ruth Institute Books, 2008).

the American Bar Association, lent national legitimacy to a process that had occurred piecemeal throughout the states beginning with California in 1968.[7]

Citizens and some legislatures have resisted no-fault unilateral divorce in what can be considered a "divorce counterrevolution." One expert lists the following attempts at state-level divorce reform: 1) mandatory mediation, 2) other forms of alternative dispute resolution, 3) therapeutic jurisprudence, 4) different procedures for parties with children than for parties without children, 5) waiting periods, 6) premarital counseling, 7) covenant marriage approaches (now adopted in Louisiana, Arizona, and Arkansas), 8) general marriage education programs, and 9) special assistance for low income or special needs couples such as those provided by the "marriage initiatives" of the Clinton and Bush welfare reforms.[8] Citizens, acting through their state and even federal legislatures—you know, the way laws are supposed to be made—have attempted to reign in the excesses of the no-fault revolution. Waiting periods for divorce have had some success in reducing divorce rates.[9] But the ALI, committed as it is to the Sexual State ideology, retains its staunch opposition to any consideration of marital fault.

Professor Lynn Wardle has shown that the American

---

[7]   MacPherson, "From No-Fault Divorce to Same-Sex Marriage," p. 131–32.

[8]   Wardle "Beyond Fault and No-Fault in the Reform of Marital Dissolution Law," in *Reconceiving the Family*, pp. 23–24.

[9]   Michael J McManus, "Confronting the More Entrenched Flow: The Disaster of No–Fault Divorce and Its Legacy of Cohabitation," *The Family in America* 25, no. 2 (Spring 2011), pp. 157–72, See esp. p. 164, chart 4.

Law Institute's *Principles of the Law of Family Dissolution* approach to fault has serious inconsistencies. If one party squanders family wealth, this fact can be considered in the property settlement, almost like an "economic fault." Allegations of assault, battery, or abuse of the children can be handled as criminal acts.

So, if the ALI's *Principles* still effectively permit the consideration of economic faults and abuse faults, what does no-fault amount to? It means that the major fault removed by "no-fault" was adultery or sexual infidelity. As Wardle says,

> Disregarding fault may make the jobs of lawyers and judges simpler, but it makes dissolution law and legal proceedings surreal, less responsive to the key issues, and less connected to what is really happening in the parties' lives, and therefore it makes dissolution law less effective, less complete, and less just. Moreover, a social consensus exists about many kinds of marital misconduct, as the drafters (of the ALI *Principles*) themselves recognize . . . in their own recommendations to consider financial misconduct and domestic violence. . . . But when it comes to sexual infidelity and other serious misbehavior, the drafters are unwilling to allow common consensus to be recognized or effectuated. This distinction between acceptable and unacceptable moral consensus considerations is both inconsistent and discriminates without justification.[10]

---

[10]   Wardle, "Beyond Fault and No-Fault in the Reform of Marital Dissolution Law," in *Reconceiving the Family*, pp. 9–27.

Adultery is consistently ranked as one of the most frequent causes of divorce. Sexual betrayal causes enormous pain to the injured spouse.[11] Parental abandonment of the family for a new love interest deeply wounds children. The prohibition on adultery is one of the Ten Commandments, to which all branches of Christianity and Judaism still pay at least lip service. For all these reasons, writing adultery out of the law was a profound and disastrous step in redefining marriage.

The reason we allowed no-fault divorce in this country is simple. The legal elite, acting through the American Law Institute and with the support of large foundations, captured the power of the State to impose their values on the rest of the country. No-fault divorce was not instituted because of a widespread demand from ordinary people for new divorce processes and procedures. The managerial class acting through the American Law Institute codified the no-fault concept in its 1974 promulgation of the Uniform Marriage and Divorce Act. The managerial class believes that financial misconduct and dissipation of assets ought to be considered in divorce settlements but "moral" issues like adultery should not.

---

[11]   Paul R. Amato and Denise Previti, "People's reasons for divorcing: gender, social class, the life course, and adjustment," *Journal of Family Issues* 24, no. 5 (July 2003), pp. 602–26, table 3 on p. 615 lists infidelity as the number one cause of divorce.

Recent Attempts at Divorce Reform
and What They Demonstrate

One might argue that the "ordinary people" acquiesced in this redefinition of marriage. No one rioted in the streets. No church raised serious public opposition. So perhaps there was a quiet desire for removing fault from divorce.

Against this claim, I make two responses. First, virtually no one, even the most conservative traditionalists, realized just how radical this legal innovation really was. No one foresaw the many new threads of laws and social practices that would come into being as the new non-permanent, non-sexually exclusive version of marriage worked its way through the culture.

Secondly, some states have attempted to reform their divorce laws. Observing the fate of these attempts is most instructive. Such an observation reveals that the elites doubled down on their prized "freedom to divorce." In 2002, the American Law Institute published its *Principles of the Law of Family Dissolution.* One commentator sympathetic to its aims stated bluntly, "By marshaling the considerable powers of the ALI in opposition to the divorce counterrevolution, the *Principles* declared the second death of marital fault as a limitation upon the freedom to divorce."[12] Note the language: "freedom to divorce."

The law of marriage and marriage dissolution has traditionally been the purview of the states. Each state has

---

[12]   James Herbie DiFonzo, "Toward a unified field theory of the family: the American law institute's *Principles of the Law of Family Dissolution*," *BYU Law Review* 923 (2001), pp. 959.

different rules about eligibility for marriage, the age of marriage, and the degree of relatedness permitted between the partners. The states also have different rules about the terms of divorce, property division, child custody, the types of evidence permitted, and many other terms of dissolution.

If states have the freedom to make their own marriage laws, states can provide a social laboratory. Some states might make some reforms of the terms of divorce; other states might choose different partial reforms. Observing how things turn out could provide a valuable lesson as to how best to proceed to provide justice for children and for mothers and fathers. We probably shouldn't have one giant reform of all divorce laws everywhere.

I mention this because I'm often asked, "So, do you want to abolish divorce?" No. I don't. This question demonstrates the thought process of the revolutionary, not the reformer. And it is quite typical of the true sexual revolutionary to be oblivious to the possibility of meaningful reform that is not revolutionary. With that in mind, let's look at a few recent attempts at divorce reform.

Shared Parenting

A few states have tried to institute a presumption of shared parenting. This is potentially a valuable reform for several reasons. The presumption of equal parenting time reduces the incentives to divorce.[13] Equal parenting time allows the

---

[13]   Margaret Brinig and Douglas Allen, "These Boots are Made for Walking: why most divorce filers are women," *American Law and Economics Review* 2, no. 1, pp. 126–69, http://aler.oxfordjour nals.org/content/2/1/126.abstract. This article shows that the

child to maintain a close bond with both parents. The presumption of equal parenting is just that: a presumption. The states that tried to enact this principle included a proviso that the presumption could be overridden under some circumstances.

In 2016, the Florida state legislature passed a custody reform bill with an equal parenting presumption. The governor vetoed it due to extensive lobbying from the Family Law section of the Bar Association.[14] The Family Law section hired emergency lobbyists to defeat the bill when a child-sharing provision was added to it. They hired two high-profile lobbyists for $105,000 on the last day of the legislative session to press the governor to veto the bill.[15]

In 2014, citizens in North Dakota placed a shared parenting bill on the ballot.[16] The bill appeared to have popular

---

probability of obtaining custody is the largest factor in determining a woman's likelihood to file for divorce.

[14]   Leslie Loftis, "Florida Governor Rick Scott Ignores Families, Protects Disastrous Divorce Law," *The Federalist,* April 18, 2016, http://thefederalist.com/2016/04/18/florida-gov-rick-scott-ignores-families-protects-disastrous-divorce-law/.

[15]   "The section already had standing lobbyists. But after a child-sharing provision was added to the bill, the section quickly engaged Rutledge Ecenia and the Rubin Group of Fort Lauderdale for $75,000 along with the Advocacy Group at Cardenas Partners, featuring prominent lobbyist Al Cardenas, for $30,000. The additions brought the section's total lobbying costs for the year to $186,996. The section opposes the bill's presumption of child sharing in divorce cases. Julie Kay, "6 Florida Bar Sections Lobbying in Tallahassee," *Daily Business Review,* April 2, 2016, http://www.dailybusinessreview.com/id=1202753914575/6-Florida-Bar-Sections-Lobbying-in-Tallahassee?mcode=0&curindex=0&curpage=ALL&slreturn=20160818222056.

[16]   "North Dakota Parental Rights Initiative, Measure 6 (2014),"

support. A committee called "Keeping Kids First" formed to oppose it. The funding for this organization came entirely from the State Bar Association and the Family Law Section of the Bar Association. In fact, the Bar Association was later sued for improper use of member funds for political lobbying but not before they had defeated the shared parenting measure.[17]

In 2016, the Alabama Family Rights Association defeated a bill that did not have shared parenting. Who had favored and, indeed, authored this bill? The Family Law Committee of the Alabama Law Institute (ALI).[18] Do you see a pattern? The family law bar, which makes money managing post-divorce conflict, opposes divorce reform.

I hasten to add: shared parenting is not a panacea. The behavior of the parents should be a significant factor in the allocation of parenting time. As one psychologist observes:

Ballotpedia, https://ballotpedia.org/North_Dakota_Parental_Rights_Initiative,_Measure_6_(2014).

[17] Rachel Alexander, "Opposition Group Turns to Stealth and Sexism to Oppose Shared Parenting in North Dakota," *Townhall*, October 12, 2014, http://townhall.com/columnists/rachelalexander/2014/10/13/opposition-group-turns-to-stealth-and-sexism-to-oppose-shared-parenting-in-north-dakota-n1904235?utm_source=thdaily&utm_medium=email&utm_campaign=nl. Rachel Alexander, "Goldwater Institute sues: state bar are unconstitutional mandatory unions," *Townhall*, February 9, 2015, http://townhall.com/columnists/rachelalexander/2015/02/09/goldwater-institute-sues-state-bars-are-unconstitutional-mandatory-unions-n1954664.

[18] Kenneth Paschal, "HB 333 was defeated," Email Campaign Archive, Alabama Family Rights Association, 2016, http://us10.campaign-archive1.com/?u=5977883b4792901a0d405fabc&id=f07950ca3e.

"Under 'no-fault,' any systemic, morally destructive behaviors engaged in by one spouse throughout a contested divorce are virtually ignored by the court. 'Shared parenting' guidelines render such behaviors even more irrelevant if that's possible. An underlying premise of shared parenting is that parental behaviors and choices, so long as they are legal, should not guide the decisions of family judges."[19]

The legal establishment strenuously opposes even modest attempts at divorce reform.

The Political Establishment and Unmarried Mothers

As we saw in the previous chapter, divorce is not the only way children are deprived of stable relationships with both their parents. Divorce dissolves the union between the parents. Unmarried parenthood, however, brings children into the world without ever having a stable bond between their parents. While the divorce revolution affected people in the middle class and above, unmarried parenthood affected people in the lowest socio-economic levels of society. Unmarried parenthood is gradually working its way up through the middle class and pretty much everyone who is not a member of the college-educated managerial class. How did this happen?

American assistance to the poor is a montage of programs. Some programs target specific people, such as the disabled.

---

[19]   Hilary Towers, "Shared parenting hurts many victims of marital abandonment," Institute for Family Studies, June 1, 2017, https://ifstudies.org/blog/shared-parenting-hurts-many-victims-of-marital-abandonment.

Others provide specific kinds of help, such as food subsidies, housing support, or medical care. Each state has its own programs. And even national programs are implemented differently from state to state. Describing the impact of all these programs on every person in every situation is obviously not possible. However, we can make a few general statements.

Some programs significantly penalize people who are or become married. For instance, some people receiving the earned income tax credit will no longer qualify if they marry a person with income of their own. Child tax credits, Medicaid, SNAP, TANF, and WIC benefits can all be affected by marriage.[20]

The benefits of marriage in alleviating poverty take some time to develop. People in these situations are sometimes better off in the short term cohabiting, or not living together at all, rather than getting married. But in the longer term, these same people may very well benefit from the stability and security that marriage can provide.[21] Counting the new

---

[20]   Elaine Maag and Gregory Acs, "The Financial Consequences of Marriage for Cohabiting Couples with Children," The Urban Institute, September 2015, https://www.aei.org/wp-content/uploads/2016/07/IFS-HomeEconReport-2016-Final-072616.pdf. W. Bradford Wilcox, Joseph P. Price, and Angela Rachidi, "Marriage, Penalized: Does Social-Welfare Policy Affect Family Formation?" American Enterprise Institute and Institute for Family Studies, 2016, https://www.aei.org/wp-content/uploads/2016/07/IFS-HomeEconReport-2016-Final-072616.pdf. Robert Rector, "How Welfare Undermines Marriage and What to Do About it," The Heritage Foundation, 2014, http://www.heritage.org/research/reports/2014/11/how-welfare-undermines-marriage-and-what-to-do-about-it.

[21]   Spencer Rand, "The Real Marriage Penalty: How Welfare Law Discourages Marriage Despite Public Policy Statements to the

spouse's income and assets immediately toward the limits set by the programs means that these couples face a large barrier to getting married: the long-term benefits of marriage never have a chance in comparison with the short-term financial losses the programs' rules impose on them.

Not surprisingly, this system has steadily increased the numbers of children born out of wedlock, especially to the lower classes. For people living well above the poverty line, these rules are not relevant for any family-forming decisions they're ever likely to make. More affluent people are not dependent on the programs.

Tragically, though perhaps well-intentioned, this is the system which has led to the multi-partner fertility phenomenon that plagues children like Elise. The separation of child-bearing from marriage has steadily moved into higher and higher income brackets as the social assistance state expands its reach into higher income classes. For instance, consider women with a high-school degree and maybe some college, whom we might call middle-American women. As of 1970, this group was marrying young—at 21—and having their first child shortly after, at 22. Over the next four decades, the age at which they became wives climbed steadily and steeply. The age at which they became mothers, however, was taking a different journey. It rose until 1990 to 24.3, right in sync with the age of marriage. Then it stopped. By the early 2000s, middle-American women were having children before they were marrying. Since then, the age gap

Contrary—and What can be done about it," *University of the District of Columbia Law Review* 18, no. 1 (2015), pp. 93–143, https://papers.ssrn.com/sol3/papers.cfm?abstract_id=2685206.

between the two events has continued to widen, and now 58 percent of their firstborn children are born out of wedlock.[22]

Let me emphasize that this is not exclusively a "race thing." This is a "class thing." Poor whites—as well as poor blacks, poor Hispanics, and poor Native Americans—have their possibilities for family life systematically distorted by this series of government programs. For instance, 37 percent of first births to white women are out of wedlock compared to 64 percent of Hispanic first births, 80 percent of African-American first births, and 8 percent of Asian-American first births according to the 2010 National Vital Statistics Birth Datafiles. This gap narrows considerably when controlling for education. Among women without a college degree, the percent having their first birth out of wedlock is 55 percent for white women, 69 percent for Hispanic women, and 87 percent for African-American women.[23]

This system of extensive social assistance was initiated under the Johnson administration's war on poverty. Did President Johnson intend to create a lower class that was continually dependent upon the government and whose families had broken down? I would not presume to say. He probably thought he was helping the poor. It may have crossed his mind that he was creating a class of people who

---

22   Kay Hymowitz, Jason Carroll, W. Bradford Wilcox, Kelleen Kay, "Knot Yet: The Benefits and Costs of Delayed Marriage in America," The National Marriage Project at the University of Virginia, The National Campaign to Prevent Teen and Unplanned Pregnancy, and The Relate Institute, accessed November 15, 2016, http://twentysomethingmarriage.org/the-great-crossover/.

23   Ibid.

would consistently vote for him and his party. I rather doubt he thought any further about it than that.

I infer this by the reaction of his administration to another part of the Sexual Revolution that they were, wittingly or unwittingly, locking into place. As the war on poverty took shape, President Johnson and his people noticed that the problems of illegitimacy were growing larger, not smaller. More children were being born out of wedlock. The government's solution? Promote contraception more aggressively to the poor.

As we've already noted in our discussion of the Contraceptive Ideology, promoting contraception itself doesn't necessarily reduce pregnancies that occur in difficult situations. People come to believe contraception will protect them from all problems. Their judgment is clouded. Their self-control is weakened. They come to think themselves entitled to sex without a baby. They have more sex in situations that cannot support a pregnancy. Sometimes their contraception fails and pregnancy results.

This is the reason for the well-established fact that non-marital pregnancy and abortion both increased dramatically during the very period that contraception came on the social scene.[24] The government officials evidently didn't realize this connection. Or perhaps they did but didn't wish to fully admit it.

In any case, it's almost amusing to read the accounts in retrospect. Policymakers continued to be surprised by increases

---

[24]   George Akerloff, Janet Yellen, and Michael Katz, "An Analysis of Out-of-Wedlock Childbearing in the United States," *The Quarterly Journal of Economics* 111, no. 2 (May 1996), pp. 277–317.

in non-marital childbearing, even though they were pro-moting contraception so heavily. In 1965, policymakers fretted over illegitimacy and rising welfare costs. The Social Security Act of 1967 made the first federal grants to private organizations like Planned Parenthood and also permitted unmarried women to receive federally-subsidized contracep-tive aid. Richard Nixon's 1970 Family Planning Services and Population Research Act passed unanimously, largely due to lawmakers' concerns about welfare costs.[25]

In 1960, roughly 5 percent of all births were to unmarried women. By 1970, the year Nixon introduced family plan-ning into US federal policy, roughly 10 percent of all births were non-marital. Since 2011, over 40 percent of all births are to unmarried women.[26] And many members of the man-agerial class still seem to believe more contraception is the answer to high welfare costs and non-marital childbearing. This policy has not worked yet: why would it start working now?

We can see in retrospect that this increase in illegitimacy took place, not despite the government's promotion of con-traception to the poor, but precisely because of it. Thus, the Contraceptive Ideology worked hand in glove with the

---

[25] Donald T. Critchlow, *Intended Consequences: Birth Control, Abor-tion and the Federal Government in Modern America* (New York: Oxford University Press, 1999): concerns in 1965, p. 75; Social Security Act of 1967, p. 79; No longer excluded single women from federal help for birth control, p. 81; Nixon's Family Plan-ning Services and Population Research Act of 1970, pp. 91–93.

[26] "The State of our Unions, 2012: Social Indicators of Marital Health and Well-Being," table 13 http://www.stateofourunions. org/2012/social_indicators.php#si-fig13.

Divorce Ideology to create a world in which the poorest, most vulnerable children in society have been deprived of a stable relationship with their father. These kids are subjected to the churning of their parents' relationships, which are constantly forming and breaking apart, and are all part of the trauma of multi-partner fertility.

Multi-partner fertility has become so common that demographers have had to modify their data collection and their analysis in order to measure it properly. Do we view multi-partner fertility from the woman's point of view, the man's, or the child's? The oldest and youngest child of a mother in a multi-partner fertility situation are likely to have very different experiences. The mother's oldest child may experience the loss of his father, being in a single parent household, and his mother's re-partnering, perhaps multiple times. In the meantime, the youngest child of the same woman is more likely to be living with his or her biological father as well as his mother. For that child, the family is "intact." For the older children, not so much.[27]

The Divorce Ideology was further enhanced, encouraged, and endorsed by radical leftists like Richard Cloward and Frances Fox Piven.[28] They actively wanted poor people to

---

[27] Karen Benjamin Guzzo and Cassandra Dorius, "Challenges in Measuring and Studying Multipartnered Fertility in American Survey Data," *Population Research Review*, 25 May 2016, http://link.springer.com/article/10.1007/s11113-016-9398-9?view=classic.

[28] Frances Fox Piven and Richard A. Cloward, "The Weight of the Poor: A Strategy to End Poverty," *The Nation*, May 2, 1966, reprinted in *Common Dreams*, March 24, 2010 http://www.commondreams.org/news/2010/03/24/weight-poor-strategy-end-poverty.

be on public assistance. They believed it would cause financial collapse and hasten the day of more comprehensive income redistribution programs. Their means of hastening that day was to encourage as many people as possible to sign up for public assistance. They worked on breaking down any reticence people might have about surrendering their independence by not working. They also criticized local welfare enforcement policies that made an "unsuitable home" grounds for discontinuing Aid to Families with Dependent Children. They criticized the fact that aid was sometimes terminated even when people were still in need. As they put it: "Upon closer examination, these 'other reasons' turned out to be 'unsuitable home' (i.e., the presence of illegitimate children), 'failure to comply with departmental regulations' or 'refusal to take legal action against a putative father.'"

The scare quotes clearly indicate Cloward and Piven's disapproval. Part of breaking down the resistance to receiving public assistance included breaking down the moral strictures people might have about having children without being married.

Obviously, not everyone in the managerial class is a radical leftist. In fact, some members of the managerial classes, sometimes in their own ironic and slightly oblivious way, try to help. They tell everyone that the absence of the father from the child's life is not such a big deal after all. The kids will be fine if we just give their mothers more money. The kids will be fine if we just create more programs that channel resources to them. The people who argue this way are in effect saying that programs run by adults unrelated to the child and money provided by strangers can take the place of their personal relationship with their fathers. Would you believe that if someone said it to you about your life?

The more ideological members of the managerial classes warn darkly about the hazards of trapping women in abusive marriages. They never get around to mentioning that cohabitation and multi-partner fertility situations are rife with domestic violence. Domestic violence, or "intimate partner violence" as we are now supposed to call it, occurs more often in the lives of unmarried couples than the lives of married couples. According to Australian, Canadian, and US data, the probability of a woman being murdered by her unmarried cohabiting partner is roughly nine times higher than the chances of a woman being killed by her husband.[29] For the record, cohabiting men are about ten times more likely to be murdered by their partners than are husbands.[30]

The most dangerous living situation for a child is to live with his or her mother and live-in boyfriend.[31] The boyfriend

---

[29]   Todd K. Shackelford and Jenny Mouzos, "Partner Killing by Men in Cohabiting and Marital Relationships: A Comparative, Cross-National Analysis of Data From Australia and the United States," *Journal of Interpersonal Violence* 20, no. 10 (October 2005), pp. 1310–24.

[30]   Todd K. Shackelford, "Partner-Killing by Women in Cohabiting Relationships and Marital Relationships," *Homicide Studies* 5, no. 3 (August 1, 2001), p. 253–66. There is now some evidence that the difference in homicide between cohabiting and married couples has diminished, along with an overall decline in intimate partner homicides. No clear explanation for this trend has emerged as definitive. Bridie James and Martin Daly, "Cohabitation Is No Longer Associated With Elevated Spousal Homicide Rates in the United States," *Homicide Studies* 16, no. 4, p. 393–403.

[31]   The risk to children from the mothers' boyfriends has been doc-

is interested in the mother, not the child. The child is a left-over from a previous relationship which neither adult really wants to be reminded of.

Some of these studies are old and out of date, you may say. Ask yourself why you think that matters. We somehow expect the passage of time to bring wider acceptance of cohabitation. We think this wider social acceptance will solve these problems. Do you have any reason to believe that is the case from watching the evening news? I don't.

Such an attitude assumes the problems have only to do

---

umented and in the literature since the 1980s. The classic work is Martin Daly and Margo Wilson, "Discriminative Parental Solicitude: A Biological Perspective," *Journal of Marriage and the Family* (May 1980), pp. 277–88. Michael Gordon and Susan J. Creighton, "Natal and Non-Natal Fathers as Sexual Abusers in the United Kingdom: A Comparative Analysis," *Journal of Marriage and the Family* 50 (February 1988), pp. 99–105 shows that the pattern is also observed in the United Kingdom among child sexual abusers: "Non-natal fathers were disproportionately represented among paternal abusers; however natal fathers were more likely to subject their victims to intercourse." Research from the 1990s includes Leslie Margolin, "Child Abuse by Mothers' Boyfriends: Why the Overrepresentation?" *Child Abuse and Neglect* 16 (1991), pp. 541–51; Robert Whelan, *Broken Homes & Battered Children: A study of the relationship between child abuse and family type* (Oxford: Family Education Trust, 1994).

More recent studies include a study of child homicides from Missouri in 2005, Patricia G. Schnitzer and Bernard G. Ewigman, "Child Deaths Resulting from Inflicted Injuries: Household Risk Factors and Perpetrator Characteristics," *Pediatrics* 116, no. 5 (November 2005), and the 2010 Report to Congress, "Fourth National Incidence Study of Child Abuse and Neglect (NIS–4) Report to Congress," (January 15, 2010), https://www.acf.hhs.gov/opre/research/project/national-incidence-study-of-child-abuse-and-neglect-nis-4-2004-2009.

with social approval. Do you suppose that less disapproval of unmarried motherhood will eliminate the stress, fatigue, and loneliness that unmarried mothers feel? Will wider social acceptance improve her judgment about what kind of guy is good for her to be involved with? Is the mere progression of time enough to make men no longer prefer their own biological children to someone else's? Will further progress of the Sexual Revolution make men less interested in sex with the mother and more interested in her child?

Sexual revolutionaries believe they can remake human nature. This is a fool's errand. "Old, outdated" studies show that we have known from the beginning that multi-partner fertility and cohabitation and non-marital childbearing are problematic. The privileged people of society —academics, social workers, judges, law enforcement officers—are all aware of these risks. But we aren't telling the

---

One exception is Richard J. Gelles and John W. Harrop, "The Risk of Abusive Violence Among Children with Nongenetic Caretakers," *Family Relations* 40 (1991), pp. 78–83, which concludes, "Data from the Second National Family Violence Survey . . . reveal NO significant difference between genetic and nongenetic parents in the rates of severe and very severe violence toward children." However, this study does not distinguish between single, cohabiting, and married parents. Hence it is only indirectly relevant to the cohabitation issue. This study is more immediately relevant to the sociobiology framing of the issue.

Against this, however, is this 2015 study which takes for granted the overrepresentation of violence against children by non-genetic caretakers and seeks only to ascertain exactly why this occurs. N. Z. Hilton, G. T. Harris, and M. E. Rice, "The step-father effect in child abuse: Comparing discriminative parental solicitude and antisociality," *Psychology of Violence* 5, no. 1, pp. 8–15.

poor, those whose lives are most likely to be disrupted and even destroyed by the loss of a "marriage culture."

Feeling jealousy over an ex's new relationships, feeling financially strapped, and feeling cheated all increase the vulnerability of the unmarried parents and their susceptibility to entering a cycle of multiple relationships. These problems are direct results of the Divorce Ideology. That is the ideology that teaches us to believe that marriage is unimportant. Kids are resilient. The way to happiness is to indulge yourself sexually. Sexual self-restraint is not necessary and, in fact, may be harmful to you. Switching sexual partners has no negative consequences worthy of mention, neither to you, nor to your children.

So the child's need for stability is sacrificed on the altar of the Divorce Ideology. The adults' need for genuine, lifelong, self-giving love is sacrificed to this very same ideology, acting in conjunction with the Contraceptive Ideology.

We cannot overlook one other fact: this social welfare system based on non-marital childbearing also created jobs for thousands of members of the managerial class. All those government payments must be processed. Programs must be administered: housing, after-school programs, educational enhancements, medical care, dental care, school lunch and breakfast programs. Applications must be taken. Eligibility must be determined. Sometimes people must be kicked out of the programs because they're no longer eligible or never were eligible in the first place. Someone, usually someone with some level of college education, must do all these jobs.

Social workers provide programs and "interventions" to deal with the problems that plague the poor due to the failure of families to form. Judges and court workers must deal with the disputes that invariably arise over the failure of parents to meet their obligations and with disputes over how to care for their children. Court-appointed psychologists do their testing and write their reports. Child protective service workers take children into custody, triggering another whole sequence of government involvement in family life.

Many college-educated professionals make a living managing the lives of the poor. The poor are disadvantaged under any social system: that is what it means to be poor. But people with few resources could more easily manage their own lives under a social system confining socially acceptable sex and childbearing to marriage. The chaos in the lives of what is now called the "underclass" is a direct result of the Divorce Ideology.

Third-Party Reproduction and the Ruling Class

We must mention one final way in which children are separated from one of their parents: third-party reproduction. Third-party reproduction means the use of sperm or egg belonging to someone who will not be involved in raising the child. Infertile heterosexual couples, same sex couples, or individuals can achieve their "reproductive goals" by using donor gametes. This process involves redefining parenthood and systematically separating the child from one of his or her parents.

This process requires changes to the legal system, the application of sophisticated technology, and lots and lots of money. For all these reasons, the use of donor gametes benefits the better educated and richer at the expense of the less educated and poorer. Not surprisingly, the American Law Institute takes these new forms of "non-traditional reproductive arrangements" for granted. The medical profession as a whole seems oblivious to the long-term consequences of their harnessing of technology. Because delayed childbearing is the price of participating in the managerial class, this class has become personally dependent on infertility treatments, including the use of third-party reproduction.

Third-party reproduction can never be exclusively a "free market" phenomenon of private individuals making agreements among themselves. Nor can we claim that if third-party reproduction is illegal, it will just go underground and a black market will develop. The law absolutely must be involved in the third-party reproduction process.

The reason I say this with such confidence is that "commissioning parents," as they are sometimes called, are not just in the market for a baby with their genetic material. They're in the market for a *baby to whom they have exclusive legal rights*. This means the force of law is necessary to keep the "third party" (who is, in fact, the child's genetic parent) away from the commissioning parents and the child. Commissioning parents must have the money to pay for the medical technology and the legal process to both produce the child they want and to keep the child's "donating" parent away.

The poor are never going to be the drivers of such a system.

In case you had any doubts, check out the publicity materials for the "Fertility Planit" conference held at UCLA in

2014.[32] The title of the event encapsulates everything one would expect from consumer culture: a snappy title with a double meaning: "Fertility for the planet" suggesting maybe, ever so subtly, that third-party reproduction is green-friendly or that you are going to "plan it" for your fertility. Get it? Suggestive, without overpromising. Very clever. I wonder how much they paid an ad agency for that.

The highlight of the conference was the roster of celebrity speakers. Actress Elisabeth Rohm spoke about her journey to motherhood via IVF and her book *Having the Child I Always Wanted (Just Not as Expected)*. I wonder if she mentioned the studies showing the increased health risks to children born through IVF procedures?[33] Model and TV host Tomiko Fraser Hines talked about being pregnant with donor eggs. I somehow doubt that Fertility Planit gave equal time to any of the women whose health has been damaged by egg "donation" as documented in the independent film *Eggsploitation*.[34]

---

[32]   "Join Marianne Williamson, Elisabeth Rohm, The Guncles, Jason Patric, Brenda Strong, Dr. Sadeghi & 200+ Health and Wellness Experts for Fertility Planit Show @UCLA Apr 4-5," press release, accessed November 14, 2016, http://www.digitaljournal.com/pr/1819443#ixzz4PzwmKrRZ.

[33]   Jennifer Roback Morse, *Children and Donor Conception and Assisted Reproduction* (San Marcos, CA: The Ruth Institute, 2016), available at http://www.ruthinstitute.org/store/ruth-survivor-series/children-and-donor-conception-and-assisted-reproduction. For the data in the brochure, see the online report: "Information for Tables in Ruth Institute brochure: Children and Donor Conception and Assisted Reproduction," The Ruth Institute, accessed November 15, 2016, http://www.ruthinstitute.org/PDFs/Donor%20Conception%20brochure.pdf.

[34]   Jennifer Lahl, producer, "Eggsploitation: the infertility industry

The managerial class is becoming deeply committed to third-party reproduction. The economic structure of the professional and technical labor market depends on delayed childbearing. Thus, that whole class of people is becoming dependent on third-party reproduction technology and the legal structures that support it.

The most recent "benefit" offered by "enlightened" employers in Silicon Valley is employer-paid egg freezing. Apple and Facebook will pay their female employees for the medical costs of freezing their eggs so they will be ready to use when the woman is ready for them. Or is it until the employer is ready for her to use them?[35]

This "benefit" is a way for employers to have access to women's labor when they are in their prime working years. When their bodies are most suited for childbearing, when childbearing is easiest and most natural for the woman, just happens to be the period when her economic productivity and her value to her employer is at its peak.

Beyond these problems lurks the issue of consumer-based eugenics. Produce multiple embryos in the lab. Destroy the ones you don't want. Genetic defects, which happen to be

---

has a dirty little secret," Center for Bioethics and Culture, 2010, http://www.eggsploitation.com/.

[35] Chris Weller, "What you need to know about egg-freezing, the hot new perk at Google, Apple, and Facebook," *Business Insider*, September 17, 2017, http://www.businessinsider.com/egg-freezing-at-facebook-apple-google-hot-new-perk-2017-9. Notice how the reporter slides past the skepticism of Mary Ann Mason, the UC Berkeley professor, who states that the companies are "doing it because it's better for business." And that is the last this upbeat story has to say about even the possibility of a downside.

more likely with assisted reproduction, can be dealt with by abortion. Too many babies surviving in utero can be dealt with through "selective reduction," another euphemism for abortion. The extra embryos can be frozen indefinitely.

In all of this, the parents have had to harden their hearts. Some of them are haunted by it long afterward.[36] Not to mention the tragedy that ensues when the clinic mixes up the embryos or the sperm. The family doesn't get the baby that has the genetic material they wanted. As is natural in a commercial transaction, they sue for damages. But no child should ever have to be in the situation of being a "defective product."[37]

---

[36] For the struggle over what to do with "extra" embryos, see Juli Fraga, "After IVF, Some Struggle With What To Do With Leftover Embryos," *Shots: Health News from NPR,* August 20, 2016, http://www.npr.org/sections/health-shots/2016/08/20/489232868/after-ivf-some-struggle-with-what-to-do-with-leftover-embryos. See also my post, Jennifer Roback Morse, "Padres: please, tell us the full truth!" The Ruth Institute, February 18, 2017, http://www.ruthinstitute.org/ruth-speaks-out/padres-please-tell-us-the-full-truth, about a man who has agonized for over a decade about what to do with his children frozen in their embryonic state. Several online groups offer support for parents struggling with selective reduction decisions. "Fertile Thoughts: Supporting your family building dreams," online forum on "The guilt and regret," http://www.fertilethoughts.com/forums/selective-reduction-and-termination-due-to-health-issues/719266-guilt-regret.html. Center for Loss in Multiple Births (Climb), accessed November 15, 2016, http://www.climb-support.org/index.html.

[37] Jennifer Roback Morse, "In an Industry that makes people, what could possibly go wrong?" *The Blaze*, April 20, 2016, http://www.theblaze.com/contributions/in-an-industry-that-makes-people-what-could-possibly-go-wrong/.

The use and misuse of the vulnerable classes is appalling. Young women are exploited for their eggs so that older, richer women can have babies, or so that men can have babies without having any relationship with a woman at all.[38] Poor women are used as surrogates to incubate the babies for rich couples or individuals. Surrogacy has been outsourced to low-income countries, such as India and Nepal.[39] Where are the anti-globalization activists when we need them?

Elites like this system of baby making and baby selling. They get the babies they want on the timetable they want. Or, wait, is it the timetable they want or that their employers demand of them?

Do we really want to say that the identity of the biological parents is of no concern at all to the child? Do we really wish to say that the identity of the woman who carries the child in her womb for nine months is completely irrelevant to the child's well-being? Do children really have no rights at all to their own parents? Most of all, do we really want to create a society in which people with money get to do anything they want? That is approximately the position of the law in the United States right now.

It is certain that the ordinary person of modest means did not create this system. It was created by the managerial class who used their influence in the law, politics, and the

---

[38]   Lahl, "Eggsploitation."

[39]   "Outsourcing Embryos," VICE HBO, January 19, 2016, https://www.youtube.com/watch?v=GED9rYPkAlQ. See also my article, Jennifer Roback Morse, "Why Everyone should oppose surrogacy," *The Blaze*, May 4, 2016, http://www.theblaze.com/contributions/why-everyone-should-oppose-surrogacy/.

formation of public opinion. As a member of that class, I feel compelled to ask: What have we done to our fellow man and fellow woman? What are we doing to the next generation? And what have we done to ourselves?

CHAPTER 10

Propaganda Defending the Divorce Ideology

A t the heart of the Divorce Ideology is one simple idea: kids are so resilient they don't need their own parents. This is the idea that allows adults to divorce, remarry, become single parents by choice, and use third party reproduction in good conscience. This idea, and all its variants, is false.

- "I can safely abandon the mother of my child, and my child."
- "I can safely kick my child's father out of the house."
- "As a judge or social worker, I can separate children from their parents, support one blameless parent against the other, and nothing bad will happen."
- "As an academic or journalist, I can safely promote the idea that marriage is unnecessary, probably oppressive, and, after all, just a piece of paper."
- "The kids will be better off if I'm happy."

Pretty much all the information we have accumulated over fifty long years of practicing the Divorce Ideology supports the contrary idea: children suffer from the loss of connection with their parents. Children suffer from their parents' divorce. Children suffer from the loss of their fathers if their parents never marry in the first place. Children suffer from their parents' remarriages and other couplings. And while the evidence is still relatively new, early indications are that the children of donor conception have serious issues with the circumstances of their conception. It takes a lot of propaganda to maintain the myth that the kids will be fine.

The victims of the Divorce Ideology number in the millions. Everyone knows someone who has been harmed by this ideology. All these people need to be silenced to maintain the fiction that the kids will be fine as long as their parents are happy. Failing that, their attention needs to be diverted. Get them focused on and angry about something else. Let them blame something or someone else: the government, the economy, racism, sexism. Focus on anything else other than the loss of the most basic human right: the right to a relationship with one's own parents and other kin, the right to know one's genetic identity and cultural heritage.

Let's analyze some of the cultural myths that have been created to sustain the Divorce Ideology. And let us call them what they are: lies.

1. *"The children will be fine as long as their parents are happy."* Sometimes also stated as: *"kids are resilient."*

In addition to all the statistical information referenced earlier, we can look at the qualitative work of clinicians. Judith

Wallerstein was a psychotherapist who initially believed that divorce would be good for adults and not too harmful to children. Her clinical experience convinced her that she was mistaken. She and her colleagues followed families for twenty-five years to learn about the long-term impact of divorce on children. Like most people of her generation, she assumed the kids would be upset in the short term by their parents' divorce but would adjust over the long term.

The heartbreaking conclusion of her twenty-five years of research convinced her otherwise. "Contrary to what we long thought, the major impact of divorce does not occur during childhood or adolescence. Rather, it rises in adulthood as serious romantic relationships move center stage. When it comes time to choose a life mate and build a new family, the effects of divorce crescendo."[1]

Besides, the claim "the kids will be fine" is a grand generalization designed to keep people from looking too closely at the facts in their own surroundings. "The kids will be fine" suggests to the person considering divorce that "*all* kids, especially *my kids*, will be fine." The statement is sneaky because it makes this suggestion without taking the responsibility for saying it.

But once a person says it aloud, we can easily see that it is a grandiose, and ultimately false, claim. It only takes one counter-example to disprove this claim. Only one person who was bitterly unhappy over their parents' divorce is sufficient to disprove it. Once we realize how underhanded

---

[1] Judith S. Wallerstein, Julia M. Lewis, and Sandra Blackslee, *The Unexpected Legacy of Divorce: The 25 Year Landmark Study* (New York: Hyperion, 2000), p. xxxv.

this statement is, we can see it for what it is: propaganda calculated to keep people from noticing that things are not going well for their own children in their own families.

2. *Restrictions on divorce will trap women in abusive marriages.*

This is a lie on several levels. To begin with, a woman in an abusive marriage could get a divorce under a fault-based system. Most states had such provisions, even under the darkest, most-medieval days of the Eisenhower administration. Whatever problems may have existed under that system could have been solved through divorce reform or greater community services for domestic violence victims. The revolutionary innovation of removing all fault from divorce proceedings wasn't necessary to solve the problem.

Furthermore, women and their children are more likely to be abused in cohabiting relationships than in marriage, as we already noted.[2] This finding has been replicated in numerous studies over time and around the world. For most women, the alternative to marriage is not a lifetime of celibacy but dating and cohabitation. Hence, frightening women out of marriage for fear of abuse is likely driving them into situations that are statistically more likely to be dangerous to them and their children.

And, finally, the claim that restrictions on divorce will trap women in abusive relationships implies, or more than implies, that we cannot back away from the failed policy

---

2   Martin Daly and Margo Wilson, "Discriminative Parental Solicitude: A Biological Perspective," *Journal of Marriage and the Family* (May 1980), pp. 277–88.

of unilateral divorce without endangering women. What is more, it implies, but does not explicitly claim, that women who can't divorce without cause are at elevated risk for spousal abuse. But most divorces don't involve physical, sexual, or emotional abuse.[3] Hence, the generalization that women who can't divorce without cause are at elevated risk for spousal abuse is almost certainly false.

This lie, "restrictions on divorce will trap women in abusive marriages," is necessary to prop up the first lie: "children will be fine as long as their parents are happy." Who needs this lie, and why? Adults who have ended non-violent marriages. Adults who want to keep their divorce options open. They need the lie because the divorce of non-offending parents is statistically likely to be harmful to their children.

---

[3]   Respectively, 6, 9, and 12 percent in the following studies. Margaret Brinig and Douglas Allen, "These Boots are Made for Walking: why most divorce filers are women," *American Law and Economics Review* 2, no. 1, pp. 126–69. The sample of divorcing couples in this paper found only 6 percent claiming some form of domestic violence as a factor in the decision to divorce (see page 149); Paul Amato and Denise Previti, "People's Reasons for Divorcing: Gender, Social Class, the Life Course, and Adjustment," *Journal of Family Issues* 24, no. 5 (July 2003), pp. 602–26, table 3. A 2014 Nebraska analysis of judicial decisions in child custody and divorce cases covering ten years of divorces found that about 12 percent of cases were classified as "high conflict." Joe Duggan, "Nebraska state senator urges action on child custody inequality," *Omaha World-Herald*, January 10, 2014, http://www.omaha.com/news/nebraska-state-senator-urges-action-on-child-custody-inequality/article_b6918430-882c-53eb-81c9-acb05bfb8d28.html.

Unstated (and Unproven) Metaphysical Claims

It's curious that the sexual revolutionaries continue to defend these all-encompassing claims. What would be so wrong with admitting that divorce harms *at least some* children? I don't feel a need to prove that the ending of their parents' low conflict marriage harms *every* child. If someone tells me they had no problem with their parents' divorce, I feel no need to argue with them or try to talk them out of their feelings. Yet the defenders of the Divorce Ideology do seem to feel a need to claim that divorce is harmless to children.

This all-encompassing claim about divorce is comparable to other claims the revolutionaries like to make. Why is it so important for them to believe that *no* woman ever regrets her abortion? Why is it so important for them to believe that pregnancy and STDs are the *only* hazards associated with sex outside of marriage? These claims and denials suggest that we aren't dealing with claims of the ordinary scientific sort but with claims ultimately about human nature itself.

The assertion that children will be fine as long as their parents are happy appears to be strictly empirical. Social scientists take some measurements of happiness, health, and well-being. They ask in a systematic and structured way, "Are the kids fine when their parents get divorced?" If the answer is no, then we adults should be willing to reevaluate our beliefs.

But that is seldom how the conversation turns out. In the shadows of what appears to be an empirical, social scientific question, moral and even metaphysical claims are lurking.

What moral obligations do parents have with respect to their children? What kind of creatures are we anyhow?

The modern world offers a series of tacit but not explicit answers to these questions. I think we'd be ashamed of ourselves if we were to state them aloud. Here are some of our answers: Adults are not allowed to physically injure their children outright. Other than that, adults have no explicit legal or implicit moral obligations to their children. We don't owe them a relationship with us. We have no obligation to facilitate our child's relationship with their other parent. We have no obligation to speak well of their other parent. It's perfectly OK for us to forget that the child's other parent is half of who the child is.

No child has identity or relational rights that an adult is bound to respect. We are inadvertently reliving the notorious *Dred Scott* decision. In it, the Supreme Court claimed that blacks descended from slaves "had no rights which the white man was bound to respect."[4]

This is all very convenient if you happen to be an adult, but not so great if you're the child. And, last time I looked, every one of us arrived on this earth as a helpless infant utterly dependent upon others for our survival. Our dependency has a personal dimension to it. As infants, we care whether we are taken care of by the same person every day or by a parade of strangers. The kind of care we need is not simply the delivery of calories to our stomach and the provision of clothing sufficient to keep us from exposure. We need someone who personally, unconditionally cares about us.

---

[4]   Dred Scott v. Sanford 60 US 393 (1857) at 408.

Digging even deeper into the claim that "the kids will be fine as long as their parents are happy," we see that this idea has a built-in hidden metaphysical claim. The natural condition of human beings is to be independent autonomous adults. We are *not* radically dependent. This has been the claim of the modern world since the beginning of modern philosophy. Man (and it is always "man" and not "woman" or "child") is assumed to be a sovereign independent autonomous agent. The fact of radical childhood dependency doesn't enter into the thinking of modern social contract theorists or political theorists.[5]

Evidently, human beings are born at age eighteen, literate, mobile, and established with bank accounts and citizenship rights. They can speak, negotiate contracts, keep promises, discern their own good, and respect the rights of others. There is some dispute about whether this autonomous contracting man acts exclusively in his own self-interest or in accordance with some notion of the general will. No matter. In all cases, man can act on his own. The radical dependence of infancy, the eventual dependence of old age, the contingent dependence of infirmity, sickness, or accident are all

---

[5]   I'm thinking of political theorists going all the way back to the immediate post-Reformation era, including thinkers as diverse as Locke, Rousseau, Hobbes, Adam Smith, David Hume, Frederick Nietzsche, Simone de Beauvoir, Karl Marx, John Stuart Mill, and modern thinkers such as John Rawls, Robert Nozick, Ayn Rand, and James Buchanan. For a thorough analysis of how modern political theory misunderstands or ignores the family, see Scott Yenor, *Family Politics: The Idea of Marriage in Modern Political Thought* (Waco: Baylor University Press, 2012.)

undeniable facts of human existence which are assumed or wished away.

If the modern claims about the human condition are true, then separating people from each other is not only a morally acceptable action of government. Separating people from their relatives might even be morally required. What appear to be empirical claims turn out to be political claims.

For instance, most people in the West believe that ensuring justice is one of the government's essential duties. One might conclude, therefore, that a dispute between a husband and wife over whether they should continue to live together as husband and wife would be none of the government's business. In cases where a marital fault has been committed, such as abandonment, abuse, or adultery, the state may need to be involved to ensure that justice is done to the injured party. But where no such faults have occurred, you'd think the government should side with the stability of the freely contracted bond. Yet under a no-fault divorce regime, the government takes sides with the party who wants the marriage the least. The government, the Sexual State, comes between a man, a woman, and their marriage vows.

That's how something as seemingly innocuous as "the kids will be fine as long as their parents are happy" generates such animosity. The discussion isn't really about, solely about, or even mainly about the empirical evidence on child well-being and how it varies with family structure. We aren't really having a discussion. We're actually tiptoeing around a set of repeated assertions about human nature. We have built our society around these assertions. We'd have to reconstruct a lot of social capital if we turned out to be wrong. Personally, I've seen enough evidence. I'm ready to do some restructuring.

Ongoing Propaganda for the Divorce Ideology

Propping up this combination of half-truths and flat-out lies requires a lot of propaganda. Every TV sitcom showing the happy fatherless family is part of this effort to remake human nature. Ditto with every movie showing jolly blended families. The Huffington Post even has a regular feature called "Blended Family Friday." They describe it this way: "As part of our Blended Family Friday series, each week we spotlight a different stepfamily to learn how they successfully blended their two families. Our hope is that by telling their stories, we'll bring you closer to blended family bliss in your own life! Want to share your own story? Email us at divorce@ huffingtonpost.com."[6]

Most of these accounts are upbeat reports from the adult's point of view. I've not seen too many written from the child's perspective. The articles tend to downplay the problems, suggesting that, with tenacity and determination, they can be overcome.

The feature outrages my friends who are adult children of divorce. They feel it diminishes the negative experiences they had as children.

---

[6]   "Meet the Blended Families We've Featured in the Past" is a montage of 156 stories of stepfamilies. The description quoted in the text appears in the tee-up of each one. http://www.huffing tonpost.com/entry/the-blended-family-motto-this-mom-swears-by_us_55fb25fce4b0fde8b0cd9012?slideshow=true#gallery/ 559ee9b3e4b05b1d02900b90/0, accessed November 16, 2016.

Some of the propaganda is subtle. It takes the form of asking some questions rather than others, emphasizing some issues over others. I noticed this tactic in an article ostensibly reporting on the increasing normalization of cohabitation. The reporter interviewed several sociologists about this trend, including Dr. Christina Gibson-Davis of Duke University. Look closely at these paragraphs.

> "The emergence of cohabitation as an acceptable context for childbearing has changed the family-formation landscape," said Christina Gibson-Davis, a sociology professor at Duke University. "Individuals still value the idea of a two-parent family but no longer consider it necessary for the parents to be married."
>
> Still, she cautions that children in cohabiting households may face more difficulties growing up if their unmarried parents are at higher risk of breaking up.
>
> In all, the share of unmarried couples who opted to have "shotgun cohabitations" — moving in together after a pregnancy — surpassed "shotgun marriages" for the first time over the last decade. [7]

Notice that Dr. Gibson-Davis seemed poised to say cohabitation isn't necessarily all roses and could be problematic. But the reporter evidently had no interest in pursuing the question further. The professor's doubts might call into question the official story line that adults are entitled

---

[7]   Hope Yen, "As cohabitation gains favor, shotgun weddings fade," *Yahoo News,* January 6, 2014, http://news.yahoo.com/cohabita tion-gains-favor-shotgun-weddings-fade-202031925.html.

to make any relationship decisions they want, for any reason they chose.

Here is another example of stealth-propaganda-by-choice-of-question. The government now collects statistics on "intimate partner violence." This choice of terminology lumps together married, cohabiting, and dating couples under the label "intimate partner." For instance, in a 1995 Department of Justice report, table 4 clearly shows the percentage of violent crimes against women committed by their spouses (9 percent), ex-spouses (4 percent), and their boyfriends or girlfriends, current or former, (16 percent). Clearly different results for different types of relationships.[8]

However, in similar reports beginning in 1998, the term "intimate partner" is used exclusively, lumping together "former or current spouses, boyfriends, and girlfriends."[9] This procedure assumes away the differences among these

---

[8]   Ronet Bachman and Linda E. Saltzman, "Violence against Women: Evidence from the Redesigned Survey," Bureau of Justice Statistics, Special Report, National Crime Victimization Survey, August 1995, NCJ-154348, https://www.bjs.gov/content/pub/pdf/FEMVIED.PDF.

[9]   For instance, Patricia Tjaden and Nancy Thoennes, "Prevalence, Incidence, and Consequences of Violence Against Women: Findings from the National Violence Against Women Survey," National Institute of Justice, Centers for Disease Control and Prevention, Research in Brief (November 1998), https://www.ncjrs.gov/pdffiles/172837.pdf; Shannan Catalano, Erica Smith, Howard Snyder, and Michael Rand, "Female Victims of Violence," NCJ 228356, Bureau of Justice Statistics, Selected Findings (September 2009), https://www.bjs.gov/content/pub/pdf/fvv.pdf; Shannan Catalano, "Intimate Partner Violence: Attributes of Victimization, 1993–2011," NCJ 243300, U.S. Department of Justice, Bureau of Justice Statistics, BJS Special Report (November 2013).

categories. In other words, these data treat an important question—"Are there differences among types of sexual relationships?"—as an assumption: "We assume there are no differences."

Deliberate choice on the part of the officials of the Sexual State? I cannot say for sure. I will say this: I act as if the officials who made that decision knew exactly what they were doing. I couldn't prove it in a court of law. But since I began operating on that assumption, I have never seen it contradicted by any facts.

The propaganda for the divorce ideology causes real pain to real people. Those who have been harmed by family breakdown feel isolated. "If only my family was cooler and more together, we could be like those people on TV and wouldn't be having all these problems." What if you and your family are more common than you believe, and the TV show characters are the unusual ones?

People who have made decisions that result in family breakdown undoubtedly sometimes do so based on the cultural narrative supporting "freedom to divorce" and "the kids will be fine." When they discover that all that freedom didn't make them happy and the kids really aren't fine, many of them feel cheated or like freaks and outliers that it did not work out that way for them. What if the difficulties they encounter are the norm and the TV characters are the freaks?

Every instance of propaganda victimizes the already-victimized. Besides being hurt by their parents' divorce or separation, children of divorce, unmarried parenthood, and donor conception are subjected to the continual claim that they are really alright. If they aren't alright, *they* are the problem, not family breakdown. We take the children for therapy and prescribe medication for them. We ask them to deny the reality that is right in front of them. No wonder they're upset and have stomach cramps, sleepless nights, psychological problems, and trouble with their schoolwork. The divorce ideology and the propaganda that supports it is crazy-making. Honestly, it's a wonder so many children of divorce do as well as they do. I can't imagine what they go through.

I don't care how often it happens or how much propaganda attempts to normalize it. I don't care what the courts say, what the "experts" say, or even what the pope in Rome says. I'll never consider it normal for children to be asked to do without one of their parents, without a really, really, good reason.

And "I want a new sexual relationship more than I want to live with your other parent" does not qualify as a really, really, good reason.

CHAPTER 11

What the Catholic Church Says About Divorce

In direct contradiction to the Divorce Ideology, the Catholic Church holds that marriage is and ought to be indissoluble. The Church bases this teaching on the plain, though radical, words of Jesus in, for instance, Mark 10:11–12: "Whoever divorces his wife and marries another, commits adultery against her; and if she divorces her husband and marries another, she commits adultery."

Based on this and related Scripture passages, the Church teaches that marriage is permanent and "remarriage" while one's spouse is living is not possible. True enough, the civil law permits this. But Catholic teaching views the second union as an attempted marriage and the first marriage as the only marriage. Having sex with someone while you are married to someone else is committing adultery against your spouse. This is the basis for the Church's disciplinary practice of telling divorced and civilly remarried Catholics that, while they can be part of the life of the Church, they cannot receive Communion.

I will not attempt to give the full theological defense of this position. Others can do so far more effectively than I. The late great Pope St. John Paul II, for instance, put forth this teaching in several documents.[1] The theology of marriage includes a thorough analysis of the opening chapters of Genesis as well as the innumerable passages in the Old Testament in which the author compares God's relationship to his people as a marriage. St. Paul's comparison of the relationship between Christ and the Church to the relationship between a husband and wife is also part of the teaching. Christ will never abandon the Church: we may not abandon each other.

My own contribution to the defense of this teaching is not to cover this well-trod theological, biblical, and pastoral ground. Rather, I point to things anyone of any faith can observe for themselves. First, by forbidding second marriages while a spouse is still living, Jesus made marriage as permanent as a biological relationship. After all, we cannot divorce our parents or siblings. We can refuse to have anything to do with them. But the identity of our blood relatives is still a primal fact of our lives, for better or for worse. Since marriage produces blood relationships—namely, between

---

[1]   The most significant of Pope St. John Paul's works on marriage and family include *Love and Responsibility* (San Francisco, CA: Ignatius Press, 1993); *Familiaris Consortio* (Boston: Pauline Books and Media, 1981); and *Male and Female He Created Them: A Theology of the Body*, trans. Michael Waldstein (Boston: Pauline Books and Media, 2006).

each parent and the child—it is fitting that the relationship between the parents be as permanent as the relationship between each parent and the child.

Second, the whole corpus of traditional Catholic teaching protects the legitimate rights of children, including their rights to a relationship with both of their parents and to know the identity of their parents. If children have rights, then parents have obligations.

We have the obligation to facilitate our child's relationship with the other parent. Since children need to feel loved and secure, we have an obligation to treat each other with love and respect. And since it is completely unreasonable to suppose we can have this type of committed relationship with more than one person at a time, we have an obligation to be sexually exclusive with our child's other parent. In fact, the first "irregular relationship" that St. John Paul II considers and rejects in *Familiaris Consortio* is polygamy.[2]

Therefore, we should not have sex with a person we cannot imagine having a lifelong loving, respectful, or at least courteous relationship with. In no case should we have sex with someone who has this type of commitment to someone else. The ordinary way of having a permanent, loving, sexually exclusive relationship with another person is to marry them.

In other words, we have an obligation in justice to our future children to have sex only with our spouse, who is not married to anyone else.

---

[2]   Pope St. John Paul II, *Familiaris Consortio* (Boston: Pauline Books and Media, 1981), no. 19.

If our spouse becomes impossible or dangerous to live with, that fact does not automatically give us the right to attempt a new relationship with another person. Separating from a dangerous spouse may be morally permissible or even required. The prohibition that Jesus lays down is not a prohibition on moving out or kicking the bum out: it is a prohibition against remarriage.

And if we listen to the children of divorce, we will see the wisdom of this prohibition. The children tell us repeatedly that it is the new relationship(s) that made them feel like leftovers. It is the new attempted "marriage" that creates the situation where the stepchild is left out of family photos. Remarriage is the thing that creates layers and layers of inequalities between the children who get to live with both parents and the children who don't. My colleague Jennifer Johnson explains it this way:

> When I was growing up, I spent my entire childhood doing the back-and-forth thing between "two homes." My parents both remarried so I had two half-time dads. I was about twelve or so when I consciously understood that my two half-time dads did not equal one dad. . . .
>
> Perhaps I came to this realization because I was eye-witness to what an intact family and a full-time dad looked like. My step-dad was a full-time dad to my half-sister. She lived with both her married parents, my mom and my step-dad. I could see that what she had and what I had were two different things.[3]

---

[3]   Jennifer Johnson, *Marriage and Equality: How Natural Marriage*

This is what the children of divorce will tell us if we will listen: the divorce was hard. The remarriage was doubly hard.[4]

The Son of God knew what he was talking about. Imagine that.

And no, contraception does not get us off the hook. We modern sophisticates tell ourselves: "We can have sex without babies now, so none of those rules apply anymore." Contraception sometimes fails. You know this. Every serious person knows this. Many, many people know someone whose contraception has failed. When that happens, these are the choices the parents face:

- Marry each other. Not ideal, perhaps, but it preserves the child's rights to both parents.

- Give the baby up for adoption to a married couple. Also not ideal because it violates the child's rights to his or her own parents. It does preserve the child's right to parents of both sexes and each parent's freedom to marry someone else. But the cost is the child losing day-to-day contact and relationship with both natural parents.

- One parent, usually the mother, parents the child alone. This is unjust to the child because it places at risk his or her relationship with the other parent.

---

upholds *Equality for Children* (Lake Charles, Louisiana: Ruth Institute Books, 2017), pp. 24–25.

[4] Leila Miller, *Primal Loss: The Now-Adult Children of Divorce Speak* (LCB Publishing, 2017).

- Have an abortion. This is obviously unjust to the child: killing an innocent person is always unjust.

I repeat: contraception does not repeal the rules. It just creates the illusion that there will be no children, which creates the further illusion that we do not have to consider their well-being. Contraception does not eliminate children's rights. The illusions it creates place their rights gravely at risk.

In short, if we begin with the rights of children, and ask what obligations these rights of children impose on adult society, we will end up with traditional Christian sexual morality. I call it "Christian" instead of "Catholic" because at one time, all the Christian churches taught pretty much the same thing about sexual morality. What is now considered the uniquely Catholic position is the common heritage of all Christians.

It is quite true that Jesus never talked about the rights of children to their parents. Neither did he talk about how hurt and humiliated the women of his day must have felt when their husbands "wrote them a bill of divorce" and sent them home.

But he was very clear about the permanence of marriage and the prohibition on attempting second marriages after divorce. And he identified closely with the suffering of the innocent.

I like to imagine him in the Garden of Gethsemane on the night before he died. He foresaw all the sins of the world and the suffering those sins would cause. I think he knew what a little child would feel when her mother got married to someone other than her father. She knows she is supposed to be happy that her mother has found happiness. But her little heart is breaking: her mother's marriage tells her that her mother and father will never get back together again.

I think Jesus knew how a little ten-year-old boy would feel when his mother asked him to walk her down the aisle to her second marriage. Jesus saw the confusion of that little boy, who was supposed to feel honored to be included in her special day. Perhaps the little boy knew there was something odd about the adult role the mother was asking him to assume.

Little did that boy know that he was embarking on a lifetime of being "mommy's little man," a parent to his mother, who would be there for her when this marriage fell apart like the last one. Little did he know that his mother would be expecting him, as her son, to be the one permanent relationship in her life. Little did he know how his mother would sabotage his attempts at marriage.

But Jesus knew. He saw it all. He suffered in solidarity with all the other suffering innocents.

One can say that the Catholic Church is cruel because this teaching is insensitive to the needs of adults. One can say the teaching is great, but the Church is hypocritical because she does not live up to this sublime teaching. But no one can deny that the Catholic Church is the last institution standing against the divorce-on-demand culture of the twenty-first century.

Yes, Pope Francis and some of his associates seem to be backing away from the teaching as it has been understood since apostolic times. The interpretation of *Amoris Laetitia*[5] which is at odds with the tradition hinges on this idea:

> So many Catholics have divorced and civilly remarried without understanding what they have done, that the only fair thing to do is to excuse them from observing the Church's teaching. Let them receive communion, if they discern that it is somehow appropriate, even though they are living a sexually active life in a civil "remarriage." It would be too hard on them, and on their children, to ask them to do what the Church has always asked of people in this situation: to live as "brother and sister," in a sexually continent life, or to separate and go back to their spouses. [6]

I do agree that many, many people, including Catholics, do not have a clue what marriage is all about and why the Church teaches what she does. The solution to that problem is simple: more and better teaching. Teaching the full truth solves the problems the flow from people's ignorance

5   Pope Francis, *Amoris Laetitia* (2016).
6   See for instance the interpretation of *Amoris Laetitia* by the bishops of Malta, Buenos Aires, and San Diego. By contrast, other bishops have chosen to interpret *Amoris Laetitia* in continuity with the traditional teaching. Archbishop Charles Chaput of Philadelphia, Archbishop Alexander Sample of Portland Oregon, and the bishops of Poland. E. Christian Brugger, "A Tale of Two Interpretations of 'Amoris Laetitia,'" *National Catholic Register*, April 25, 2017, http://www.ncregister.com/daily-news/a-tale-of-two-interpretations-of-amoris-laetitia; and Carl Olsen "A Malta Laetitia," *Catholic World Report*, January 14, 2017, http://www.catholicworldreport.com/2017/01/14/a-malta-laetitia/.

of the truth. It also prevents the suffering that divorce and attempted remarriages cause.

I always wonder about the children of the original, valid marriages. No one ever seems to be worried about their feelings. How do they feel if even the Church tells one of their parents that it was acceptable for them to abandon the family for a new love interest? In the *Amoris Laetitia* controversies, it is always the children of the new union whose feelings are considered, never the children of the original, presumably valid union.

The radical teaching of Jesus changed civilization for the better: it equalized relations between men and women and between the generations. Adult men no longer got to do whatever they wanted. In fact, historian and sociologist of religion Rodney Stark attributes the rapid growth of Christianity in its early centuries to the fact that women found Christian teaching attractive. They knew if they married a Christian man, he would not abandon her for another woman. She knew he would not force her to "expose" her children to the elements.[7]

In my opinion, the worst crime of the Catholic Church about marriage today is that she does not teach it and observe it as she ought. In today's Catholic culture, there are too many annulments, too little preaching from the pulpit, and too many perfunctory marriage preparation programs. Catholics themselves scarcely know what their own Church teaches and why she teaches it.

---

[7]   Rodney Stark, *The Triumph of Christianity: How the Jesus Movement Became the World's Largest Religion* (New York, NY: Harper Collins, 2011), pp. 124–29.

And our non-Catholic neighbors? They desperately need to hear the life-giving message of Jesus from us. They will not hear it from anyone else, that is for sure. The Church's teaching is so good that we have no right to keep it to ourselves.

PART IV

The Gender Ideology

CHAPTER 12

The Gender Ideology and the Managerial Class

The third "big idea" of the Sexual Revolution, after the Contraception and Divorce Ideologies, is the Gender Ideology, which posits that men and women are completely interchangeable. All differences we observe between them are social constructs that a good and decent society should strive to remove. As a society, the ideology holds, we can succeed and progress if only we have sufficient commitment to do the necessary re-engineering of our social framework.

As the Gender Ideology has worked its way through the institutions of society, it has morphed into an even more radical form. The radicals now insist that any individual can reconstruct his or her own personal gender identity. The sex of the body is not a reality that each person must accept as a given of their lives. We're now supposed to believe that gender is a construct merely assigned at birth. The outward appearances of genitalia are not sufficient to classify people into male or female.[1] All differences between men and women, including the seemingly natural differences, can be reconstructed with enough re-engineering of the human biological hardware and social cultural software. The modern Sexual State will, of course, be on hand to ensure that the entire society conforms itself to each individual's newly chosen identity.

The Gender Ideology is truly revolutionary. It hides behind the reasonable idea that men and women be treated with equal dignity and goes far beyond it. The Contraceptive Ideology attempts to separate sex from babies. The Divorce Ideology separates children from their parents. The Gender Ideology separates individuals from their own bodies, which are regarded as unreasonable constraints on one's freedom and self-determination.

Unlike the Contraceptive and Divorce Ideologies, the origins and implementation of the Gender Ideology can't be detected in a few simple and easily identifiable policies. A whole series of public policies and social practices are based on and reinforce the premise that all differences between men and women are morally suspect. Examples of such policies include:

- Title IX which requires equality between men and women in university sports programs,[2]

---

[1] Christin Scarlett Milloy, "Don't Let the Doctor Do This to Your Newborn," *Slate*, June 26, 2014, http://www.slate.com/blogs/outward/2014/06/26/infant_gender_assignment_unnecessary_and_potentially_harmful.html.

[2] Eliza Beeney, "Women Wrestlers Go to the Mat for Equal Rights," ACLU (blog), August 8, 2011, https://www.aclu.org/blog/womens-rights/women-wrestlers-go-mat-equal-rights.

- laws regulating and limiting the use of physical fitness requirements for law enforcement officers,[3]
- subjecting single-sex educational programs to regulation to ensure that they are not "stereo-typed,"[4]
- banning women in military combat roles is now considered unlawful and unnecessary sexual stereotyping,[5]
- the government encouraging and subsidizing special opportunities for women to participate in the "STEM" disciplines: Science, Technology, Engineering, and Mathematics—these are the only disciplines which remain male-dominated—[6]
- father-daughter dances are considered unlawful gender stereotyping and, hence, are banned in some places,[7]

---

[3] "Physical Ability Tests for Police Departments and SWAT Teams: Know Your Rights in the Workplace," ACLU fact sheet, https://www.aclu.org/sites/default/files/assets/kyr_physicalabilities-rel1.pdf.

[4] "Teach Kids, not Stereotypes," ACLU fact sheet, https://www.aclu.org/womens-rights/teach-kids-not-stereotypes.

[5] Kellan Howell, "Defense Secretary Ashton Carter OKs final strategy for women in combat," *Washington Times,* March 11, 2016, http://www.washingtontimes.com/news/2016/mar/11/ash-carter-approves-final-strategy-women-military-/.

[6] See for instance, the "Women in STEM" page from the White House, "Office of Science and Technology Policy," https://www.whitehouse.gov/administration/eop/ostp/women. The website *Engineer Girl* lists page after page of enrichment and scholarship opportunities for girls, http://www.engineergirl.org/9539.aspx, accessed December 15, 2016.

[7] "Rhode Island bans father daughter dances: says they break the law," NBC News, September 18, 2012, http://usnews.nbcnews.com/_news/2012/09/18/13938087-rhode-island-school-bans-father-daughter-dances-says-they-break-the-law?lite. My commentary on this issue can be found here: John J. Miller, "Home Economics," *Home Front* (blog), September 25, 2012 http://

- and the Obama-era US Department of Justice issuing an Executive Order mandating that every public school in America accommodate self-described "transgender" students by eliminating single sex bathrooms, locker rooms, and shower rooms.[8]

Please notice that all of the above examples involve the power of the government. Regulations, rulings from administrative agencies, court cases: all were involved in creating the social infrastructure that makes it difficult to say "men and women are different, and that's OK." Also notice that these examples go far beyond anti-discrimination law in the ordinary sense of mandating equal pay for equal work. These policies aim to drive men and women into job categories or even leisure activities or personal preferences in equal numbers. Finally, please notice, that these changes were not driven by the demands of ordinary people fighting injustice. These are policies that came about because ideologues captured the power of the State and bent it to their own purposes.

---

www.nationalreview.com/home-front/328429/father-daughter-dance-banned/jennifer-roback-morse last.

[8] U.S. Department of Justice "U.S. Departments of Justice and Education Release Joint Guidance to Help Schools Ensure the Civil Rights of Transgender Students," May 13, 2016, https://www.justice.gov/opa/pr/us-departments-justice-and-education-release-joint-guidance-help-schools-ensure-civil-rights.

The Managerial Class and the Sexual Revolutionary Ideology in General

Earlier in this book, I alluded to the concept of a managerial class based on economic or educational distinctions. The managerial class goes beyond the purely class designation in this respect: it's built upon the idea that society is something that needs to be managed. Earlier aristocracies viewed themselves as superior to the lower classes and expected obedience and deference. Seldom have the privileged classes taken it upon themselves to "nudge"[9] their neighbors and fellow citizens about their eating habits, sex lives, spending habits, personal safety, and even their thoughts. Using the force of law, the power of the regulatory state, the economic power of large corporations, and the influence of the mass media, today's elite class views itself as the guardian of the public weal or common good.

Legal historian Joseph Dellapenna observes that the rise of the managerial class was not unique to the United States in the twentieth century. "The managerial class rose to dominance in the U.S. with the New Deal in the 1930s, and has continued to dominate ever since. . . . Evidence of the transition to social domination by a managerial class can be traced back to the nineteenth century, particularly in England. Nor was this transition limited to western or capitalist nations.

---

9   Cass Sunstein and Richard Thaler, *Nudge: Improving Decisions about Health, Wealth and Happiness* (New York: Penguin Books, 2009). Richard Thaler was awarded the Nobel Prize in economics in 2017.

In a real sense, the rise of Communism and Socialism was nothing more or (less) than a rise of the managerial class."[10]

The managerial class and the Sexual Revolution have risen together. Maybe it's a coincidence, but the class and ideological interests overlap and support one another to a perhaps surprising extent. The ideological regime of the Sexual Revolution has delivered benefits to both employers and employees in the managerial class.

- Separating sex from reproduction means that the employer need not be inconvenienced by worker turnover generated by pregnancy. Women workers who can work uninterrupted at their jobs for longer periods of time are more valuable to employers.

- The kind of careerist feminism that has become culturally dominant planted within women the idea that their value as persons depends on their work. Any person who believes their value depends on their wage, status, and job performance is getting something from their job other than money. Economists call this a "psychic benefit." This amounts to a form of compensation to the worker *that costs the employers nothing.* This form of compensation is delivered to women workers by the careerist feminist ideology at absolutely no charge to any employer.

- Unilateral divorce removed the presumption of permanence from marriage. This keeps men and women

---

10   Joseph W. Dellapenna, *Dispelling the Myths of Abortion History* (Durham, NC: Carolina Academic Press, 2006), p. 620. Ponder that last sentence for a while.

alike off-balance as to whether their spouses will stay married to them. This reduction in security of the marriage increases the workers' commitment to the work force.

- Unilateral divorce also increases the woman's incentive to postpone having children until she is ready to take care of them independently should the need arise. The insecurity surrounding marriage also increases her incentive to stay at work longer than she might otherwise prefer.

It's true that some forms of feminism insisted on many new labor regulations and anti-discrimination rules. These rules created new costs for employers, no doubt. However, if we ignore the benefits employers receive indirectly from marital instability and other cultural changes, we would be unable to explain how quickly employers adapted to the Sexual Revolution.

Managerial class employers prefer employees whose work is not disrupted by activities that are irrelevant to the company's mission. Activities like getting pregnant and taking care of babies fit that description for most businesses. Feminist Joan Williams defines this as the "ideal worker:" a person who never takes time off, is never sick, whose mental and psychological focus is entirely on the job.[11]

At one time, men behaved like ideal workers. They treated their jobs as their source of identity and pride. They made

---

[11] Joan Williams, *Unbending Gender: Why Family and Work Conflict and What We Can Do About It* (Oxford: Oxford University Press, 2000.)

themselves available to their employers pretty much on demand. The employers may or may not have realized that these male ideal workers were motivated by their desire to provide for the people they loved: their wives, children, and possibly elderly parents. Men took pride and found their identity in being successful breadwinners. Love and relationship was quietly but firmly in the background of the male ideal worker. Perhaps they appeared to be working for money and their egos, but many of them were, at least in part, working for love.

The kind of feminism that demanded income equality strove to transform women into ideal workers as well. Today's managerial class woman finds her identity and self-worth more in her career than in her relationships. At the same time, the instability of modern marriage means that the modern woman needs the income her job brings her. The desire and need for independent income and career achievement benefits employers. Feminism delivered a whole new class of women workers eager to prove themselves and, in many ways, desperate for work.

While any employer might desire this arrangement, such gender-neutral ideal workers are, relatively speaking, more significant to the employers of the highly educated, highly skilled workers than to other classes. Managerial class jobs require formal education, experience, and skill. More experience on the job improves a person's intuition and judgment. These traits are difficult to replicate in another worker. By contrast, employers can more easily find a substitute worker for jobs that require less education, skill, or experience. An employer can more easily replace the receptionist than the chief financial officer.

This is how the new managerial class transcends Left and Right. This new class supported certain kinds of capitalism. A significant subset of this class promoted the notion that every woman intellectually able to do so should get an advanced degree and join the workforce. Otherwise, she risks social ostracism. How else to explain the enthusiasm of the establishment media for a book with the charming title *Get to Work: A Manifesto for Women of the World*?[12]

We've built a society around the premise that our educated women must be permitted to time their 1.6 pregnancies right down to the minute when it's most convenient. But convenient for whom? All too often, it means the convenience of the employer, or the interests of the career path, or of those who hold the student debt which the young woman or young couple must pay down. The convenience in question is quite often not really what the woman would choose for herself. The social structures we've created put unbelievable pressure on her to conform to the educational and career ladder that's been laid out for her. That ladder was created for the interests of the employers, universities, and radical ideologues, not necessarily for the interests of the average woman.

---

[12]   Linda Hirschman, *Get to Work: A Manifesto for Women of the World* (New York: Viking Adult, 2006).

The Managerial Class and the Gender Ideology in Particular

The Gender Ideology, the blurring of distinctions between male and female, has been in the background of the advance of the Sexual Revolution. The idea that women can do anything a man can do has been one of the ideological drivers of the massive shift of married women into the labor force, as has the idea that society should, as a matter of gender justice, structure itself so women can compete in the labor force on the same terms as men. The preferred means of making men and women equal has been to neutralize the impact of having and raising children on women's employment opportunities. This is why the Contraceptive Ideology has been so significant to establishment feminists.

For the members of the managerial class, the Gender Ideology is plausible. Sitting comfortably in their offices, formulating regulations, implementing policies, enforcing rules, passing judgments, writing reports, holding press conferences, and arguing in front of commissions are activities that can be readily performed by men or women. In this kind of work environment, a woman can work for a lifetime and never be confronted with the reality of sex differences (unless she has the misfortune to work for or encounter someone like Harvey Weinstein, Matt Lauer, or Charlie Rose). The kinds of differential treatment one encounters in these environments might be, and often are, chalked up to some form of illegitimate discrimination. Questioning the gender-neutral lifestyle and the gender-neutral ideology never enters the mind. Men and women alike can do the jobs assigned.

However, when a person decides to become a parent, the significance of his or her gendered body becomes unavoidable. It came as a shock to me that the experience of infertility affected my husband in a different way than it did me. Only after that experience did I look back over our life together and realize that he had always been acting and reacting differently. I hadn't allowed myself to see it. In this way, as in many others, infertility proved to be good preparation for parenthood. As our lives as parents unfolded, we became aware that we had different strengths, weaknesses, sensitivities, and blind spots. We came to learn that these differences were valuable to us. Each of us brought something unique to the parenting process, things we would have overlooked or underemphasized. We had to learn to appreciate our differences rather than see them as nothing but sources of conflict or unfairness.

The larger point is that the gender ideology is more plausible for the managerial class than for anyone else. People who do manual labor aren't deluded for a moment that men and women are interchangeable. Men are highly overrepresented in the "death professions," occupations that have significant risks like lumberjacks, crop dusters, coal miners, and window washers on high-rise buildings. Men suffer 92 percent of deaths that take place on the job.[13] The men in

---

[13]   Warren Farrell, *Why Men Earn More: The Startling Truth about the Pay Gap, and What Women Can Do About It* (New York: American Management Association, 2005). Citing statistics from the Bureau of Labor Statistics, the top most dangerous jobs as

these occupations face risk that is literally unimaginable to the members of the managerial classes sitting safely at their desks. People who work in and around these dangerous jobs accept gender differentiation with far less of the ideological angst that plagues the managerial class.

The Gender Ideology has been successful in its objective of moving large numbers of women into the labor force at roughly the same ages and on the same terms as men. Among managerial class jobs, only in a handful of fields does a considerable gender dichotomy still exist. Those fields requiring controlled aggression, such as trial lawyers[14] and stockbrokers,[15] still tilt toward men. And fields that require what one psychiatrist calls the "high systemizing abilities," such as engineering, math, and hard sciences, are still male-dominated.[16]

of 2003 were timber cutters, fishers, pilots and navigators, and structural metal workers, pp. 27–29.

[14] Stephanie A. Scharf and Roberta D. Liebenberg, *First Chairs at Trial: More Women Need Seats at the Table: A Research Report on the Participation of Women Lawyers as Lead Counsel and Trial Counsel in Litigation* (American Bar Association, 2015), http://www.americanbar.org/content/dam/aba/marketing/women/first_chairs2015.authcheckdam.pdf.

[15] Stephanie Wilcox, "Building a Better Wall Street: Training Female Traders," *The Glass Hammer* (n.d.), accessed December 8, 2016, http://theglasshammer.com/2011/02/22/building-a-better-wall-street-training-female-traders/. "Though the hedge fund industry is a $2.5 trillion industry, a mere three percent of the assets are managed by women, according to Lauren Templeton, hedge fund manager and founder and principal of Lauren Templeton Capital Management and Maximum Pessimism, LLC."

[16] Simon Baron-Cohen, *The Essential Difference: The Truth about the Male and Female Brain* (New York: Basic Books, 2003), ch. 6.

The managerial class can't all be plausibly called "elites," especially in comparison with people like Warren Buffet and George Soros. But compared with truck drivers, supermarket cashiers, offshore oil rig workers,[17] and hotel housekeepers, yes, all members of the educated classes are elites. It is true enough that some blue-collar workers earn more money than some managerial class professionals. But even a well-paid plumber has no authority or opportunity to "manage" other people or society. Ordinary people who cook, clean, repair, and build didn't invent the Gender Ideology, nor did they exert themselves to impose it on the rest of society.

Any honest person must admit that the Gender Ideology needed a push, and that help was provided directly through the power of the State. In cases where the law can't enter, the Gender Ideology uses the power of the elite members of society to shame people who don't conform to its strictures.

For example, Dr. Larry Summers is a distinguished economist who became president of Harvard University after serving as secretary of the treasury under President Bill Clinton. Dr. Summers lost his job as president of Harvard because he noted the underrepresentation of women in the sciences.[18] He suggested, in a private meeting, that perhaps the question of gender differences in mathematizing and systematizing skills was a subject that ought to be studied.

---

[17]   Offshore oil rig workers are 95 percent male. Ron White, "Offshore Jobs That Hire Women," *The Nest* (n.d.), accessed November 29, 2016, http://woman.thenest.com/offshore-jobs-hire-women-20337.html.

[18]   Scott Jaschik, "What Larry Summers Said," *Inside Higher Education*, February 18, 2005, https://www.insidehighered.com/news/2005/02/18/summers2_18.

The establishment feminists went into overdrive to push him from his post.[19] I'd guess that the custodians, cooks, and groundskeepers at Harvard weren't too worried about Dr. Summers' ideological transgression and supposed insensitivity. I don't know for sure, of course, as no one thought to ask them what they thought.

Conclusion

Capturing the power of the State was essential in implementing the Gender Ideology. The elites, not the people, drove this process of State capture. Elite institutions, not grassroots movements, sustain and maintain these ideologies through disinformation, incomplete information, and outright propaganda. The managerial class keeps the fantasy ideology going along. Without their help and cooperation, the whole structure would crumble.

The class interests of the managerial class are not monolithic. Some of its members have suffered from their acquiescence in the Gender Ideology. (Remember Lynette, the heartbroken career woman from chapter 1?) That's because the Gender Ideology is a fantasy based upon untruth. Of course, it's bad for society and harmful to anyone who attempts to live by its tenets. The Gender Ideology is just as false as the Divorce Ideology that children don't really need their own parents, and the Contraceptive Ideology that sex

---

[19]   Stuart Taylor, Jr., "Why Feminist Careerists Neutered Larry Summers," *The Atlantic*, February 2005, http://www.theatlantic. com/magazine/archive/2005/02/why-feminist-careerists-neu tered-larry-summers/303795/.

does not really make babies. But some readers might still be wondering, "Is the Gender Ideology really false?" After all, aren't sexual stereotypes outdated, old-fashioned, and wrong?

CHAPTER 13

Are Men and Women Different After All?

The differences between human males and females begin at conception and continue throughout their lifetimes. Scientists and scholars have known since at least 1949 that male babies are more likely to be stillborn than female babies.[1] Please note: this research was done when parents didn't know the sex of their children until birth. Neither parents nor society were engaging in any differential treatment of boys and girls. The most plausible explanation is that these differences in the in utero experience of boy and girl infants are biologically-based.

Psychiatrist Sebastian Kraemer summarizes a mass of evidence in his short but significant work "The Fragile Male."

---

[1]   Herluf H. Strandskov and Henry Bisaccia, "The Sex Ratio of Human Stillbirths at each month of uterogestation and at conception," *American Journal of Physical Anthropology* 7, no. 2 (June 1949), pp. 131–44.

> At conception, there are more male than female
> embryos. . . . External maternal stress around the time
> of conception is associated with a reduction in the male
> to female sex ratio, suggesting that the male embryo is
> more vulnerable than the female. From this point on
> it is downhill all the way. The male fetus is at greater
> risk of death or damage from almost all the obstetric
> catastrophes that can happen before birth. Perinatal
> brain damage, cerebral palsy, congenital deformities of
> the genitalia and limbs, premature birth, and stillbirth
> are commoner in boys, and by the time a boy is born,
> he is on average developmentally some weeks behind
> his sister. . . . At term the excess has fallen from around
> 120 male conceptions to 105 boys per 100 girls.[2]

Attributing all these differences to cultural conditioning is highly implausible. Not that the gender ideologues would say otherwise. Rather the gender ideologues simply ignore biological realities which do not support their grand narrative.

Dr. Kraemer continues his literature review throughout the child's life. Boys are more likely to have developmental and behavioral disorders. Included on this list of "male privilege" is the boys' greater likelihood of reading delays, hyperactivity, autism, Tourette's syndrome, clumsiness, stammering, and conduct and oppositional disorders. As one scholar put it, "Males are attempting something extra, all through life."[3]

---

2   Sebastian Kraemer, "The Fragile Male," *British Medical Journal* 321 (2000). p. 1609, http://dx.doi.org/10.1136/bmj.321.7276.1609.

3   Ibid.

Studies of toddlers and children show that boys are more vulnerable than girls to stressors in their social environments. Boys are more likely to be disruptive in school.[4] Boys, more than girls, are likely to suffer if they're born to mothers under the age of 19.[5] Too much day care harms boys more than girls.[6] Boys are more likely than girls to be aggressive if they live in mother-only homes.[7]

When mothers are depressed during their child's first year of life, boys, but not girls, are at risk for having their intellectual abilities impaired. The author of that study observed poignantly, "Because infant boys are already developmentally delayed compared with girls, their abilities to regulate their attention and emotion and find order in the world are particularly in need of help from a sensitive healthy caregiver."[8]

Popular sites like What to Expect verify that some aspects of child development differ by gender, yet even such sites advise parents to try to equalize or neutralize the differences.

---

[4] Marianne Bertrand and Jessica Pan, "The Trouble with Boys: Social Influences and the Gender Gap in Disruptive Behavior," *Applied Economics* 5, no. 1 (2013), pp. 32–64.

[5] Greg Pogarksy, Terence P. Thornberry, and Alan J. Lizotte, "Developmental Outcomes for Children of Young Mothers," *Journal of Marriage and Family* 68 (May 2006), pp. 332–44.

[6] Jay Belsky and Michael j. Rovine, "Non-maternal Care in the First Year of Life and the Security of Infant-Parent Attachment," *Child Development* 59 (1988), pp. 157–67.

[7] Nancy Vaden-Kiernan et al., "Household Family Structure and Children's Aggressive Behavior: A Longitudinal Study of Urban Elementary School Children," *Journal of Abnormal Child Psychology* 23, no. 5 (1995).

[8] Deborah Sharp et al., "The Impact of Postnatal Depression of Boys' Intellectual Development," *Journal of Child Psychology and Psychiatry* 36, no. 8 (1995), pp. 1315–36.

We're so influenced by the Gender Ideology that we don't seem to consider the possibility of embracing the children's own preferences for activities that are "stereotypically" male or female. We can't allow ourselves to imagine that accepting these differences might just allow the kids to be more authentically themselves.[9]

Studies of animal brains reveal sex differences. "Neuroscientists have generated considerable data demonstrating sex influences on brain function at all levels, including the molecular and ion-channel level." These mammalian brains are filled with sex influences that obviously can't be explained by human culture.[10] Neuroscience has been reluctant to study the question of whether male and female brains differ from each other. One prominent neuroscientist explains: "Studying sex differences in the brain was for a long time distasteful to large swaths of academia. Regarding sex differences research, Gloria Steinem once said that it's 'anti-American, crazy thinking to *do* this kind of research.' Indeed, in about the year 2000, senior colleagues strongly advised me against studying sex differences because it would 'kill' my career."[11]

Yet, he continues, this reluctance hardly means that men and women are being treated equally:

---

[9]   "8 Differences Between Boys and Girls," *What to Expect* (n.d.), accessed November 29, 2016, http://www.whattoexpect.com/ first-year/photo-gallery/differences-between-boys-and-girls. aspx#09.

[10]   Larry Cahill, "Equal ≠ The Same: Sex Differences in the Human Brain," *Cerebrum* 5 (March-April 2014), http://www.ncbi.nlm. nih.gov/pmc/articles/PMC4087190/.

[11]   Ibid.

For a long time, for most aspects of brain function, sex influences hardly mattered to the neuroscience mainstream. The only sex differences that concerned most neuroscientists involved brain regions (primarily a deep-brain structure called the hypothalamus) that regulate both sex hormones and sexual behaviors. Neuroscientists almost completely ignored possible sex influences on other areas of the brain, assuming that the sexes shared anything that was fundamental when it came to brain function. Conversely, the neuroscience mainstream viewed any apparent sex differences in the brain as not fundamental—something to be understood after they grasped the fundamental facts. By this logic, it was not a problem to study males almost exclusively, since doing so supposedly allowed researchers to understand all that was fundamental in females without having to consider the complicating aspects of female hormones. To this day, neuroscientists overwhelmingly study only male animals.

In other words, some neuroscientists study male brains exclusively. They do this in the name of "equality," without the slightest tinge of irony. The Gender Ideology has influenced even the hard sciences so profoundly that the "no difference" concept is treated as an assumption, not a testable hypothesis.

Dr. Cahill titles his article "Equal ≠ The Same." I first encountered the notion that "equal" might not mean "the same" in 1991 when my husband and I became parents, first to a two-and-a-half-year-old badly neglected Romanian orphan boy and then six months later when I gave birth to a seemingly miraculously conceived daughter. In the beginning, I was troubled that our son absorbed much more of my time. Was it because he was older, or needier? Or could it be, (gasp!) that I was secretly favoring him because he was a boy?

Eventually, I realized that my ideological angst was unnecessary. Our son legitimately needed more care and attention from my husband and me. Taking our daughter to speech therapy twice a week because I was taking our son to speech therapy twice a week would've been stupid. Neither child would benefit from that kind of "equality." I knew in my heart that I was equally ready to meet each child's genuine needs, whatever they might be. That is the "equality" that both kids needed from me.

The Gender Ideology makes this commonsense attitude unnecessarily difficult. At the time, I did not know any of this material about the general developmental differences between boys and girls. All I knew was that I had two very different children, and the boy was exceptionally needy. It should never have even crossed my mind that I was secretly "favoring" the boy with more attention because of deep-seated hidden gender-based, culturally-constructed favoritism. Honestly, I had other things to worry about. Yet there I was, dealing with an unnecessary ideologically-driven drain on my time and attention.

Much more is at stake than my little personal episode of angst. This ideological resistance to studying sex differences has real consequences. Only recently have we allowed ourselves to notice that women and men react differently to medications. The FDA recently cut the recommended dosage of a popular sleeping pill, but only for women. Prescribing the same dosages for men and women amounted to over-medicating women. After twenty years of this, the FDA finally admitted that women's brains processed the drug differently.[12]

Under the influence of the Gender Ideology, important issues such as whether men and women process drugs differently are not treated as scientific questions but as assumptions. Fortunately, thanks to the work of brave men and women willing to step outside the reigning ideology, Dr. Cahill continues, "the National Institutes of Health has—for the first time—announced that all research they support will soon be required to carefully address potential sex differences. This is a remarkable development for research and medicine, and one that I, and everyone who appreciates the importance of sex influences, have been working toward for years."[13] No more studying women as if they were "men with pesky hormones."[14]

Is the "Gender Binary" Real?

Despite this glimmer of scientific progress, the Gender Ideology continues its march through society. The latest concept

---

[12]   Lesley Stahl, "Sex Matters: Drugs can affect the sexes differently," *CBS News*, May 25, 2014, http://www.cbsnews.com/news/sex-matters-drugs-can-affect-sexes-differently-2/

[13]   Dr. Cahill's response to Cordelia Fine et. al, "Reaction to 'Equal ≠ The Same: Sex Differences in the Human Brain,'" *Cerebrum*, December 15, 2014, http://www.dana.org/Cerebrum/Default.aspx?id=115816.

[14]   Stahl, "Sex Matters."

is challenging the "gender binary" of male and female. The popular social media site Facebook allows users to describe themselves as any one of seventy-one gender options. People can also select their preferred pronouns.[15] The idea is that a person's biological sex is not an objective reality but something "assigned at birth."

Some people do have ambiguous combinations of chromosomes and secondary sex characteristics. These are medically diagnosable conditions collectively known as intersex conditions or disorders of sex development. The Intersex Society of North America defined the term *intersex* as: "a general term used for a variety of conditions in which a person is born with a reproductive or sexual anatomy that doesn't seem to fit the typical definitions of female or male."[16]

In 2008, a new organization called the Accord Alliance replaced the Intersex Society of North America. This is approximately when the preferred terminology switched from intersex to disorders of sex development (DSD). The new organization addresses the same set of medical conditions.[17] The Accord Alliance defines DSD as "congenital conditions in which development of chromosomal, gonadal or anatomic sex is atypical," so DSD is an umbrella term

---

[15]   Rhiannon Williams, "Facebook's 71 gender options come to UK users," *UK Telegraph*, June 27, 2014, http://www.telegraph.co.uk/technology/facebook/10930654/Facebooks-71-gender-options-come-to-UK-users.html.

[16]   "What is intersex?" Intersex Society of North America, accessed December 3, 2016, http://www.isna.org/faq/what_is_intersex.

[17]   Intersex Society of North America (website), accessed December 3, 2016, http://www.isna.org/. The description of the new organization is at the bottom of the page.

covering a wide variety of conditions in which sex develops differently from typical male or typical female development.[18] They distinguish between DSD and transgenderism
this way: "'Transgender' means a person feels the gender
assigned to him or her at birth was not the right one for him
or her. DSD is, by definition, about atypical development of
a person's body, not about how a person feels about herself
or himself."[19]

Thus, the Accord Alliance, the most significant advocacy group for people who might be described as outside
the "gender binary," defines disorders of sex development
as medically diagnosable conditions. The transgender experience need not have anything at all to do with a medical
condition. The Accord Alliance continues: "Although it is
certainly possible that a child born with DSD will eventually
identify as a transgender person, it is also possible for children born without DSD to eventually identify as transgender. Most people with DSD are not transgender, and most
transgender people have no identifiable DSD."[20]

Now, one might think that people with these atypical
characteristics would be of interest and concern to those who
"reject the gender binary." People with unusually formed

---

18   Accord Alliance, "Frequently Asked Questions" in response to
      the question "What are the differences between sex, gender, and
      sexual orientation?" (n.d.), accessed December 5, 2016, http://
      www.accordalliance.org/learn-about-dsd/faqs/.

19   Accord Alliance, "Frequently Asked Questions," in response to
      the question, "Does having a DSD make a person transgender?"
      (n.d.), accessed December 5, 2016, http://www.accordalliance.
      org/learn-about-dsd/faqs/.

20   Ibid.

genitalia, people whose chromosomes are not the simple XX or XY, and people in other statistically unusual situations would bolster the case that "gender" is something other than the simple dichotomy between male and female. Oddly enough, however, the most public opponents of the "gender binary" don't seem to assign much significance to DSD.

For instance, the Obama-era Department of Justice sent a "Dear Colleague Letter on Transgender Students" to every public school in America mandating gender-neutral bathrooms and locker rooms. But the Department of Justice definition of "transgender students" specifically states: "Under Title IX, there is no medical diagnosis or treatment requirement that students must meet as a prerequisite to being treated consistent with their gender identity."[21]

On page two, the guidelines explain that the student may present themselves as transgender to their peers, teachers, and school staff. "The Departments interpret Title IX to require that when a *student or the student's parent or guardian, as appropriate,* notifies the school administration that the student will assert a gender identity that differs from previous representations or records, the school will begin treating the student consistent with the student's gender identity."[22]

A commonsense interpretation of this passage might be that a minor child could not "appropriately" present themselves with a different gender without the permission of his

---

[21]   US Department of Justice, US Department of Education, May 13, 2016, accessed November 22, 2016, http://www2.ed.gov/about/offices/list/ocr/letters/colleague-201605-title-ix-transgender.pdf.

[22]   Ibid., emphasis added.

or her parents. Only a student who has reached the age of majority, or a legally emancipated minor, would be allowed to specify a different gender in opposition to his or her parents' wishes. However, the guidelines never specify what they mean by "as appropriate."

Recent events suggest that "common sense" is not so common. A mother sued a Minnesota school district because it assisted her minor son in obtaining hormonal therapy without her permission or even knowledge.[23] Eventually, she lost her case: a federal judge threw it out.[24]

On page four, the Department of Justice guidelines inform the school districts: "The Departments may find a *Title IX violation* when a school limits students' educational rights or opportunities by failing to take reasonable steps to protect students' privacy related to their transgender status, including their *birth name or sex assigned at birth. Nonconsensual disclosure* of personally identifiable information (PII), such as a *student's birth name or sex assigned at birth,* could be harmful to or invade the privacy of transgender students and

---

[23]　　Mary Emily O'Hara, "Minnesota Mom Sues Her Trans Child Over Gender Reassignment," *NBC Out,* November 17, 2016, http://www.nbcnews.com/feature/nbc-out/minnesota-mom-sues-her-trans-child-over-gender-reassignment-n685266.

[24]　　Notice the very different reports of the same set of facts from these two sources: "Minnesota Mom loses fight against teen's sex change," *Courthouse News Service,* May 24, 2017, https://www.courthousenews.com/minnesota-mom-loses-fight-teens-sex-change/; and "Mom loses lawsuit against school that secretly gave her son 'transgender' treatment," *LifeSiteNews,* May 26, 2017, https://www.lifesitenews.com/news/federal-judge-to-mom-school-not...liable-for-secretly-helping-your-son-beco.

may also violate the Family Educational Rights and Privacy Act (FERPA)."[25]

The highlighted passages, taken together with the undefined "as appropriate" mentioned before, strongly suggest that the Department of Justice leaves its options open. It may consider revealing the child's transgender status even to his or her own parents as a violation of the child's privacy. So students can call themselves male or female as they wish without medical evaluation or parental oversight. They can change their self-identification for any reason or no reason. The guidelines offer no guidance whatsoever to the schools on how to deal with this situation. The United States Department of Justice reveals itself, in this case, to be a part of the Sexual State.[26]

While this push was taking place in the public schools, various municipalities and states have been persuaded or pressured to create transgender bathroom policies. The revolutionaries have enlisted the help of major corporations[27]

---

[25]   US Department of Justice, US Department of Education, May 13, 2016, accessed November 22, 2016, http://www2.ed.gov/about/offices/list/ocr/letters/colleague-201605-title-ix-transgen der.pdf, emphasis added.

[26]   The Trump administration overturned some of these policies. Jeremy W. Peters, Jo Becker, and Julie Hirschfeld Davis, "Trump Rescinds Rules on Bathrooms for Transgender Students," *New York Times*, February 22, 2017, https://www.nytimes. com/2017/02/22/us/politics/devos-sessions-transgender-stu dents-rights.html.

[27]   Brooke Sopelsa, "Major Corporations Join Fight Against North Carolina's 'Bathroom Bill,'" *NBCNews*, July 8, 2016. http://www. nbcnews.com/feature/nbc-out/major-corporations-join-fight-against-north-carolina-s-bathroom-bill-n605976.

and even professional sports[28] in their cause of redefining the human body. The Democratic Party is completely committed to these policies. Even the Republican Party, while ostensibly opposing the legal implementation of the full Gender Ideology, barely knows how to defend its position on this issue.

Young people are not fully developed in their sense of identity, including their sense of gender identity. Children who are so confused about who they are that they identify as something other than their bodily gender need more adult supervision and greater bodily privacy, not less of each. Mandating genderless bathrooms to be accessed by any student is not helpful even to the "transgender" student as defined by these guidelines. Open access restrooms and changing facilities aren't necessary for the benefit of self-defined "transgender" students. Changing and restroom facilities that can only be used by one person at a time could solve the privacy problems for the student who self-identifies as transgender, as well as the other students.

DSD children with intersex conditions don't need bathrooms that are open to everyone of any gender. Nor do they need school administrators concealing information from their parents in the name of respecting their "civil rights." The role of the schools should be confined to respecting the treatment plan the child's parents and doctors have developed for that child.

---

[28]   Jon Schuppe, "NBA Tells North Carolina Changes to LGBT Law HB2 Aren't Enough," *NBCNews,* July 1, 2016, http://www. nbcnews.com/news/us-news/nba-tells-north-carolina-changes-lgbt-law-hb2-aren-t-n602411.

The Intersex Society of North America, the forerunner of the Accord Alliance, did *not* necessarily embrace the idea that society must "break down the gender binary" to accommodate their unique situation or that intersex individuals be treated as a third gender or as having no gender.[29]

> There are at least two problems with trying to raise kids in a "third gender." First, how would we decide who would count in the "third gender"? How would we decide where to cut off the category of male and begin the category of intersex, or, on the other side of the spectrum, where to cut off the category of intersex to begin the category of female? . . . Second, and much more importantly, we are trying to make the world a safe place for intersex kids, and we don't think labeling them with a gender category that in essence doesn't exist would help them. What we *do* advocate is providing parents of intersex newborns—and within a couple of years, intersex children themselves—honest and accurate information about intersex, psychological counseling by professionals who are not intersexphobic, medical help for any real medical problems, and especially referrals to other people dealing with the same issues.[30]

No mention of genderless bathrooms.

---

[29] The Intersex Society of North America (website), accessed November 3, 2016, http://www.isna.org/.

[30] The Intersex Society of North America (website), http://www.isna.org/. See the FAQ page on third gender: accessed November 3, 2016, http://www.isna.org/faq/third-gender.

When pressed, the radicals retreat to the position that not everyone is born unambiguously male or female. They hold that the variety of intersexed conditions is conclusive proof that "assigning gender at birth" is intrinsically harmful to children. These radicals never mention that DSD or "intersex" is a medically diagnosable condition while "transgender" is a self-diagnosed, self-applied identity label.

GLAAD (formerly the Gay & Lesbian Alliance Against Defamation) defines *transgender* this way: "Transgender is a term used to describe people whose gender identity differs from the sex the doctor marked on their birth certificate. Gender identity is a person's internal, personal sense of being a man or a woman (or someone outside of that gender binary). For transgender people, the sex they were assigned at birth and their own internal gender identity do not match."[31]

GLAAD publishes a Media Reference Guide explaining their preferred terminology for various people and situations. The 2016 version, the most recent edition, gives this definition for *intersex*: "An umbrella term describing people born with reproductive or sexual anatomy and/or a chromosome pattern that can't be classified as typically male or female. Those variations are also sometimes referred to as Differences of Sex Development (DSD.) Avoid the outdated and derogatory term 'hermaphrodite.' While some people can have an intersex condition and also identify as transgender, the two are separate and should not be conflated."[32]

---

[31]   "Transgender FAQs," GLAAD, n.d., accessed December 2, 2016, http://www.glaad.org/transgender/transfaq.

[32]   "GLAAD Media Reference Guide," GADD, 10th ed., October

This is the sum total of the mentions of the terms *intersex* and DSD out of the forty-page media guide.

Please notice that GLAAD redefined the DSD initialism to mean "Differences of Sex Development." When the Accord Alliance uses DSD, they mean "disorders of sex development." Substituting *difference* for *disorder* may sound like an affirming, sensitive improvement in language. However, this substitution masks the fact that while most DSDs are medically benign, some DSDs are serious, even life-threatening medical conditions.[33] The term *disorder* calls attention to this fact.

By contrast, transgender persons are a major concern of GLAAD. In fact, GLAAD changed its name to position itself to advocate for "transgender" people.[34] The sex radicals insist that this divergence between one's "internal sense" and their biological identity is perfectly healthy. Even asking the question of whether the person might be mistaken or emotionally disturbed is tantamount to insensitivity, discrimination,

---

2016, http://www.glaad.org/sites/default/files/GLAAD-Media-Reference-Guide-Tenth-Edition.pdf.

[33] Accord Alliance, "Frequently Asked Questions," in response to the 23 questions under the heading, "Specific conditions" (n.d.), accessed December 8, 2016, http://www.accordalliance.org/learn-about-dsd/faqs/. DSDs with serious medical complications include congenital adrenal hyperplasia (CAH) and cloacal exstrophy. Conditions that should be watched for the possible development of cancer include dysplastic gonads and undescended testicles.

[34] "GLAAD will no longer be an acronym for the Gay and Lesbian Alliance Against Defamation," GLAAD, March 24, 2013, https://www.glaad.org/news/glaad-will-no-longer-be-acronym-gay-and-lesbian-alliance-against-defamation.

or harassment. As GLAAD puts it, "Trying to change a person's gender identity is no more successful than trying to change a person's sexual orientation—it doesn't work. So most transgender people seek to bring their bodies more into alignment with their gender identity."[35]

No objective medical criteria exist for diagnosing this condition. It depends entirely on the individual's self-perception. An individual can pump his or her body full of artificial hormones and undertake life-changing irreversible surgery with only minimal psychological counseling. In fact, counselors are sometimes fearful of challenging a person's gender identity for fear of being viewed as "transphobic."

Some people have a divergence between their bodies and their internal sense of gender identity. Suppose we accept for the sake of argument that for some of these people an immutable, medically unverifiable condition known as transgenderism causes this divergence.[36] How would we verify the existence of such a condition if the only criteria is the person's internal sense?

Is it theoretically possible that some traumatic event caused the mismatch between a person's biological sex and their "internal sense" of their gender identity? Could a

---

[35]   "Transgender FAQs," GLAAD, (n.d.), accessed December 2, 2016, http://www.glaad.org/transgender/transfaq.

[36]   For the record, I do not concede this point. See Lawrence Mayer and Paul McHugh, "Sexuality and Gender: Findings from the Biological, Psychological and Social Sciences," *The New Atlantis*, no. 50 (Fall 2016), https://www.thenewatlantis.com/docLib/20160819_TNA50SexualityandGender.pdf; and The American College of Pediatricians, "Gender Dysphoria in Children," June 2017, https://www.acpeds.org/the-college-speaks/position-statements/gender-dysphoria-in-children.

person reject his or her biological gender for socially constructed reasons that cannot be described as "immutable?" A single counter-example is sufficient to disprove the statement that "all persons who feel the gender assigned to him or her at birth was not the right one for him or her are otherwise perfectly healthy." I can cite at least one case of trauma-induced and one case of social-conditions-induced feelings of mismatch between gender identity and the body.

Walter Heyer attributes his desire to be a girl to abuse by his grandmother and uncle: repeated cross-dressing by his grandmother and sexual abuse by his uncle. Heyer transitioned to living as a woman but had no lasting peace. He finally discovered that he had developed a dissociative disorder due to the abuse. Eventually, he detransitioned back to living as a man. But by that time, he had lost years of his life to a misdiagnosis that left him permanently sterile.[37]

Nancy Verhelst's misdiagnosis cost her her life. Her mother wanted a boy and rejected Nancy as a child. One of her brothers abused her.[38] Nancy transitioned to a male body, hated the way she looked, and asked to be euthanized. The ever-so-progressive government of Belgium, where she lived, permitted this request to be honored.[39] The press reported

---

[37]   Walter Heyer, "I was a Transgender Woman," *The Public Discourse*, April 1, 2015, http://www.thepublicdiscourse. com/2015/04/14688/.

[38]   Roel Nollet "Nathan — Free as a Bird," IDFA, 2014, https:// www.idfa.nl/en/film/a9a2b9b7-9c9b-4407-b195-1c6f374babdd/ nathan-free-as-a-bird.

[39]   Jennifer Roback Morse, "Euthanizing the Unhappy: The Urgent Need for Love," *The Public Discourse*, November 7, 2013, http:// www.thepublicdiscourse.com/2013/11/11113/.

her story as if a "botched" sex change operation led to Nancy's (who renamed herself Nathan) request for euthanasia.[40]
However, the operation was not botched in any medically
defined sense of the term. She didn't like the way she looked
and felt. The surgery didn't solve her problem. She had herself killed.

Walter Heyer's case shows that it's possible that, for some
people at least, trauma is the underlying cause of mismatch
between biological sex and gender identity. The underlying
trauma should be treated as the cause. The feeling of a mismatch is a symptom.

Similarly, Nancy Verhelst's case shows that some people,
at least, experience a socially-generated rejection of their
body or sexual identity. This rejection, not an immutable
biological condition, is the source of the mismatch between
the person's internal sense of sexual identity and his or her
own body. This is not a healthy situation that the medical
profession and all of society should be affirming. The helping professions should have assisted Nancy in addressing the
underlying issue of self-rejection. The rest of society, concerned friends, relatives, and neighbors should have supported her in accepting herself. (And somebody should have
slapped her mother and her brother.)

In cases like these, isn't changing the body to fit the mind
counterproductive and not healthy at all? If this is at least

---

[40]   Bruno Waterfield, "Belgian killed by euthanasia after a botched
        sex change operation," *UK Telegraph,* October 1, 2013,
        http://www.telegraph.co.uk/news/worldnews/europe/bel-
        gium/10346616/Belgian-killed-by-euthanasia-after-a-botched-
        sex-change-operation.html.

theoretically possible, how can we clinically distinguish between a case of an "immutable" transgender condition and a case of a socially-caused, unhealthy transgender condition? Any honest person should be able to conclude from the publicly available facts that neither Walter Heyer nor Nancy Verhelst should have been approved for sex reassignment surgery. They had other problems that someone should have addressed.

Indeed, some in the helping professions are becoming alarmed by the casual way very young people are taking the life-changing steps involved in embracing the "transgender" identity. A site called "Youth-Transcritical Gender Professionals" has "First, do no harm" as its motto. But these concerns are socially invisible in today's world, dominated as it is by the Gender Ideology.

If an individual decides to transition, regrets it, and decides to de-transition, the advocates of the Gender Ideology and their creation, the Sexual State, have nothing helpful to say to that person. Walter Heyer transitioned to female and back to male. He maintains a website called Sex Change Regret to offer some help for people who are otherwise invisible to the world so influenced by the Gender Ideology.[41] Like other phases of the Sexual Revolution, hiding the people who have been harmed is crucial to keeping the ideology functioning. Mr. Heyer is a thorn in the side to the truly committed gender ideologues.

As for Ms. Verhelst, I have yet to see a single person from

---

[41]   Sex Change Regret (website), accessed December 2, 2016, http://www.sexchangeregret.com/.

the Gender Ideology advocacy groups utter a word about her tragic life and death. A filmmaker documented the last three years of her life, including her ultimate death. The synopsis of this film states, "Recordings of Nathan, conversations with his close friends, Nathan's own audio recordings from the past and news reports about Nathan's case all serve to complete an inhumanly tragic story that ends humanely."[42]

In my opinion, Nancy's story should be a cautionary tale against the Gender Ideology. Instead, her life has been pressed into the service of that ideology as well as euthanasia advocacy.

Conclusion: Who Benefits From Confusion?

For a long time, I had trouble understanding the push for transgender policies. How does it help people who have a diagnosable medical condition, DSD, to be lumped together with people who have no such condition but who want to alter their own bodies? But now, I'm pretty sure I understand who is helped by this deliberate conflation of people in very different types of medical and psychological situations. Look at what these transgender policies accomplish:

- Young people can define and redefine their gender identities, with or without parental supervision. This creates a separation between children and their parents and inserts the State between them.

---

42 Roel Nollet "Nathan — Free as a Bird," IDFA, 2014, https://www.idfa.nl/en/film/a9a2b9b7-9c9b-4407-b195-1c6f374babdd/nathan-free-as-a-bird.

- People of any age can define and redefine their gender identities. The State sets itself up as the public enforcer of their new identities. New York has redefined sexual harassment to include failing to use the correct pronouns. This can carry a fine of up to $250,000.[43]

The Gender Ideology empowers the State.

But the State is not the only entity empowered by the Gender Ideology. Members of the managerial class in both private academic settings and the corporate world who are ideologically connected or at least ideologically compliant find themselves with a large new portfolio of managerial activities. Was this student's behavior really harassment? Was this employee really creating a hostile work environment?

By contrast, the common-sense policy of providing

---

[43] Eugene Volokh, "You can be fined for not calling people 'ze' or 'hir,' if that's the pronoun they demand that you use," *Washington Post*, May 17, 2016, https://www.washingtonpost.com/news/volokh-conspiracy/wp/2016/05/17/you-can-be-fined-for-not-calling-people-ze-or-hir-if-thats-the-pronoun-they-demand-that-you-use/?utm_term=.0bdaa7b58345.

The *Gothamist*'s attempt to debunk Professor Volokh's article falls flat. It insists that the fine cannot be applied for "accidently" using the wrong pronoun but can only be applied for "intentionally and repeatedly" using the wrong pronoun. This statement and headline, while perhaps technically and currently accurate, do not get to the heart of Professor Volokh's concerns. Using the wrong pronoun can be treated as harassment, which has serious penalties attached to it. Volokh did not claim that people would be fined for accidents. His concern is with the government forcing people to say things they do not believe. Miranda Katz, "No, NYC Did Not Just Introduce A $250,000 Fine For Any Incorrect Use Of Gender Pronouns," *Gothamist*, May 19, 2016, http://gothamist.com/2016/05/19/gender_pronouns_false_fine.php.

individual-use bathrooms and changing rooms doesn't empower the State, any of its allied advocacy groups, or the managerial class. Likewise, children who have a disorder of sexual development do not present the opportunity for large-scale ideological social management. These children, and the adults they later become, need individualized, personal care involving their parents, doctors, and other helping professions. They don't need any one-size fits all, federally imposed regulations.

This accounts for the regulators at the Department of Justice overlooking them in their "Guidelines for Transgender Students." This accounts for the short shrift that advocacy organizations like GLAAD give to intersexed people. Persons with DSDs are not politically useful to the gender ideologues. This massive accumulation of power for the ideologically connected is precisely the motivation for continuing the inhuman policy of de-gendering the entire society.

Yes, the gender binary is real. Some people have intersexed medical conditions. Their lives don't in any way contradict the gender binary. They can have good lives without insisting that the rest of society "break down the gender binary."

The human species is a mammalian species. Our reproduction requires one male and one female. Our young are born alive and dependent. The Gender Ideology is an attack on these basic, biological facts. The Gender Ideology makes war on the human body. That means the Gender Ideology makes war on the human race. This deadly ideology has got to be stopped.

CHAPTER 14

On the Controversy Over the Definition of Marriage

The reader may be surprised that in a book on marriage, family, and human sexuality, I have not yet said a word about the most divisive controversy of our time: the definition of marriage. I made a deliberate decision to postpone this topic until the end of the book.

In 2015, the United States Supreme Court ruled in a 5-4 decision that the US Constitution requires so-called gay marriage. The court held that any requirement that marriage be confined to one man and one woman violates the due process and equal protection clauses of the Fourteenth Amendment to the US Constitution.[1] Henceforth, marriage is legally independent of gender. (That is why I refer to it as "genderless marriage.")

The Sexual Revolution has three foundational ideologies: the Contraceptive Ideology, the Divorce Ideology, and the

---

[1]   Obergefell v. Hodges, 135 S.Ct. 2071 (2015).

Gender Ideology. In order to believe that genderless marriage is desirable or even possible, one must already believe all three of these ideas. We've redefined sex to be a sterile recreational activity, so sex is not particularly important. We've redefined our understanding of children and their needs, so a lasting marriage between children's biological parents, one man and one woman, is not important. We've redefined our understanding of our very identities as men and women, so the sex of the body is not important. So why not remove the gender requirement from marriage?

In other words, the earlier phases of the Sexual Revolution laid the groundwork for genderless marriage. Indeed, gay marriage is the logical outcome of the Sexual Revolution. This is why the elites are convinced that the marriage issue is no longer debatable. In their minds, they have already redefined marriage. They can't understand why anyone is still holding out.

But all three of the foundational ideas of the Sexual Revolution are false. Experience has shown these ideas to be pernicious and harmful. Redefining marriage solidifies and further institutionalizes these untruths. We never should have embraced them in the first place. That is why I am convinced we must oppose the idea of embedding them even further into law and society. That is why I am opposed to the redefinition of marriage imposed by the US Supreme Court.

The Sexual Revolution has been the creation of the elites. It could not have survived and metastasized as it has without the active support of the government's ability to coerce, tax, manipulate, and regulate. And so it is with the gay marriage issue.

No honest person can deny that the elites of society have foisted this social innovation on the rest of us. Elites of the entertainment and media worlds created and sustained the campaign to normalize homosexual practice and soften us up for a redefinition of marriage. These industries shamelessly exploit the vast power of the media to manipulate public opinion and perceptions. The academic elites piled on with phony "studies," advocacy research bought and paid for by sexual revolutionary foundations. They also piled on with trumped-up attacks on studies that did not produce the results they wanted.

When marriage was an issue on the ballot, when ordinary citizens could express their views, man-woman marriage routinely won. Up until the 2012 elections, man-woman marriage had won thirty-two out of thirty-two contests.[2] As the controversy continued, the sexual revolutionaries harnessed their greater wealth and influence. The 2012 election saw the first time that voters rejected ballot measures favoring man-woman marriage. And the revolutionaries began focusing their attention on courts and state legislatures. They reasoned, correctly, that their superior resources could obtain the outcomes they wanted more easily there than in popular referenda.

I first noticed the disparity in resources in 2011, in the New York state legislature. One wealthy businessman with a gay son dumped money in the campaign coffers of select

---

[2]   Erik Eckholm, "One Man Guides the Fight Against Gay Marriage," *New York Times*, October 9, 2012, http://www.nytimes. com/2012/10/10/us/politics/frank-schubert-mastermind-in-the-fight-against-gay-marriage.html.

assemblymen to get them to vote for the redefinition of
marriage. That businessman happened to be Republican.[3]
I began to see that the elite support for the redefinition of
marriage was a bipartisan phenomenon.

I witnessed another version of the same story when I testified in Rhode Island in January 2013.[4] When I arrived at
the state house in Providence, the size of the crowds stunned
me. About one thousand people showed up to support natural marriage. The place was packed with African-American
and Hispanic Evangelicals who opposed the marriage redefinition bill.[5] There were so few people advocating gay "marriage" that the media could barely find anyone to interview.[6]

---

3   Frank Bruni, "Paul Singer's Equality Efforts," *New York Times*,
     June 9, 2012, https://bruni.blogs.nytimes.com/2012/06/09/
     paul-singers-equality-efforts/; Sean Sullivan, "Meet the billion-
     aire hedge fund manager quietly shaping the GOP gay marriage
     debate," *Washington Post*, May 3, 2013, https://www.washing
     tonpost.com/news/the-fix/wp/2013/05/03/meet-the-billionaire-
     hedge-fund-manager-quietly-shaping-the-gop-gay-marriage-de
     bate/?utm_term=.36e34a0d1dcd.

4   My testimony can be viewed here: Steve Ahlquist, "2013-01-
     15 RI House Marriage Equality Testimony 006 Jennifer Ro-
     back Morse," January, 21, 2013, https://www.youtube.com/
     watch?v=IRTvl0-ifXI.

5   I took some (very amateur) photos and videos. I had a feeling no
     one in the elite media would show those images. RuthInstitute,
     "Dr J at the Rhode Island legislature building with Marriage
     Supporters," January 21, 2013, https://www.youtube.com/
     watch?v=VqVFZh0qDgw.

6   Alissa Graham, "My experience at the HB5015 Hearing in Prov-
     idence Rhode Island," January 28, 2013, http://www.ruthblog.
     org/2013/01/28/my-experience-at-the-hb5015-hearing-in-prov
     idence-rhode-island/. Full disclosure: this story, published by
     the Ruth Institute, was written by a local student of mine who
     attended the hearings.

But the crowds of ordinary people with their homemade amateur signs were not the whole story. The professional side of the political equation tells the story.

One can track the number of lobbyists registered for each side of each bill using information from the Rhode Island secretary of state. The House version of the marriage redefinition bill, H5015A, had one lobbyist opposed: my buddy Chris Plante of the National Organization for Marriage, Rhode Island. The other side had twelve registered lobbyists. On the Senate side, the proponents of the marriage redefinition bill, S0038, had eighteen registered lobbyists. Opposed? You guessed it. Chris Plante, all by his lonesome.[7]

On one side, one thousand people of modest means with homemade signs and one registered lobbyist. One the other side, a handful of people and eighteen professional lobbyists.

I thought back to the California Proposition 8 campaign in 2008, which defined marriage as the union of a man and a woman in the California state constitution. I was a campaign spokeswoman for the campaign, so I had a ringside seat. The financial resources on both sides were roughly equal: each side spent about $40 million.[8]

---

[7] To find the lobbyists, go to this page: https://www.lobbytracker. sos.ri.gov/Public/LobbyingReports.aspx. Click on "legislative session 2013." Click on "bills." Type in H5015A for the House side and S0038 for the Senate side. You will see 13 registered lobbyists for House bill and 19 registered lobbyists for the Senate bill. Inspection will show that all except Chris Plante are associated with organizations that support gay marriage.

[8] To be precise, the man-woman marriage advocates raised $39 million while the gay marriage advocates raised $44 million. "Proposition 8: Who gave in the gay marriage battle?" *Los Angeles Times,* (n.d.), accessed April 30, 2018, http://projects.latimes.com/prop8/.

However, the man-woman marriage campaign had one hundred thousand volunteers. According to campaign manager Frank Schubert, the campaign visited 70 percent of all California households in person and contacted another 15 percent by phone. Schubert also recounted how many individual contributors the campaign had. Their mandated reporting of donations to the state government "was so large that it literally crashed the secretary of state's Web page. . . . They couldn't accept it — there were over 5,000 *pages* of contributors." Meanwhile, the gay marriage supporters had a total of six thousand individual contributors.[9]

The "Yes on 8" campaign was arguably the largest grass-roots campaign in history: the sort of thing the progressives of the early twentieth century would've celebrated. Ordinary people were dissatisfied with the way the elites were treating them on the marriage issue, so they took matters into their own hands. The non-establishment used the initiative procedure of which the early progressives were so proud.[10]

None of that history seemed to matter to the modern Progressives. They took Proposition 8 to court on flimsy pretexts and rich people's money. Hollywood icon and multi-millionaire Rob Reiner used his money and influence to hire the "dream team" of attorneys from the *Bush v. Gore* days.[11]

---

[9]   Schubert was quoted in Tim Dickinson, "Same-Sex Setback," *Rolling Stone*, December 11, 2008, https://www.rollingstone. com/politics/news/same-sex-setback-20081211, emphasis added.

[10]   Wikipedia, s.v. "Initiative and referendums in the United States," last modified April 29, 2018, https://en.wikipedia.org/wiki/Initiatives_and_referendums_in_the_United_States.

[11]   In this video, Chad Griffin describes the American Foundation for Equal Rights, of which he is the president, as "sole sponsor of the Perry case." Also, you can see Rob Reiner in the video

According to *Hollywood Insider*, "Reiner used his Hollywood insider status to court a handful of millionaires and billionaires including Norman Lear, Steve Bing, and David Geffen, who provided the $3 million-$5 million in seed money that allowed the foundation to support the work of high-powered lawyers Ted Olson and David Boies."[12] The mainstream media loved being able to say that now "marriage equality" was a bipartisan issue with prominent attorneys from both parties attacking Proposition 8.

Along the way, they were gutting the citizens' initiative process. This was particularly obvious in the challenge that landed in the California Supreme Court. The people of California had voted to amend their own constitution. The attorney general has the responsibility to defend the laws of the state. However, when the activists staged their challenge to the constitutionality of Proposition 8, California's attorney general refused to defend it in court. By doing nothing, the attorney general, in effect, pocket vetoed the duly enacted citizens' initiative.

But not defending the initiative established a dangerous precedent. Anytime an initiative passed that the elite

at 6:30. Ted Olsen thanks him and his wife for their support around 7:30 on the video. American Foundation for Equal Rights, "Prop. 8 Standing Oral Arguments before California Supreme Court," September 6, 2011, https://www.youtube.com/watch?v=Mmmy1fqeF0Y&feature=youtu.be. Reiner and his wife are board members of the American Foundation for Equal Rights, as can be seen on the organization's tax filings: http://www.afer.org/wp-content/uploads/2011/03/2010-03-31_AFER_IRS-990.pdf.

12   Gregg Kilday, "How Rob Reiner became anti-Prop. 8 kingpin," *The Hollywood Reporter*, August 5, 2010, https://www.hollywoodreporter.com/news/how-rob-reiner-became-anti-26362.

political classes disliked, they could get their friends to challenge it in court. If the political elites, such as the attorney general, then refused to defend the ballot initiative in court, the courts could then overturn it pretty much by default.

The gay marriage advocates claimed that the Proposition 8 proponents had no "standing" to even defend the measure in court. The California Supreme Court threw out this challenge to Proposition 8, but not because they disliked gay marriage. They had already written an opinion stating that the California constitution required it. That California Supreme Court decision was the event that triggered the Propositon 8 campaign in the first place.

I was in the courtroom for oral arguments at the California Supreme Court. The justices' disdain for the arguments of their fellow members of the legal establishment was unmistakable in the courtroom. The tension was palpable. But the sexual revolutionaries didn't care about the initiative process, which was once considered the crown jewel of citizen reforms from the Progressive era. They cared only about getting the result they wanted. Thankfully, the California Supreme Court threw out the "standing" challenge. They, at least, wanted to preserve the integrity of the initiative process.[13]

The Sexual Revolution, through its three foundational

---

13   "In analyzing the standing issue under California law, the court
      noted that because the fundamental purpose of the initiative
      process in California is 'to enable the people to amend the state
      Constitution or to enact statutes when current government
      officials have declined to adopt (and often have publicly op-
      posed) the measure in question, the voters who have successfully
      adopted an initiative measure may reasonably harbor a legiti-

ideologies—the Contraceptive Ideology, the Divorce Ideology, and the Gender Ideology—has harmed millions of people. Will "gay marriage" create victims? I believe it will, just as every earlier round of the Sexual Revolution has produced victims. People have been harmed because they or someone close to them built their lives around lies and half-truths. Those people are socially invisible. The elites make sure that no one ever hears any downsides, risks, or harms associated with their fantasy ideology.

The same is and will continue to be true of the victims of the normalization of homosexual practice and the redefinition of marriage. Adult children of same-sex couples who believe they were harmed by the way they were raised are considered social pariahs. Dr. Robert Oscar Lopez was raised by his mother and her lesbian lover. He has been an outspoken critic of genderless marriage and a passionate advocate for the rights of children to both parents. Gay activists harassed him and his university. He ultimately lost his job as a tenured English professor.[14] He collected stories from

---

mate concern that the public officials who ordinarily defend a challenged state law in court may not, in the case of an initiative measure, always undertake such a defense with vigor or with the objectives and interests of those voters paramount in mind. As a consequence, California courts have routinely permitted the official proponents of an initiative to intervene or appear as real parties in interest to defend a challenged voter-approved initiative measure "to guard the people's right to exercise initiative power."" "California Supreme Court Rules on Proposition 8 'Standing' Issue," California Courts News Release, November 17, 2011, https://newsroom.courts.ca.gov/news/california-supreme-court-rules-on-proposition-8-standing-issue.

[14]   Mirah Riben, "End the Witch-hunt: In Defense of Robert

other adult children of gay parents. They submitted amicus briefs to the Supreme Court. These adult children of gays were ignored at best and ruthlessly hounded at worst.[15]

We're only permitted to hear sanitized, pre-screened testimony as to the wonderful upbringing children received from their two moms, for example. Just as the adult children of divorce are socially invisible, so too must the adult children of same-sex parents be rendered socially invisible.

Same-sex couples who utilize third party reproduction are following a pre-packaged script or "perfect narrative" too. In that script, they have a child that looks like both of them, perhaps by selecting a gamete donor who looks like the social parent. If the couple uses a known donor, that person (who is, after all, the child's other parent) always wants exactly the same amount of participation in the child's life that the same-sex couple wants them to have. Or, if they have an anonymous gamete donor, the child never has any psychological issues with not knowing his or her missing parent. And they all live happily ever after.

We already know that every part of that script is misleading. Plenty of cases have emerged where the promised

---

Oscar Lopez," *Huffington Post*, November 13, 2015, https://www.huffingtonpost.com/mirah-riben/end-the-witch-hunt-in-def_b_8539402.html.

[15]   Rivka Edelman reports on the attacks and threats she received. Rivka Edelman, "This lesbian's daughter has had enough," *The American Thinker*, October 20, 2014, http://www.american thinker.com/articles/2014/10/this_lesbians_daughter_has_had_ enough.html. Austin Ruse also reports on Rivka Edelman and others. Austin Ruse, "Real Victims of the Gay Bullyboys," *Crisis*, October 10, 2014, https://www.crisismagazine.com/2014/re al-victims-gay-bullyboys.

fairy tale doesn't materialize. A lesbian couple in Ohio had a mix-up at the sperm bank. These two white women ended up with a mixed-race baby.[16]

A Canadian lesbian mother discovered that her child's sperm donor dad was none of the things he claimed to be. He was not working on a PhD in neuroscience engineering hoping to become a professor of biomedical robotics at a medical school. In fact, he has had run-ins with the law and serious mental illness, including schizophrenia and bipolar disorder. Believe it or not, this guy who lied on his sperm bank intake form also had a narcissistic personality disorder.[17]

And don't get me started on the cases of "known" sperm donors that fall apart and require court intervention. For some strange reason, these well-crafted plans of a lesbian couple and a gay couple sharing parenting contentedly forever don't seem to work out. In this heartrending British case, the judge is beside himself trying to figure out what to do. He can't figure it out because there is no just solution: a solution that is fair to the biological parents, their partners, and, most of all, to the children.[18]

---

[16]   Jennifer Roback Morse, "Gay Activist Elites at Fault: Why I am Not Angry at Lesbians Who Sue the Sperm Bank," *Christian Post*, October 9, 2014, https://www.christianpost.com/news/gay-activist-elites-at-fault-why-i-am-not-angry-at-lesbians-who-sue-the-sperm-bank-127822/.

[17]   Jennifer Roback Morse, "In An Industry That Makes People, What Could Possibly Go Wrong?," *The Blaze*, April 20, 2016.

[18]   Steve Doughty, "High Court judge's blast for four gay parents fighting over two little sisters," *Daily Mail*, October 10, 2011, http://www.dailymail.co.uk/news/article-2047671/High-Court-judges-blast-gay-parents-fighting-little-sisters.html#ixzz54e

I do not entirely blame these parents. They were follow-ing the grand sexual revolutionary narrative. This narrative is laid out for them very publicly and prominently. Any caveats or concerns are carefully buried under the rhetoric of "hate." Dr. Lopez and his friends "hate gay people," you see. That is the only possible reason they could have for saying anything negative about their childhood experiences.

Even if nothing spectacular goes wrong with same-sex parenting, the whole premise is unjust to children. Children have a right to their own parents. A same-sex couple can only have children through some form of third party reproduc-tion. The law separates the child from one of his or her bio-logical parents. In this case,[19] a child is in foster care due to neglect by both her mother and her mother's female partner. The child's known sperm donor father wants to be involved in the child's life. The judge forbade him from even doing a paternity test, saying, "A paternity test for an outsider, who merely donated sperm, belatedly asserting parental rights would effectively disrupt, if not destroy, this family unit and nullify the child's established relationship with the wife, her

---

QED9Y2. This is possibly the same case three years later. It is difficult to be sure because the earlier story does not include identifying information. Eleanor Harding, "£500,000 custody battle between gay parents after a sperm donation deal went wrong wrecked childhoods of two little girls, says judge," *Daily Mail*, November 4, 2014, http://www.dailymail.co.uk/news/arti cle-2821113/Custody-battle-gay-parents-wrecked-childhoods-2-girls-says-judge.html#ixzz54eNks3zs.

[19]   Brandy Zadrozny, "Lesbian Couple's Sperm Donor Sues for Pa-rental Rights," *The Daily Beast*, January 31, 2018, https://www. thedailybeast.com/lesbian-couples-sperm-donor-sues-for-paren tal-rights?source=facebook&via=mobile.

other mother. Testing in these circumstances exposes children born into same-gender marriages to instability for no justifiable reason other than to provide a father-figure for children who already have two parents."

Very real people have built their lives around the fantasy ideology. When the inevitable problems arise, the revolutionaries are nowhere in sight. The only thing the revolutionaries offer is more radicalism. In this case, the family law director of the National Center for Lesbian Rights stated, "A significant portion of cases that we work on include a parent who might not be a biological parent but planned for conception and birth as any parent would, and whose rights are in question. . . . The unfortunate reality for same-sex couples . . . is depending on the state you live in, you don't really know if the law is going to ultimately protect you."[20]

The presumption of the radicals is that the law must protect the interests of the commissioning parents to the child they planned for, not the interests of the child to having her own parents. The radicals offer more separation of the child from the parent, more rights for the non-biological, socially constructed parent, and more power for the State and the advocacy groups to flex their muscles and impose their will on the powerless individuals involved and society as a whole.

As to same-sex attraction itself, there is only one socially acceptable script for a person who experiences same-sex attraction. That person must "come out," accept his or her true self, and engage in an active sex life. That person should become an activist in favor of all the political causes that the

---

20   Ibid.

LGBT wing of the Sexual Revolution currently favors. Look at the rancor directed at gay men and lesbian women who deviate from the party line.[21]

This repeats the earlier revolutionary pattern too. The establishment feminists gave women one socially acceptable script. Get on the pill as soon as possible. Have an active sex life. Get educated as if you had to take care of yourself financially for a lifetime. Disregard or suppress any desires you may feel for marriage, husband, children, and stability. That's not the real you. And by all means, become a political activist for every cause favored by the feminist wing of the Sexual Revolution. Women who don't follow the feminist script aren't real women.

Likewise, same-sex attracted persons who don't follow the script are lying to themselves. Living a chaste, sexually-abstinent life? Unthinkable to the gay activist, even though some same-sex attracted men and women choose that life and live it happily.[22] Marrying a person of the opposite sex, being faithful to that person, and having a family together is a betrayal of your true self. If anyone raises a hand and says, "But I've done it, and I'm having a great life," the full

---

[21]   Claire Chretien, "Ex-gays: California 'stay gay' bill denies our existence," *LifeSiteNews*, May 30, 2018. https://www.lifesitenews.com/news/ex-gays-californias-stay-gay-bill-denies-our-existence; Stella Morabito, "The Trans Lobby hates this man for proving sex change regret is real," *The Federalist*, January 9, 2018, http://thefederalist.com/2018/01/09/walt-heyer-proves-sex-change-regret-real-thats-trans-lobby-hates/.

[22]   Daniel Mattson, *Why I Don't Call Myself Gay* (San Francisco: Ignatius Press, 2017) makes the case for the sexually abstinent life.

weight of the gay establishment goes into overdrive to discredit that person and his or her testimony.[23] Why? Because it goes against the narrative.

The narrative continues: You were born that way. Get over it. You can't change. Efforts to change will hurt you.

Sexual revolutionaries breathlessly and innocently proclaim: "Conversion therapy laws prohibit licensed mental health practitioners from subjecting LGBT minors to harmful 'conversion therapy' practices that attempt to change their sexual orientation or gender identity."[24]

But what exactly is "conversion therapy?" What exactly is "harmful?" One California therapist, explains: "The effect of the current ban on 'sexual orientation change efforts' for minors is to make it impossible for these patients to pursue any treatment goal that involves the possibility of change, no matter how mainstream the interventions may be."[25]

How does this blanket ban on treatment help the same sex attracted young person? It doesn't. It only helps the narrative.

The science does not support the claim that people are

---

[23]   Doug Mainwaring is a same-sex attracted man who is married to a woman and living a good and, may I say, holy life. Doug Mainwaring, "I'm a gay man, happily married to a woman. And I'm not the only one," *LifeSiteNews,* March 27, 2017.

[24]   "Conversion Therapy Laws," Movement Advancement Project, (n.d.), accessed May 1, 2018, http://www.lgbtmap.org/equality-maps/conversion_therapy.

[25]   Christopher Rosik, "Sexual orientation change efforts and the campaign to ban them," interview with Dr. Christopher Rosik, *MercatorNet,* July 17, 2015, https://www.mercatornet.com/arti cles/view/sexual-orientation-change-efforts-and-the-campaign-to-ban-them/16522.

"born that way." People do change their patterns of attraction, their self-identification, and their behaviors.[26] Even the American Psychological Association has admitted: "There is no consensus among scientists about the exact reasons that an individual develops a heterosexual, bisexual, gay or lesbian orientation. Although much research has examined the possible genetic, hormonal, developmental, social and cultural influences on sexual orientation, no findings have emerged that permit scientists to conclude that sexual orientation is determined by any particular factor or factors. Many think that nature and nurture both play complex roles; most people experience little or no sense of choice about their sexual orientation."[27]

---

[26]   Lisa Diamond's extensive research shows that women's patterns of sexual attraction and behaviors can change over time. Lisa Diamond, "Female Bisexuality From Adolescence to Adulthood: Results From a 10-Year Longitudinal Study," *Developmental Psychology* 44, no. 1 (2008), pp. 5–14, https://psych.utah.edu/_documents/people/diamond/diamond-female-bisexuality-adolescence-to-adulthood.pdf; and her book-length treatment, *Sexual Fluidity: Understanding Women's Love and Desire* (Cambridge MA: Harvard University Press, 2009). Likewise, Ritch Savin-Williams has written extensively about sexual fluidity among men. His book-length treatment is *Mostly Straight: Sexual Fluidity among Men* (Cambridge MA: Harvard University Press, 2017). One representative article is Zhana Vrangalova, "Mostly Heterosexual and Mostly Gay/Lesbian: Evidence for New Sexual Orientation Identities," *Archives of Sexual Behavior* 41, no. 1 (February 2012), pp. 85–101.

[27]   American Psychological Association, "Sexual Orientation and Homosexuality," (n.d.), accessed January 19, 2018, http://www.apa.org/topics/lgbt/orientation.aspx, in response to the question "What causes a person to have a particular sexual orientation?"

Who benefits from the belief that no one can ever change their patterns of attraction? The ideologues, that's who.

Conclusion: Closing Old Doors. Opening New Ones.

I recall the first time I defended Proposition 8 at an editorial board. I showed a Canadian birth certificate to the editors of the *Los Angeles Times*. I said, "Look, they have gay marriage in Canada. The birth certificate still says 'mother's name.' But where it should say 'father's name,' it now says 'father or co-parent.' Fatherhood is reduced to a check-off box. They are marginalizing fathers from the family."

The editor replied, "So what? Lots of kids don't have dads."

Her callousness shocked me. It shocks me still.

A few years ago, I debated gay marriage at a major law school. My opponent was a professor deeply committed to the full gay agenda. He took offense that I referred to his partner as "partner." "He is not my partner. He is my husband!" he said indignantly.[28] I replied that under the laws he advocated, there would be no husbands or wives. I wouldn't have a husband. Neither would he. Everyone would have generic "spouses." I was surprised that a professional advocate for gay marriage hadn't considered that removing the

---

[28]   My debate opponent was Dr. Gary Gates, a fine demographer, probably the best in the world at collecting accurate population data on sexual minorities. The debate took place at the UCLA Law School on August 29, 2012. A recording is here: http://ruthinstitute.libsyn.com/dr-j-dr-gary-gates-ucla. This exchange took places around 42 minutes. My response is around 52–55 minutes. Of course, you can't see his facial expression. But I can report that he did seem to be genuinely surprised by this news. (Last accessed November 18, 2016.)

gender requirement from marriage would in turn require removing gendered language from the law. Less than two years after our debate, and less than a year after the *Obergefell* decision, this is exactly what took place.[29]

I've heard all the efforts to dodge the issues. The most commonly used tactic is to call me names. Revolutionaries love to change the subject from their policy and its consequences to the moral character (or supposed lack thereof) of their opponents. They do this whether the subject is contraception, abortion, divorce, or, now, gay marriage and transgenderism. They do this because, as this book shows, their policies are indefensible. Their policies are destructive. They *must* change the subject.

Another dodge levels the accusation that opposing genderless marriage singles out gay people.

"You say you are worried about children losing their relationship with their parents. Why don't you talk about all the children harmed by divorce?"

That door is now closed. This book has closed it.

"Why do you criticize same-sex couples who use assisted reproduction technologies when most of the people who use those technologies are straight?"

That door is now closed. This book has closed it.

No one can say I've singled out same-sex attracted persons for special hatred or mistreatment. No one can claim that I'm making excuses for the sexual misbehavior of straight

---

29   "California governor signs bill replacing words 'husband' and 'wife' in state law," *Fox News Politics*, July 7, 2014, http://www.foxnews.com/politics/2014/07/07/california-bill-replacing-words-husband-wife-in-marriage-law-signed-by-gov.html.

people. No one can seriously maintain that I am holding gay people to an impossibly higher standard.

It's time to face up to the harms the Sexual Revolution has caused. Whether you you're male or female, straight or gay, young or old, religious or irreligious: what kind of world do you want to help create? A world in which every child has a legally recognized right to a relationship with both parents? Or a world in which some children have these legally recognized rights and others do not? Or more radical still, a world in which no children at all have legally recognized rights to their own parents?

Do you want to help create a world in which adults have obligations to provide a relationship and identity to children? Or a world in which adults get to do whatever they want sexually and kids just have to accept whatever the adults choose to give them? A world that lives in harmony with our bodily existence as male and female rational creatures? Or a world at war with our bodies, with all creation, and with God?

The choice is ours. No more dodging or changing the subject. If children don't have a right to their own parents, no one has a right to anything. If you disagree, please explain to me why. Someday, the kids are going to grow up. Someday, the kids are going to ask.

I'm ready with my answer. Will you be?

CHAPTER 15

What the Catholic Church
Says About Male and Female

Then God said, "Let us make man in our image, after our like-
ness; and let them have dominion over the fish of the sea, and over
the birds of the air, and over the cattle, and over all the earth,
and over every creeping thing that creeps upon the earth." So God
created man in his own image, in the image of God he created
him; male and female he created them.

Genesis 1:27–28

We could summarize Catholic teaching in these points:

- God created us male and female.
- Sex differences are real. Not all differences between men and women are socially constructed.
- Not all differences in social treatment of men and women are justifiable.

God Created Us Male and Female

Pope Francis recently said, "Let us not fall into the sin of trying to replace the Creator. We are creatures, and not omnipotent. Creation is prior to us and must be received as a gift."[1] I realize that this claim makes no sense for the truly committed atheist. However, since we are spelling out the Church's teaching, we must state this. Its implications are deeper than one might first suppose. "Receiving" ourselves as part of creation is precisely what the Gender Ideology, in all its forms, resists.

One might reply, "God created people with intersexed conditions that are not typically male or female." The Church teaches that attempting to correct physical anomalies, particularly those that have serious health implications, is perfectly moral. As I have already shown, the transgender ideology goes way beyond this.

The mutilation involved in so-called "transitioning" surgeries indicates a despising of God's gift of the body. The Catechism's general principle addresses this. "Except when performed for strictly therapeutic medical reasons, directly intended amputations, mutilations, and sterilizations performed on innocent persons are against the moral law."[2] Bear in mind, the Catechism was promulgated in 1994, well before the current transgender craze. The Church may not have been contemplating the surgeries of today, but the principle stands.

---

[1]   *Amoris Laetitia*, no. 56.

[2]   *Catechism of the Catholic Church* 2297.

Sex Differences Are Real

I showed in an earlier chapter the scientific evidence for believing that some differences between men and women are prior to any possibility of social construction. The Church has always accepted sex differences, even before modern science revealed so many of the mysteries of man and woman. The Catholic priesthood is all-male, possibly the last all-male institution remaining in the modern world. The Church recently reaffirmed this position, which dates to apostolic times.[3]

This is not the time and place to go into a thorough theological explanation. Suffice to say, the defense of the all-male priesthood is based on Catholic teaching on the sacraments, creation, ecclesiology (that is, the science of the Church), and the priesthood itself.[4] No change in society's views or structures is going to induce the Catholic Church to change on this issue.

At the same time, women have always had leadership and teaching roles in the Catholic Church. Some Christian Churches hold very rigid views about sex roles, often based on St. Paul's statements about women not teaching in church.[5] We don't interpret those passages so rigidly that

---

[3] Christopher Lamb, "Vatican's doctrine prefect says Church teaching on male-only priesthood is 'definitive,'" *The Tablet*, http://www.thetablet.co.uk/news/9167/vatican-s-doctrine-prefect-says-church-teaching-on-male-only-priesthood-is-definitive-.

[4] Sara Butler, "Embodied Ecclesiology: Church Teaching on the Priesthood," in *Women, Sex, and the Church: A Case for Catholic Teaching*, edited Erika Bachiochi, (Boston: Pauline Books and Media, 2010).

[5] "I permit no woman to teach or to have authority over men;

women are not allowed to teach little boys their catechism. (Yes, I've heard of that from some of my Evangelical friends. I find it creepy, honestly.) Literally millions of Catholics have learned the basics of their faith from religious sisters. And if I start listing the contributions of women saints to the spiritual, intellectual, and institutional life of the Church, we'd be here all day.

My point is simply this: affirming the real differences between men and women does not automatically demean or diminish women. Which brings me to the next point.

Sex Differences are real, but not all differences in social treatment of men and women are justifiable.

We can give one instance of this general point by citing a document from 1930. *Casti Connubii* was Pope Pius XI's response to the issues of his time, which included birth control and new roles for women. Here is how Pius XI interprets St. Paul's teachings on family roles:

> The order of love (as St. Augustine called it) includes both the primacy of the husband with regard to the wife and children, the ready subjection of the wife and her willing obedience, which the Apostle commends in these words: "Let women be subject to their husbands

---

she is to keep silent," (1 Tm 2:12) and "the women should keep silence in the churches. For they are not permitted to speak, but should be subordinate, as even the law says. If there is anything they desire to know, let them ask their husbands at home. For it is shameful for a woman to speak in church" (1 Cor 14:34–35).

as to the Lord, because the husband is the head of the wife, and Christ is the head of the Church."

This subjection, however, does not deny or take away the liberty which fully belongs to the woman both in view of her dignity as a human person, and in view of her most noble office as wife and mother and companion; nor does it bid her obey her husband's every request if not in harmony with right reason or with the dignity due to wife; nor, in fine, does it imply that the wife should be put on a level with those persons who in law are called minors, to whom it is not customary to allow free exercise of their rights on account of their lack of mature judgment, or of their ignorance of human affairs.[6]

In other words, the husband's authority is legitimate, but not unlimited.

In fact, a bit of reflection will show that the husband's role carries the greater danger. The husband is charged with leading the family. If he neglects this responsibility, he is morally culpable. If he exploits his authority, bossing his wife around, for his own comfort and benefit, while neglecting her legitimate needs, he is spiritually liable for the consequences. If his abuses lead his wife or children to decide they don't want anything to do with religion, well, let's just say there is a dark place in hell for him.

(I realize that a lot of non-Catholic Christians have

---

6   Pope Pius XI, *Casti Connubii*, December 31, 1930, nos. 26–27. His citation is from Ephesians 5:22–23.

trouble with the concept of a "dark place in hell." This is not the time to go into it, but: the justice of God must somehow include gradations of punishment and reward. You don't have to believe in every detail of Dante's visions of heaven, hell, and purgatory to get the point. Viewing salvation as a simple "on-off" switch, either "saved or not-saved" or worse "once-saved, always saved," can't be right. The Catholic Church is right about this too. We'll have to talk about this some other time.)

The pope continues, and makes a point we dearly need to hear:

> But it [the subjection of the wife] forbids that *exaggerated* liberty which cares not for the good of the family; it forbids that in this body which is the family, the heart be separated from the head to the great detriment of the whole body and the proximate danger of ruin. For if the man is the head, the woman is the heart, and as he occupies the chief place in ruling, so she may and ought to claim for herself the chief place in love.[7]

The husband is the head. The wife is the heart. The body needs both. And both, in their separate ways, image God.

The Catechism makes a point like Pius XI's in language that may be easier for modern sensibilities to hear.

> Each of the two sexes is an image of the power and tenderness of God, with equal dignity though in a different way. The union of man and woman in marriage is

---

[7]   Pope Pius XI, *Casti Connubii*, December 31, 1930, nos. 26–27.

a way of imitating in the flesh the Creator's generosity and fecundity: "Therefore a man leaves his father and his mother and cleaves to his wife, and they become one flesh."[8]

God is the logos: reason writ large. Today, we have a tendency to view the ability to reason as the one and only defining characteristic of the human person. A person who cannot reason is not fully human and is therefore disposable. This is our rationalization for abortion, euthanasia, and assisted suicide.

We tend to forget that God is also love. Scripture is quite clear on this point. Seeing the woman as the heart of the family while the husband is the head does not diminish either of them. I believe it is only in our hyper-rationalized world that we have forgotten that the capacity to love and be loved is every bit as defining of our humanity as is the capacity to reason.

It is the modern world that has diminished the feminine, not the Church.

---

[8] *Catechism of the Catholic Church* 2335.

PART FIVE

Conclusion

CHAPTER 16

From the Ruling Class to the Leadership Class

When I point out that our sexual culture is not working for the vast majority of people, I often hear responses like these:

- "Nothing can be done about it."
- "Government cannot legislate morality."
- "No one has the right to impose their morality on anyone else."

These slogans are supposed to end the discussion. We're supposed to be cowed into silence. After all, no one wants to "impose" anything on others.

But honestly, can anyone seriously claim that the State is acting as a purely neutral referee among differing, equally acceptable points of view? This is no longer a credible claim. It is now obvious that the Sexual State today has absolutely no intention of allowing competing worldviews the space

341

they need to function. Those in power within the State have demonstrated that they intend to use its full authority and might to impose their views on the rest of society, to create cultural hegemony, and to wipe out all remaining pockets of resistance.

One of the peculiarities of American political culture is that no one, Left or Right, will admit to being part of the ruling class. One of our favorite images of ourselves is that we don't need rulers. We rule ourselves. We pride ourselves on being able to stand up to whatever pressures may come our way. At the same time, we Americans resent people whom we perceive to have power over us, whether economic, political, or social. *Elite* is a dirty word, something nobody wants to be identified as no matter how accurate such a label might be. American politicians compete vigorously for the most powerful offices in the world, all the while trying to convince us that they are utterly indifferent to power.

The most visible class divide for family issues is the divide between the college-educated members of the managerial class and everyone else. Members of the managerial class wait until they are married to have children. They get married and stay married. Today's educated classes have divorce rates and non-marital childbearing rates comparable to those from the dreaded 1950s. All that is good.

In other words, today's educated classes and their children have the benefits of stable family life. The sexual revolutionary ideology keeps those benefits carefully hidden, even from those who are reaping them. Meanwhile, members of the lower classes, including what used to be called the middle class, are bearing the full brunt of this inhuman ideology.

It doesn't have to be this way. True Believers in the entire Sexual Revolution are not very numerous. I've met lesbians who are disgusted with the pornography culture, pro-choice feminists who are appalled by middle schoolers "sexting," committed career women who are fed up with the sex education their children are taught, and divorce lawyers who quit in disgust and finish out their careers doing wills and trusts. Few people agree with every single precept of the Sexual Revolution.

Who Benefits?

Who ultimately benefits from the Sexual Revolution? First, rich and powerful men who want to have sex on their own terms. Second, the scores of people who make money from family breakdown. The presence of millions of such people and the billions of dollars they earn creates a powerful inertia for any kind of serious systemic change.

But most of these people could earn a living some other way. Lawyers don't have to make a career out of managing post-divorce conflict: they could do wills and trusts. Yes, someone makes money selling a formerly married couple the furnishings for a complete new household. But those same people could make money selling baby furniture and larger dining room tables to the couples who trust one another enough to have more children. Psychologists who work for the family court system producing reports about parental fitness could be making a living as life coaches, building up happy, stable marriages. Doctors treating the mental and physical health issues associated with the hook-up culture would probably prefer to deliver healthy babies and treat healthy children.

As for pornographers and abortionists (both worldwide industries with revenues in the billions), yes, they would have to find another way to make a living. So what? They *should* find another way. Does anyone today care that the owners of slave markets lost their livelihoods after 1863?

That leaves the educated career woman as a beneficiary of the Sexual Revolution. She seemingly gets to "have it all." But it isn't really working for her either. She could have many of the benefits attributed to the Sexual Revolution without the ideology.

As noted in an earlier chapter, the trend toward the increased labor force participation of married women began well before the key features of the Sexual Revolution. It began to increase around the turn of the twentieth century and accelerated in the 1940s. A large percentage of women workers continued to work after WWII. In fact, the increase in married women's labor force participation was so strong in the 1940s that economic historians dispute not so much the timing of this shift but its cause.[1] The rise of the modern feminist ideology and its demand for "reproductive freedom" cannot be the primary cause.

The landmark structural features of the Sexual Revolution can't be the cause of these shifts in labor force participation and education either. *Griswold v. Connecticut* struck down all state restrictions on contraception for married couples in

---

[1]   Claudia D. Goldin, "The Role of World War II in the Rise of Women's Employment," *The American Economic Review* 81, no. 4 (September 1991), pp. 741–56.

1965. No-fault divorce was first introduced in California in 1968. *Roe v. Wade* became the nationwide law in 1973. But women's labor force participation and higher education had already been increasing since the beginning of the twentieth century. Whenever we hear the phrase "The Sexual Revolution has been great because . . . ," you can be sure that women's career and educational achievements will be one of the items on the other side of the dots. The costs women have endured are never factored into the calculation. Nor do we consider that we could have achieved what was good using other, more humane, more genuinely pro-woman means.

The Sexual Revolution hid behind a peculiar version of Marxist-inspired secular feminism. This vision insisted on identical incomes for men and women at every point in their lives. This misguided concept of justice has shaped fifty years of public and corporate policy. I call this concept misguided because it disregards the fact that traditional male career trajectories demand the most intense investment early in life. In other words, we have been ignoring the basic biological fact that men and women are different, particularly with respect to anything relating to having and raising children. We would all be better off if we faced reality rather than fight it.

Up until now, too many women have defined their goal as being equal participants in a labor market designed for people who don't give birth. We've made a devil's pact under the influence of the sexual revolutionary ideology that men and women are interchangeable and that sex and babies can be radically disconnected. Here is the bargain we made:

We're allowed to participate in the public sphere as long as we chemically neuter ourselves during our peak childbearing years. We agree to participate in a market in which the commercial production and care of children are both considered normal parts of an educated woman's life. When our children are the smallest and most vulnerable, we agree to place them in the care of others, often strangers; that is, if we're lucky enough to have children. If we're unable to conceive when we're finally ready professionally and financially, we agree to submit our bodies to the expensive, degrading, and possibly dangerous trauma of artificial reproductive technology. These technologies may include artificially over-stimulating our ovaries, retrieving our eggs, creating embryos, freezing them for unspecified periods of time, and watching a large percentage of our tiny children not survive these processes. Maybe, just maybe, at the end of all this, we might give birth to a healthy baby.

I am no longer willing to accept this bargain. I claim the right to participate in the labor market as women, not as men in skirts. Up until now, we've taken the labor market as a given and tried to adapt our bodies to its needs. I say: we women should take our bodies as given and insist that the labor market accommodate us. I claim the right to get married and stay married, not the right to raise our children alone and to spend larger and larger portions of our lives alone. Up until now, we've defined our personal goal as being financially independent of men. I say we find ways to strengthen our collaboration with our husbands.

Many self-proclaimed champions of women have insisted that we need to have sex on the same terms as men: no more "double standard." I claim that these demands have not liberated women from sexual exploitation and domination by men. In fact, the attempt to "eliminate the double standard" has delivered women into the hands of men at their very worst, men like Harvey Weinstein and Matt Lauer and all the rest. I claim the right to have sex on terms that benefit women and their unique needs. I am convinced that these very same terms would benefit men at their very best.

The Judeo-Christian Alternative

Fortunately, the Judeo-Christian tradition proposes an alternative vision of life and of what is truly valuable and worth pursuing. Christianity offers a different path to women's participation in higher education and work, and an alternative vision of the kind of relationships that are possible between men and women. Christianity also offers a different vision of the place of human sexuality in our lives and the meaning of the human body itself.

Educated women would be better off if they accepted that their fertility peaks during their twenties and planned their lives around this fact. Go to college for a liberal, not necessarily a vocational, education. Get married. Have kids. Use your higher education by being involved in your kids' education. Let your husbands support you. Trust them. Be grateful for them. Don't compete with them, but work together for the good of the whole family. When the kids are older, maybe then go back to school for an advanced degree. Go to work. Help support the kids' college education and your joint retirement. And, since women live longer than men, you could work longer and let your husbands relax a bit.

Of course, this vision of the workplace also involves an alternative vision of marriage and family. Marriage is a life-long institution for mutual cooperation and support rather than the unenforceable non-contract it has become. I need not say that cooperation between spouses would be far better for children. Nor need I say that this is the exact opposite of the sexual revolutionary vision, which replaced marital stability with employment stability.

Christianity and Judaism also offer a different vision of the differences between men and women. The sexual revolutionary true believer resents sex differences, viewing them as evidence of cosmic injustice. The Judeo-Christian vision embraces these differences as part of the divine plan for teaching love and drawing us out of our natural self-centeredness. Marriage is inherently a gender-based institution because it helps men and women bridge the natural differences between them. Marriage is the school and household of love. Within the household, men and women learn to help, cooperate with, and understand each other.[2]

---

[2]   See for instance, from the Catholic perspective, Joseph Cardinal Ratzinger "Letter to the Bishops of the Catholic Church on The Collaboration of Women and Men in the Church and in the World." From a Jewish perspective, see David P. Goldman, "It Takes a Congregation," *First Things* (blog), June 26, 2009, accessed December 2, 2012, http://www.firstthings.com/on thesquare/2009/06/it-takes-a-congregation. "The human bride and bridegroom unite in mystical emulation of God's espousal of Israel, and the very mountains of Israel dance in joy with each wedded pair."

This is quite different from the all too common modern secular image of husbands and wives at each other's throats, in competition for dominance and power inside their own homes. The modern sexual revolutionaries insist that love, sex, and reproduction be separated from each other for the sake of making men and women equal. But this pursuit of "equality" places men and women at odds with each other. Men exploit women for sex, seeing them as objects that give pleasure. Women exploit men for reproduction, treating them as a combination of wallet and sperm bank.

The Judeo-Christian vision insists that marriage is the proper context for both sexual activity and childrearing. The man's sexual desire for woman turns him toward love for her. Christianity demands that he love his wife "as Christ loves the Church," which is to say, a completely self-emptying, self-giving love.[3] The husband's love for his wife builds upon and reinforces his love for the children she bears. The woman's desire for children turns her heart toward the man who will be the father of her children. Love, sex, and childbearing are integrated under the umbrella of marriage.

Finally, the Judeo-Christian vision of sexuality contrasts with the sexual revolutionary view in the most fundamental way. The revolutionary vision is that sex has no meaning apart from the meaning that an individual might happen to assign to it. In both the Christian and the Jewish traditions, every sexual act has cosmic significance whether the individuals recognize it or not.

---

3   Ephesians 5:25. See also Karol Wotyla, *Love and Responsibility* and John Paul II, *Male and Female He Created Them: Human Love in the Divine Plan.*

Which vision appeals to you? The vision of use and be used or the vision of love and be loved? The vision of intrinsic meaning, which implies and imposes some responsibility upon us, or the vision of intrinsic meaninglessness, which frees us from responsibility but offers us nothing?

What Is to Be Done?

If the legitimate goals of the educated professional woman could be better met some other way, and if most of the people making money from the Sexual Revolution could earn a living some other way, who does that leave as the main beneficiary of the Sexual State? The rich and powerful men who want to have unlimited sex on their own terms.

These men attempt to use that influence to fill the upper level positions of power in society with true believers in the Sexual Revolution. But true believers are not numerous enough to implement their fantasy ideology without the help, or at least cooperation, of the rest of the managerial class. What if we stopped cooperating?

Yes, I put myself in this category of the managerial class because, truthfully, anyone with a college degree and a white-collar job is part of this class. We're the social workers, teachers, school principals, college professors, and administrators. We're the judges, lawyers, editorial writers, radio producers, and video game makers. We decide what stories count as news and what stories to spike, what headlines to write and what photos will accompany those headlines.

We're the doctors, nurses, and pharmacists. We write insurance policies, employee handbooks, and government regulations. We exercise our discretion in implementing and enforcing these codes. We decide what reading material will be in the doctor's office waiting room and what the school play will be. Right now, members of the managerial class are deciding how much time perfectly responsible parents are permitted to spend with their own children. Yes, members of the managerial class have quite a few opportunities to make a difference.

In our society, as in every known society, people have different gifts and talents. Each person has a unique personal and human history. Our parents, our situation in life, and the stability and wealth of our families all go into making us unique individuals. Yet we didn't create our basic genetic and cultural endowments; our very lives are gifts to us. Yes, we have worked hard for our positions. Lots of people with less privilege work hard too. How many of us could have the positions of influence and status we now have without any assistance from our parents, teachers, mentors, and the structures of society?

We can feel cheated that someone somewhere has more than we do and blame someone for this unfairness. We can rail against the injustice of these inequalities, or we can recognize that no one creates him or herself. We can recognize that our life is a gift. We may be angry at the source of this gift if we think we didn't get enough, or we can choose to be grateful for our life.

Your life may be a mess. You may have started from an unfair position compared with someone else. You may have had a good start and made a mess of things along the way.

In either case, or any case in between, your existence itself is still a gift.

Our minds have been so clouded by the totalitarian ideologies of our time that we either succumb to or overreact against them. Some people do have more power, gifts, and talents than others. The Communists are correct about that. But that doesn't mean we can reconstruct society to equalize everything for everyone. The only way this can be done is by empowering the managerial class enough to manage everyone into equality. What kind of equality is that, really? The equality of the gulag.

No one has the right to demand that we spend ourselves for the good of others; the Randians and Libertarians are correct about that. On the other hand, what is the point of our gifts? Do we believe the most fulfilling use of our gifts is to consume them for our own ends and purposes? Will we not find some joy and satisfaction in using what we've been given for the common good? My husband and I each have gifts and talents which the other doesn't have. As a team, we each use our gifts for the benefit of our little society of the family. Our children continually surprise us with their gifts and talents. (Especially our adopted son, as in, "Where did he get that talent? Not from us!") They, too, have learned to place their blessings at the service of the whole family, not because they must, or because anyone makes them, but because they are grateful to be part of something that is life-giving and good. They want to contribute. I bet you do too.

Our current set of gifted and talented people are not leading, they're ruling. They're an elite ruling class in the worst sense of the term. They're using their positions of power, influence, wealth, and authority to dominate people, to reconstruct the social universe in their own ideological image, and for their own economic and social benefit. This must stop.

Are we going to continue down this path? Or are we going to use the power and influence that we possess to make a positive difference? What if teachers refused to teach the Gender Ideology in schools? What if judges and lawyers refused to enforce the Divorce Ideology and told the warring couples to go home and straighten up? What if doctors said: "Hell no, we aren't keeping parents in the dark about their children's sexual activity, contraceptive use, pregnancies, and abortions. If we really think parents are likely to abuse their child because of something we tell them about their child's activities, we'll report them to the child protective authorities. We will not go along with withholding necessary information from all parents because of the small probability of abuse by a small number of parents."

Every one of us can do something positive to build up the civilization of love within our own sphere of influence. The first and most basic thing you can do if the sexual revolutionary ideology has harmed you is to tell your story. The ideology cannot withstand scrutiny. The mismatch between the publicly proclaimed benefits and the carefully hidden costs is what allows the ideology to survive. Do your part by telling your story, at least to those closest to you.

If you're a disappointed, even heartbroken career woman, tell younger women that putting off childbearing until age thirty-five is not a plan without cost. If you're a reluctantly divorced person, let others know that not all divorces are desired by and beneficial to both parties. If your husband is an unrepentant pornography addict whom you finally had to kick out of the house for the good of the family, or if you are a repentant pornography addict, tell people pornography is not a victimless crime. If you lived with someone for years who ultimately would not marry you, tell people that marriage is more than "just a piece of paper," that living together is different from marriage, and that you learned too late that he was not opposed to marriage, he just didn't want to marry you. If you're a child of divorce, by all means, let people know what that was like for you. Let people know that your real heart's desire was not for your parents to be happy so much as it was for them to pull themselves together and be appropriate parents.

The managerial class does not need to be a ruling class. We could be a leadership class. We can use our gifts and talents for the good of others, not to manage other people's lives. Together, we can build a civilization of love.

CHAPTER 17

From the Sexual State to a Civilization of Love: A Manifesto for the Family

I hope I've convinced you that some people are using their power to promote and impose the fantasy ideology of the Sexual Revolution against the wishes of the vast majority of people. Our society is rife with structural injustices to children and cultural barriers to marriage. When we begin to tell the whole truth of the Sexual Revolution, we'll finally be ready to enact the public policies that will change course.

Many of the policies of the Sexual State were imposed on society by judges. Many people, including well-meaning social conservatives, concluded that we must therefore make sure to elect a president who will select good people for the judiciary. The only problem with this strategy has been the candidate pool: the available candidates with appropriate qualifications have all been marinated in the same cultural sauce. Just what is that sauce? The idea that society is composed of independent sovereign adults who negotiate among themselves for the right to create laws that bind them all. This idea doesn't recognize dependency as a legitimate part of the human condition.

Within this framework, the only way women could find dignity for themselves was to insist that they too be permitted in the managerial class. Women, too, wanted to be part of the collection of independent sovereign individuals making decisions for the whole. Since delayed childbearing, or no child-bearing, is a prerequisite for entry into the managerial class, our policy-making is dominated by people with few or no children. With women's demand to take their place in the world outside the home, children and the private sphere of the home have lost their last defenders.

Once a subset of women decided that their goal was equality within the managerial class, the next logical step was to equalize everything within their sexual-social lives that has to do with children, which turns out to be, well, just about everything. The next logical step was to institutionalize the ideology of the Sexual Revolution throughout society. Hence, we have the idea that sex and babies can and should be separated from each other and from marriage, the sex of the body ought to have no implications for our social lives, and gender is a social construct to be changed at will.

We have no choice but to step outside this framework and make room for the concept that the dependency of childhood is legitimate. We must show respect for the gendered nature of our bodies. We must purge ourselves of our fears and suspicions of the people closest to us.

I've composed a Manifesto for the Civilization of Love to

guide us. The first part spells out changes in public policies. As you look at these policies, you'll see that they don't require government programs, spending, or coercion. Instead, the first ten steps insist that the government stop doing things it never had any business doing in the first place.

1. **End sex education in the public schools.** It's none of the State's business to teach children how to put condoms on bananas, instruct them on sexual techniques, or tell them the meaning of the human body. This is pure propaganda for the sexual revolutionary State. Children should learn sexual information from their families in the privacy of their homes, not from strangers in a public place.

2. **Abolish taxpayer-funded women's studies and gender studies programs in colleges and universities.** These departments are also propaganda-creation machines for the sexual revolutionary State. Women's studies professors who have something of value to say can find jobs in other academic departments.

3. **Reform divorce laws.** Allow the State to take notice of adultery and other forms of marital fault so that sexual exclusivity becomes reintroduced as a social norm. Introduce some form of mutual consent for divorce so that the presumption of permanence is reinforced, not undermined. Marriage is the only institution we have that connects mothers and fathers to their children and to one another, to say nothing of their extended family. Separating children from either of their biological parents without compelling reason is a structural

injustice to the child, which no civilized society should allow. Needless to say, "because I don't want to have a relationship with my child's other parent" is *not* a compelling reason to deprive a child of his or her birthright.

4. **Remove the "marriage tax" from all welfare programs.** If we really mean to help the poor, we should not penalize them financially for getting married. And yes, eliminating marriage penalties may cost the government money in the short run. But over time, fewer people will need financial assistance, so the change may pay for itself. Even if it doesn't, creating incentives for non-marital childbearing and multiple-partner fertility, is grossly unjust. The government needs to stop undermining marriage for the poorest and most vulnerable citizens.

5. **Cease governmental promotion and subsidization of contraception.** Contraception is legally available. It doesn't need to be free. The government has no business promoting its use or attempting to influence people's family planning decisions.

6. **Abolish abortion.** The health and social problems that abortion was supposed to solve can be solved another way. The business of the Civilization of Love is to do exactly that. The vast network of pregnancy care centers that provide material, emotional, and spiritual assistance to women during their pregnancies and for the first year of their children's lives is a good and noble start.

7. **Restore an unapologetic gender requirement to marriage.** Men and women are different, especially with respect to childbirth and child-rearing.

8. **End all government funding for population control in foreign countries.** This includes both direct population control and indirect "nudges" with financial incentives. U.S. taxpayers should not be in the business of steering the reproductive decisions of women in the Philippines, China, India, and other countries.

9. **Abolish the Third-Party Reproduction Industry.** Children are not commodities. Infertility is not fatal. The government should not be in the business of creating legally binding contracts that separate children from their parents. Let us end this slippery slope once and for all. Encourage research into cures for infertility that enhance natural processes.

10. **Make legal provision for the adoption of all frozen embryos** and ensure that no new tiny human beings are frozen ever again.

Here are two things the government should start doing.

11. **Tax pornography.** Regulate pornography. Then tax it some more. Pornography addiction is a soul-destroying, family-destroying evil, that should be discouraged. If you think you can figure out a plan for banning it altogether, I'm listening.

12. **Adopt a Family Impact Analysis (like an Environmental Impact Statement) for all new public policies.** Will this proposal strengthen or weaken the

family in doing its jobs: supporting itself, having and educating children, and building relationships inside the family? Many of our welfare state programs would not have been enacted in their current form if anyone had thought to raise these questions.

A tall order, you say? Yes, indeed. This just shows how deeply entrenched the Sexual State has become. If the State had been confined to its proper boundaries in the first place, none of these policies would be in place.

Now, the personal, non-governmental, side of the equation. The final three steps have nothing to do with government. Creating a social and cultural environment favorable to marriage requires more than public policies. It also demands much of us in all spheres of our lives.

13. **Create social forms of encouragement for long-lasting love inside the family.** Ask this question of economic and social practices: will this practice help families sustain themselves, be accountable to one another, and build lasting relationships?

14. **Create social structures to support people who fall between the cracks or who have fallen short of the ideals of life-long married love.** Support people in exceptional situations without undermining the general rules.

15. **Overall, and finally, as St. Paul said, put on love.** When we have decisions to make, let us ask ourselves, "Is this the way of love or the way of something else?"

It's time for each of us to use such power as we have within our sphere of influence to build a better world. Let's stop lording it over each other, trying to manage or rule each other. Let's refuse to be ruled by our self-appointed "betters" and "thought-leaders" who have done so much damage. Revelations about the behavior of many of them show clearly they are not better than the rest of us. Let us all—men and women, young and old, married or unmarried—use our gifts and talents to build up our families and our communities. Together, we can lead our families, our neighbors, and our country toward a Civilization of Love.

Bibliography and Further Resources

Further Resources

Book publishing has an entirely different rhythm from Internet publishing. In the time that has elapsed since I composed this manuscript, a few significant items have been published. I offer them here as additional references.

Darel Paul's *From Tolerance to Equality: How Elites Brought America to Same-Sex Marriage* (Waco TX: Baylor University Press: 2018) supports my argument that the cultural elites created large parts of the Sexual Revolution, especially the support for genderless marriage. This work rigorously documents the argument that business and the professions embraced the normalization of homosexual practice and have been systematically imposing their views on the rest of the population.

Moira Greyland Peat's *The Last Closet: The Dark Side of Avalon* (Castalia House Publishing, 2017) is the author's memoir of growing up in a household of famous gay activists and apologists in 1970s Berkeley. Moira's mother was Marion Zimmer Bradley, author of the Avalon series. Her father was Walter Breen, a famous numismatic author. They were both child molesters. Moira's story illustrates how fame, wealth, and power covered up the abuse her parents inflicted on her, her brothers, and other children.

We may also mention the revelations of sexual abuse of power in Hollywood, the media, and politics that began in 2017 and are continuing to unfold. I wrote about this a few times late in 2017. "The Toxic Ideas that Enabled Harvey Weinstein and Others," *Crisis*, October 26, 2017, and "Here is What is Fishy About Al Franken's Resignation and Selective Outrage," *Clash Daily*, December 19, 2018.

https://www.crisismagazine.com/2017/toxic-ideas-enabled-harvey-weinstein-enablers

https://clashdaily.com/2017/12/heres-whats-fishy-al-frankens-resignation-selective-outrage/

Bibliography

"2013-01-15 RI House Marriage Equality Testimony 006 Jennifer Roback Morse." Posted by Steve Ahlquist, January 21, 2013. YouTube. https://www.youtube.com/watch?v=IRTvl0-ifXI

"8 Differences Between Boys and Girls." *What to Expect,* March 17, 2015. http://www.whattoexpect.com/first-year/photo-gallery/differences-between-boys-and-girls.aspx#09

"Abortion Surveillance — United States, 2012, Surveillance Summaries, November 27, 2015 / 64 (SS10); 1-40."

Adler, N. E., H. P. David, B. N. Major, S. H. Roth, N. F. Russo, and G. E. Wyatt. "Psychological Factors in Abortion: A Review." *American Psychologist* 47.10 (1992): 1194-2012.

Adler, N. E., H. P. David, B. N. Major, S. H. Roth, N. F. Russo, and G. E. Wyatt. "Psychological Responses after Abortion." *Science* 248.4951 (1990): 41-44.

Akerloff, George, Janet Yellin and Michael Katz. "An Analysis of Out-of-Wedlock Childbearing in the United States." *The Quarterly Journal of Economics* 111.2 (1996): 277-317.

Alexander, Rachel. "Goldwater Institute sues: state bars are unconstitutional mandatory unions." *Townhall*, February 9, 2015. http://townhall.com/columnists/rachelalexander/2015/02/09/goldwater-institute-sues-state-bars-are-unconstitutional-mandatory-unions-n1954664

Alexander, Rachel. "Opposition Group Turns to Stealth and Sexism to Oppose Shared Parenting in North Dakota." *Townhall*, October 12, 2014. http://townhall.com/columnists/rachelalexander/2014/10/13/opposition-group-turns-to-stealth-and-sexism-to-oppose-shared-parenting-in-north-dakota-n1904235?utm_source=thdaily&utm_medium=email&utm_campaign=nl

"Alexandra L. Rowan Foundation Overview." *Alexandra Rowan Foundation*. http://www.alexrowanfoundation.org/

"Amanda Gessleman, Ph.D." *Kinsey Institute* https://www.kinseyinstitute.org/about/profiles/agesselman.php

Amato, Paul and Alan Booth. *A Generation at Risk: Growing up in an Era of Family Upheaval*. Cambridge: Harvard University Press, 1997.

Amato, Paul R. and Denise Previti. "People's reasons for divorcing: gender, social class, the life course, and adjustment." *Journal of Family Issues* 24.5 (2003): 602-626.

American Academy of Ophthalmology. "Long-Term Oral Contraceptive Users Are Twice as Likely to Have Serious Eye Disease." *Ophthalmology Web*, November 19, 2013. http://www.ophthalmologyweb.com/1315-News/150975-Long-Term-Oral-Contraceptive-Users-Are-Twice-As-Likely-To-Have-Serious-Eye-Disease/

"American Humanist Association." *Wikipedia*. https://en.wikipedia.org/wiki/American_Humanist_Association

Andersen, Kirsten. "27 Dutch women's deaths linked to controversial birth control pill." *Life Site News,* October 28, 2013. https://www.lifesitenews.com/news/27-dutch-womens-deaths-linked-to-controversial-birth-control-pill

Anderson Moore, Kristen, Susan M. Jekielek, and Carol Emig. "Marriage from a Child's Perspective: How Does Family Structure Affect Children and What Can We Do About It?" *Child Trends Research Brief,* June 2002.

Bachman, Ronet and Linda E. Saltzman. "Violence against Women: Evidence from the Redesigned Survey." *Bureau of Justice Statistics*, Special Report, National Crime Victimization Survey, August 1995, NCJ 154348. https://www.bjs.gov/content/pub/pdf/FEMVIED.PDF

Baillargeon, Jean-Patrice, Donna K. McClish, Paulina A. Essah, and John E. Nestler. "Association between the Current Use of Low-Dose Oral Contraceptives and Cardiovascular Arterial Disease: A Meta-Analysis." *The Journal of Clinical Endocrinology & Metabolism* 90.7 (2005). DOI: http://dx.doi.org/10.1210/jc.2004-1958

Baldwin, Alec. *A Promise to Ourselves*. New York: St. Martin's Press, 2008.

Baron-Cohen, Simon. *The Essential Difference: The Truth about the Male and Female Brain*. New York: Basic Books, 2003.

Baskerville, Stephen. *Taken Into Custody: The War Against Fathers, Marriage and the Family*. Nashville, TN: Cumberland House Publishing, 2007.

Beckford, Martin. "The last Catholic adoption agency faces closure after Charities Commission ruling." *The Telegraph*, August 19, 2010. http://www.telegraph.co.uk/news/religion/7952526/Last-Catholic-adoption-agency-faces-closure-after-Charity-Commission-ruling.html

Beckman, Linda and S. Marie Harvey, eds. *The New Civil War*. Washington, DC: American Psychological Association, 1998.

Beeney, Eliza. "Women Wrestlers Go to the Mat for Equal Rights." *ACLU*, August 8, 2011. https://www.aclu.org/blog/womens-rights/women-wrestlers-go-mat-equal-rights

Beksinkska, Mags E., Jenni A. Smit, Immo Kleinschmidt, Cecilia Milford, and Timothy M. M. Farley. "Prospective Study of weight change in new adolescent users of DMPA, NET-EN, COC's, non-users and discontinuers of hormonal contraception." *Contraception* 8.1 (2010): 30-34. http://www.ncbi.nlm.nih.gov/pmc/articles/PMC3764463/

Belsky, Jay and Michael J. Rovine. "Non-maternal Care in the First Year of Life and the Security of Infant-Parent Attachment." *Child Development* 59 (1988): 157-167.

Benjamin Guzzo, Karen and Cassandra Dorius. "Challenges in Measuring and Studying Multipartnered Fertility in American Survey Data." *Population Research Review*, May 25, 2016. http://link.springer.com/article/10.1007/s11113-016-9398-9?view=classic

Bennett, Saye. "A Lesbian Psychologist Speaks Out." *Youth Trans Critical Professionals,* July 22, 2016. https://youthtranscriticalprofessionals.org/2016/07/22/a-lesbian-psychologist-speaks-out/

Bertrand, Marianne and Jessica Pan. "The Trouble with Boys: Social Influences and the Gender Gap in Disruptive Behavior." *Applied Economics* 5.1 (2013): 32-64.

Black, Dan, Gary Gates, Seth Sanders, and Lowell Taylor. "Demographics of the Gay and Lesbian Population in the United States: Evidence from Available Systematic Data Sources." *Demography* 37.2 (2000): 139-154.

Blankenhorn, David. *The Future of Marriage.* New York: Encounter Books, 2007.

Blessed Pope Paul VI. *Humanae Vitae* (Of Human Life). July 25, 1968. http://www.vatican.va/holy_father/paul_vi/encyclicals/documents/hf_p-vi_enc_25071968_humanae-vitae_en.html

Boyles, Salynn. "Heart, Stroke Risk Low with Birth Control Pills." *WebMD,* June 13, 2012. https://www.webmd.com/sex/birth-control/news/20120613/heart-stroke-risk-birth-control-pills#1

Bradshaw, Zoe and Pauline Slade. "The effects of induced abortion on emotional experiences and relationships: A critical review of the literature." *Clinical Psychology Review* 23 (2003): 929-958.

"Breast Cancer Prevention, Patient Version." *National Cancer Institute*. http://www.cancer.gov/types/breast/patient/breast-prevention-pdq#section/_12

Brind, Joel. "Early Reproductive Events and Breast Cancer: A Minority Report." *Breast Cancer Prevention Institute,* March 10, 2003. http://www.bcpinstitute.org/papers/NCI_minority%20report-3_2003-brind.pdf

Brinig, Margaret and Douglas Allen. "These Boots are Made for Walking: why most divorce filers are women." *American Law and Economics Review* 2.1 (2000): 126-169. http://aler.oxfordjournals.org/content/2/1/126.abstract

Bruni, Frank. "Paul Singer's Equality Efforts." *New York Times,* June 9, 2012. https://bruni.blogs.nytimes.com/2012/06/09/paul-singers-equality-efforts/

Buckles, K. and D. M. Hungerman. "The Incidental Fertility Effects of School Condom Distribution Programs." NBER Working Paper, no. w22322, June 2016. http://papers.ssrn.com/sol3/papers.cfm?abstract_id=2794728

Burke, Theresa. *Forbidden Grief: The Unspoken Pain of Abortion.* Springfield, IL: Acorn Books, 2002.

Burwell v Hobby Lobby 573 US 2014, 40. https://www.supremecourt.gov/opinions/13pdf/13-354_olp1.pdf

Butler, Sara. "Embodied Ecclesiology: Church Teaching on the Priesthood," in *Women, Sex, and the Church: A Case for Catholic Teaching.* Edited Erika Bachiochi. Boston: Pauline Books and Media, 2010.

Cahill, Larry. "Equal ≠ The Same: Sex Differences in the Human Brain." *Cerebrum* (March-April 2014): 5. http://www.ncbi.nlm.nih.gov/pmc/articles/PMC4087190/

"California governor signs bill replacing words 'husband'
and 'wife' in state law." *Fox News Politics,* July 7, 2014.
http://www.foxnews.com/politics/2014/07/07/califor-
nia-bill-replacing-words-husband-wife-in-marriage-law-
signed-by-gov.html

"California Supreme Court Rules on Proposition 8 'Standing' Issue." *California Courts News Release,* November
17, 2011. https://newsroom.courts.ca.gov/news/califor-
nia-supreme-court-rules-on-proposition-8-standing-issue

Carlson, Allan C. *Godly Seed: American Evangelicals Confront Birth Control, 1873-1973.* New Brunswick, NJ:
Transaction Publishers, 2012.

Carlson, Allan C. "The Bipartisan blunder of Title X."
Family Policy, September-October 2000.

Catalano, Shannan, Erica Smith, Howard Snyder, and
Michael Rand. "Female Victims of Violence." *Bureau of
Justice Statistics, Selected Findings,* September 2009, NCJ
228356. https://www.bjs.gov/content/pub/pdf/fvv.pdf

Catalano, Shannan. "Intimate Partner Violence: Attributes
of Victimization, 1993–2011." *Bureau of Justice Statistics,
Special Report,* November 2013, NCJ 243300.

Catechism of the Catholic Church, Double Day; 2nd edition
(March 4, 2003).

Center for Loss in Multiple Births (Climb), Inc. http://
www.climb-support.org/index.html

"Child of surrogacy campaigns to outlaw the practice."
New York Post, June 16, 2014. http://nypost.com/2014/
06/16/children-of-surrogacy-campaign-to-outlaw-
the-practice/.

Christian Legal Society v Martinez 561 US 661. https://
www.law.cornell.edu/supct/html/08-1371.ZS.html

CIA World Factbook. https://www.cia.gov/library/publica-
tions/the-world-factbook/rankorder/2127rank.html#ja

Cochran, William Gemmell, W. O. Jenkins, Frederick
Mosteller, and John Wilder Tukey. *Statistical problems of
the Kinsey Report on Sexual Behavior in the Human Male:
A report of the American Statistical Association, National
Research Council (U.S.), Committee for Research in Prob-
lems of Sex—Psychology.* Boston: American Statistical
Association, 1954.

Cohen, I. Glen. "Regulating Reproduction: The Problem with Best Interests." *Minnesota Law Review* 96
(2012): 423. https://papers.ssrn.com/sol3/papers.
cfm?abstract_id=1955292

Coleman, B. "Birth Control Pill Could Cause Long-Term
Problems with Testosterone." *Medical News Today*,
January 4, 2006. http://www.medicalnewstoday.com/
releases/35663

Coleman, Priscilla K. "Abortion and mental health: quantitative synthesis and analysis of research published
1995–2009." *The British Journal of Psychiatry* 199.3
(2011): 180-186. http://bjp.rcpsych.org/content/bjprc-
psych/199/3/180.full.pdf

"Combined Estrogen-Progestogen Contraceptives and
Combined Estrogen-Progestogen Menopausal Therapy."
*IARC Monographs on the Evaluation of Carcinogenic Risks
to Humans* Vol 91 (2007): 175.

Connelly, Matthew. *Fatal Misconceptions: The Struggle to
Control World Population.*

Cambridge: Belknap Press of Harvard University Press, 2008.

"Conversion Therapy Laws." *Movement Advancement Project.* http://www.lgbtmap.org/equality-maps/conversion_therapy

Cordell-Whitney, Dionne. "Minnesota Mom loses fight against teen's sex change." *Courthouse News Service,* May 24, 2017. https://www.courthousenews.com/minnesota-mom-loses-fight-teens-sex-change/

"Counting the Cost of Family Failure: Update 2016." *Relationships Foundation.* http://knowledgebank.oneplusone.org.uk/wp-content/uploads/2016/03/Counting-the-Cost-of-Family-Failure-2016-Update.pdf

Crane, Barbara. "The Transnational Politics of Abortion." *Population and Development Review* Vol. 20 Supplement, *The New Politics of Population: Conflict and Consensus in Family Planning* (1994): 241-262.

Critchlow, Donald T. *Intended Consequences: Birth Control, Abortion and the Federal Government in Modern America.* New York: Oxford University Press, 1999.

Daly, Martin and Margo Wilson. "Discriminative Parental Solicitude: A Biological Perspective." *Journal of Marriage and the Family* 42.2 (1980): 277-288.

"Dear Colleague Letter on Transgender Students." *U.S. Department of Justice, U. S. Department of Education,* May 13, 2016. http://www2.ed.gov/about/offices/list/ocr/letters/colleague-201605-title-ix-transgender.pdf

"Dear ISNA friends and supporters." *ISNA: Intersex Society of North America.* http://www.isna.org/

Dellapenna, Joseph W. *Dispelling the Myths of Abortion History.* Durham, NC: Carolina Academic Press, 2006.

"Demographic Transition." *Wikipedia.* http://en.wikipedia. org/wiki/Demographic_transition#cite_note-marathon. uwc.edu-6

Department of Reproductive Health and Research. "Carcinogenicity of combined hormonal contraceptives and combined menopausal treatment." *World Health Organization,* September 2005. http://www.who.int/reproductivehealth/topics/ageing/cocs_hrt_statement.pdf

Diamond, Lisa. "Female Bisexuality From Adolescence to Adulthood: Results From a 10-Year Longitudinal Study." *Developmental Psychology* 44.1 (2008): 5-14. https:// psych.utah.edu/_documents/people/diamond/diamond-female-bisexuality-adolescence-to-adulthood.pdf

Diamond, Lisa. *Sexual Fluidity: Understanding Women's Love and Desire.* Cambridge, MA: Harvard University Press, 2009.

Dickinson, Tim "Same sex setback." *Rolling Stone,* December 11, 2008. https://www.rollingstone.com/politics/ news/same-sex-setback-20081211

DiFonzo, James Herbie. "Toward a unified field theory of the family: the American Law Institute's Principles of the Law of Family Dissolution." *BYU Law Review* 923 (2001): 959.

"Divorce Stories." *Marriage Ecosystem.* http://www.marriage-ecosystem.org/divorcestories.html

Doran, Matt. *Donor Children.* http://www.donorchildren. com/about-us

Doughty, Steve. "High Court judge's blast for four gay parents fighting over two little sisters." *Daily Mail,* October 10, 2011. http://www.dailymail.co.uk/news/article-2047671/High-Court-judges-blast-gay-parents-fighting-little-sisters.html#ixzz54eQED9Y2

Dred Scott v Sanford 60 US 393 (1857).

"Dr. J at the Rhode Island legislature building with Marriage Supporters." *Ruth Institute,* January 21, 2013. YouTube. https://www.youtube.com/watch?v=VqVFZh0qDgw

"Dr. J & Dr. Gary Gates @ UCLA." *Ruth Institute,* August 29, 2012. http://ruthinstitute.libsyn.com/dr-j-dr-gary-gates-ucla

Duggan, Joe. "Nebraska state senator urges action on child custody inequality." *Omaha World Herald,* January 10, 2014. http://www.omaha.com/news/nebraska-state-senator-urges-action-on-child-custody-inequality/article_b6918430-882c-53eb-81c9-acb05bfb8d28.html

Eckholm, Eric. "One Man Guides the Fight Against Gay Marriage." *New York Times,* October 9, 2012. http://www.nytimes.com/2012/10/10/us/politics/frank-schubert-mastermind-in-the-fight-against-gay-marriage.html

Edelman, Rivka. "This lesbian's daughter has had enough." *The American Thinker,* October 20, 2014. http://www.americanthinker.com/articles/2014/10/this_lesbians_daughter_has_had_enough.html

"Effectiveness of Family Planning Methods." *Centers for Disease Control.* http://www.cdc.gov/reproductivehealth/

contraception/unintendedpregnancy/pdf/contraceptive_
methods_508.pdf

Eggsploitation: the infertility industry has a dirty little secret.
Produced by Jennifer Lahl, Center for Bioethics and
Culture, 2010. http://www.eggsploitation.com/

Eig, Jonathan. *The Birth of the Pill: How Four Crusaders
Reinvented Sex and Launched a Revolution.* New York:
Norton, 2014.

Emerson, Thomas. "Nine Justices in search of a doctrine."
Michigan Law Review 64 (December 1965).

Engineer Girl. http://www.engineergirl.org/9539.aspx

Ertelt, Steven. "Obama Proposes Rule Prohibiting
States from Defunding Planned Parenthood." *Life
Site News,* September 6, 2016. http://www.lifenews.
com/2016/09/06/admin-proposed-rule-prohibit-
ing-states-from-defunding-planned-parenthood/

"Estradiol." *Drugs.com.* https://www.drugs.com/estradiol.
html

"Estrogen Levels." *She Cares.* http://www.natural-hor-
mones.net/estrogen-levels.htm

"Estrogen: Pregnancy, Menopause, Estrogen and Disease."
Medical News Today. http://www.medicalnewstoday.
com/articles/277177.php?page=3

Fagan, Patrick and Aaron Churchill. "The Effects
of Divorce on Children," *Marriage and Religion
Research Institute,* January 11, 2012. http://marri.us/
effects-divorce-children

Farrell, Warren. *Why Men Earn More: The Startling Truth
about the Pay Gap, and What Women Can Do About It.*
New York: American Management Association, 2005.

Fesler, Leah. "A lot of women don't enjoy the hook-up culture: so why do we force ourselves to participate?" *Quartz,* May 17, 2016. https://qz.com/685852/hookup-culture/

Fine, Cordelia, Daphna Joel, Rebecca Jordan-Young, Anelis Kaiser, and Gina Rippon. "Reaction to 'Equal ≠ The Same: Sex Differences in the Human Brain.'" *Cerebrum,* December 15, 2014. http://www.dana.org/Cerebrum/Default.aspx?id=115816

Form 990 for Open Society Institute for 2014, Part XV, Line 3. http://www.guidestar.org/FinDocuments/2014/137/029/2014-137029285-0c25cf2f-F.pdf

Form 990 for Susan Thompson Buffett Foundation, Part XV, Line 3. http://www.guidestar.org/FinDocuments/2014/476/032/2014-476032365-0b9faf84-F.pdf

"Fourth National Incidence Study of Child Abuse and Neglect (NIS–4), 2004-2009." *Office of Planning, Research, and Evaluation,* January 15, 2010. https://www.acf.hhs.gov/opre/research/project/national-incidence-study-of-child-abuse-and-neglect-nis-4-2004-2009

Fox Piven, Frances and Richard A. Cloward. "The Weight of the Poor: A Strategy to End Poverty." *The Nation,* May 2, 1966, reprinted at *Common Dreams,* March 24, 2010. http://www.commondreams.org/news/2010/03/24/weight-poor-strategy-end-poverty

Fraga, Brian. "Blue States target Little Sisters of the Poor." *National Catholic Register,* November 29, 2017. http://www.ncregister.com/daily-news/blue-states-target-little-sisters-of-the-poor

Fraga, Juli. "After IVF, Some Struggle With What To Do With Leftover Embryos." *Shots: Health News from NPR,* August 20, 2016. http://www.npr.org/sections/health-shots/2016/08/20/489232868/after-ivf-some-struggle-with-what-to-do-with-leftover-embryos

Franks, Angela. *Margaret Sanger's Eugenic Legacy: The Control of Female Fertility.* Jefferson, NC: McFarland & Co. Publishers, 2005.

Freeborn, Donna, and Chad Haldeman-Englert. "Sex Hormone Binding Globulin (Blood)." *University of Rochester Medical Center: Health Encyclopedia.* https://www.urmc.rochester.edu/encyclopedia/content.aspx?ContentTypeID=167&ContentID=shbg_blood

"Frequently Asked Questions." *Accord Alliance.* http://www.accordalliance.org/learn-about-dsd/faqs/

"Frequently Asked Questions: What is Reproductive Health?" *United Nations Population Fund.* http://www.unfpa.org/frequently-asked-questions#rh

Fu, Haishan, Jacqueline E. Darroch, Taylor Haas, and Nalini Ranjit. "Contraceptive Failure Rates in the US: New Estimates from the 1995 National Survey of Family Growth" Table 2. *Family Planning Perspectives* 31.2 (1999). https://www.guttmacher.org/about/journals/psrh/1999/03/contraceptive-failure-rates-new-estimates-1995-national-survey-family

Gallagher, Maggie and Joshua Baker. "Do Moms and Dads Matter? Evidence from the Social Sciences on Family Structure and the Best Interests of the Child." *Margins* 4 (2004): 161-180.

Garrow, David J. *Liberty and Sexuality: The Right to Privacy and the Making of Roe v Wade.* New York: Macmillan Publishing, 1994.

Gaudiosi, John. "Virtual Reality Livestreams come to the porn industry." *Fortune,* December 16, 2015. http://fortune.com/2015/12/16/vr-livestream-porn/

Gelles, Richard J. and John W. Harrop. "The Risk of Abusive Violence Among Children with Nongenetic Caretakers." *Family Relations* 40.1 (1991): 78-83.

Gesselman, A. N., G. D. Webster, and J. R. Garcia. "Has Virginity Lost Its Virtue? Relationship Stigma Associated with Being a Sexually Inexperienced Adult." *Journal of Sex Research* 54.2 (2016): 202-213. http://www.ncbi.nlm.nih.gov/pubmed/26983793

GLAAD Media Reference Guide, 10th Edition, October 2016. http://www.glaad.org/sites/default/files/GLAAD-Media-Reference-Guide-Tenth-Edition.pdf

"GLAAD will no longer be an acronym for the Gay and Lesbian Alliance Against Defamation."

GLAAD, March 24, 2013. https://www.glaad.org/news/glaad-will-no-longer-be-acronym-gay-and-lesbian-alliance-against-defamation

Goldin, Claudia D. "The Role of World War II in the Rise of Women's Employment." *The American Economic Review* 81.4 (1991): 741-756.

Goldman, David P. "It Takes a Congregation." *First Things*, June 26, 2009. http://www.firstthings.com/onthesquare/2009/06/it-takes-a-congregation

Gordon, Michael and Susan J. Creighton. "Natal and Non-Natal Fathers as Sexual Abusers in the United

Kingdom: A Comparative Analysis." *Journal of Marriage and the Family* 50.1 (1988): 99-105.

Graham, Alissa. "My experience at the HB5015 Hearing in Providence Rhode Island." *Ruth Institute Blog,* January 28, 2013. http://www.ruthblog.org/2013/01/28/my-experience-at-the-hb5015-hearing-in-providence-rhode-island/

Green, Richard. "Hugh Hefner, the International Academy of Sex Research, and Its Founding President." *Archives of Sexual Behavior* 46.8 (2017): 2211-2212. https://doi.org/10.1007/s10508-017-1098-y

Grigg-Spall, Holly. *Sweetening the Pill: or How We Got Hooked on Hormonal Birth Control.* Winchester, UK: Zero Books, 2013.

"The guilt and regret." *Fertile Thoughts: Supporting your family building dreams* on-line forum, June 3, 2013. http://www.fertilethoughts.com/forums/selective-reduction-and-termination-due-to-health-issues/719266-guilt-regret.html

Hall, Sarah. "Schizophrenia much more likely in children of single parents." *UK Guardian,* November 2, 2006.

Harding, Eleanor. "£500,000 custody battle between gay parents after a sperm donation deal went wrong wrecked childhoods of two little girls, says judge." *Daily Mail,* November 4, 2014. http://www.dailymail.co.uk/news/article-2821113/Custody-battle-gay-parents-wrecked-childhoods-2-girls-says-judge.html#ixzz54eNks3zs

Harper, Cynthia C. and Sara S. McLanahan. "Father Absence and Youth Incarceration." *Journal of Research on Adolescence* 14.3 (2004): 369-397.

Hartmann, Betsy. *Reproductive Rights and Wrongs: The Global Politics of Population Control.* Boston: South End Press, 1995, Revised Edition.

Henshaw, R., S. Naji, I. Russell, and A. Templeton. "Some problems caused by not having a conceptual foundation for health research: An illustration from studies of the psychological effects of abortion." *Psychology and Health* 5 (1994): 13-23.

"Her Story." *Gianna Jessen.* http://giannajessen.com/

Heyer, Walter. "I was a Transgender Woman." *The Public Discourse*, April 1, 2015. http://www.thepublicdis course.com/2015/04/14688/

Hilton, N. Z., G. T. Harris, and M. E. Rice. "The step-father effect in child abuse: Comparing discriminative parental solicitude and antisociality." *Psychology of Violence* 5.1 (2015): 8-15.

Hirshman, Linda. *Get to Work: A Manifesto for Women of the World.* New York: Viking, 2006.

Hobbs, Jay. "Two of California's most dangerous cities targeting pro-life centers." *Life Site News,* August 5, 2016. https://www.lifesitenews.com/news/two-of-californias-most-dangerous-cities-targeting-pro-life-centers

Hodges, Fr. Mark. "17-year-old ballerina's death caused by birth control pills, doctors believe." *Life Site News,* April 27, 2016. https://www.lifesitenews.com/news/17-year-old-ballerinas-death-caused-by-birth-control-pill-doctors-believe

Hodges, Fr. Mark. "Mom loses lawsuit against school that secretly gave her son 'transgender' treatment." *Life Site News*, May 26, 2017. https://www.lifesitenews.

com/news/federal-judge-to-mom-school-not...
liable-for-secretly-helping-your-son-beco.

Hodgson, Dennis and Susan Cotts Watkins. "Feminists and Neo-Malthusians: Past and Present Alliances." *Population and Development Review* 23.3 (September 1997): 486.

Howell, Kellan. "Defense Secretary Ashton Carter OKs final strategy for women in combat." *Washington Times,* March 11, 2016. http://www.washingtontimes.com/news/2016/mar/11/ash-carter-approves-final-strategy-women-military-/

Hu, Claire. "Nancy took the Pill at 16—and Died." *Evening Standard,* March 4, 2002. https://www.standard.co.uk/news/nancy-took-the-pill-at-16-and-died-6311225.html

Hymowitz, Kay, Jason Carroll, W. Bradford Wilcox, and Kelleen Kay. "The Great Crossover." *Knot Yet: The Benefits and Costs of Delayed Marriage in America.* http://twentysomethingmarriage.org/the-great-crossover/

"I am a product of surrogacy." *The Other Side of Surrogacy.* www.theothersideofsurrogacy.blogspot.com

"Initiative and referendums in the United States." *Wikipedia.* https://en.wikipedia.org/wiki/Initiatives_and_referendums_in_the_United_States

"Intelligent or Unintelligent Birth Control?" *The Birth Control Review,* reprinting an editorial from *American Medicine.* http://library.lifedynamics.com/Birth%20Control%20Review/1919-05%20May.pdf

Issues 4 Life Foundation. "In 163 Years the Total Black Fertility Rate Dropped 77% --God Help Us!"

Christian News Wire. http://christiannewswire.com/news/5004578195.html

"IVF doctors misleading women about success rates, industry experts say." *ABC News,* May 30, 2016. http://www.abc.net.au/news/2016-05-30/ivf-doctors-misleading-patients-about-success-rates-experts-say/7457750

James, Bridie and Martin Daly. "Cohabitation Is No Longer Associated With Elevated Spousal Homicide Rates in the United States." *Homicide Studies* 16.4 (2012): 393-403.

Jaschik, Scott. "What Larry Summers Said." *Inside Higher Education,* February 18, 2005. https://www.insidehighered.com/news/2005/02/18/summers2_18

Johnson, Angela. "My beautiful cheerleader daughter died in agony all because she took this acne drug: Heartbroken mother fights to ban dangerous pill." *Daily Mail,* June 8, 2013. http://www.dailymail.co.uk/news/article-2338072/Dianette-My-beautiful-cheerleader-daughter-died-agony-took-acne-drug.html

Johnson, Jennifer. *Marriage and Equality: How Natural Marriage upholds Equality for Children.* Lake Charles, Louisiana: Ruth Institute Books, 2017.

"Join Marianne Williamson, Elisabeth Rohm, The Guncles, Jason Patric, Brenda Strong, Dr. Sadeghi & 200+ Health and Wellness Experts for Fertility Planit Show @UCLA Apr 4-5." *Digital Journal,* March 29, 2014. http://www.digitaljournal.com/pr/1819443#ixzz4PzwmKrRZ

Jones, E. Michael. *Libido Dominandi: Sexual Liberation and Political Control.* South Bend, IN: St. Augustine's Press, 2000.

Jones, James H. *Alfred C. Kinsey: A Life*. New York: Norton, 1997.

Jones, Rachel K., Jacqueline E. Darroch, and Stanley K. Henshaw. "Contraceptive Use Among U.S. Women Having Abortions in 2000-2001." *Perspectives on Reproductive and Sexual Health* 34.6 (2002): 294-303. https://www.guttmacher.org/about/journals/psrh/2002/11/contraceptive-use-among-us-women-having-abortions-2000-2001

"Judge: Speaking Spanish at Home is Child Abuse." *New York Daily News,* August 30, 1995. http://www.nydailynews.com/archives/news/judge-speaking-spanish-home-child-abuse-article-1.698045

Katz, Miranda. "No, NYC Did Not Just Introduce a $250,000 Fine for Any Incorrect Use of Gender Pronouns." *Gothamist*, May 19, 2016. http://gothamist.com/2016/05/19/gender_pronouns_false_fine.php

Kay, Julie. "6 Florida Bar Sections Lobbying in Tallahassee." *Daily Business Review*, April 2, 2016. http://www.dailybusinessreview.com/id=1202753914575/6-Florida-Bar-Sections-Lobbying-in-Tallahassee?mcode=0&curindex=0&curpage=ALL&slreturn=20160818222056

Kemmeren, Jeanet M., Bea C. Tanis, Maurice A. A. J. van den Bosch, Edward L. E. M. Bollen, Frans M. Helmerhorst, Yolanda van der Graaf, Frits R. Rosendaal, et al. "Risk of Arterial Thrombosis in Relation to Oral Contraceptives (RATIO) Study: Oral Contraceptives and the Risk of Ischemic Stroke." *Stroke,* May 1, 2002. http://stroke.ahajournals.org/content/33/5/1202

Kengor, Paul. *Takedown: From Communists to Progressives, How the Left has Sabotaged Family and Marriage.* Washington, D.C.: World Net Daily Books, 2015.

Kern, Jessica. "Kern Testimony." *CBC Network.* http://www.cbc-network.org/wp-content/uploads/2013/06/Kern_TestimonyDC20-32.pdf

Kinsey, Alfred, Wardell B. Pomeroy, and Clyde E. Martin. *Sexual Behavior in the Human Male.* Philadelphia: W. B. Saunders, 1948.

Kinsey, Alfred, Wardell B. Pomeroy, Clyde E. Martin, and Paul H. Gebhard. *Sexual Behavior in the Human Female.* Philadelphia: W. B. Saunders, 1953.

"Kinsey Institute's Commercial Connections." *Ruth Speaks Out*, July 14, 2016. http://www.ruthinstitute.org/ruth-speaks-out/kinsey-institutes-commerical-connections

"Kinsey Reports." *Rockefeller Foundation.* http://rockefeller100.org/exhibits/show/health/kinsey-reports

Kost, Kathryn, Susheela Singh, Barbara Vaughan, James Trussell, and Akinrinola Bankole. "Estimates of contraceptive failure from the 2002 National Survey of Family Growth." *Contraception* 77.1 (January 2008): 10-21. https://www.ncbi.nlm.nih.gov/pmc/articles/PMC2811396/pdf/nihms164460.pdf

Kotz, Deborah. "Birth control pills raise risk of heart attacks and strokes, but only slightly." *Boston,* June 13, 2012. http://www.boston.com/dailydose/2012/06/13/birth-control-pills-raise-risk-heart-attacks-and-strokes-but-only-slightly/G3wQiKMFSVbc9W7HKJeWqO/story.html

Kraemer, Sebastian. "The fragile male." *British Medical Journal* 321:1609 (2000). http://dx.doi.org/10.1136/ bmj.321.7276.1609

Lamb, Christopher. "Vatican's doctrine prefect says Church teaching on male-only priesthood is 'definitive,'" *The Tablet*. http://www.thetablet.co.uk/news/9167/vatican-s-doctrine-prefect-says-church-teaching-on-male-only-priesthood-is-definitive-.

Lanfranchi, Angela, Ian Gentles, and Elizabeth Ring-Cassidy. *Complications: Abortion's Impact on Women.* Toronto: The deVeber Institute for Bioethics and Social Research, 2013.

Lanfranchi, Angela. "The Federal Government and Academic Texts as Barriers to Informed Consent." *Journal of American Physicians and Surgeons* 13.1 (2008): 12-15.

LaPlante, Joseph R. "Tough times for Catholic adoption agencies." *Our Sunday Visitor,* May 7, 2014. https:// www.osv.com/OSVNewsweekly/ByIssue/Article/ TabId/735/ArtMID/13636/ArticleID/14666/Tough-times-for-Catholic-adoption-agencies.aspx

Laumann, Edward O., John H. Gagnon, Robert T. Michael, and Stuart Michaels. *The Social Organization of Sexuality: Sexual Practices in the United States.* Chicago: University of Chicago, 1994.

Lauzon, P., D. Roger-Achim, A. Achim, and R. Boyer. "A comparison of medical and surgical methods of termination of pregnancy: Choice, psychological consequences and satisfaction with care." *British Journal of Obstetrics and Gynaecology* 105 (2000): 1288-1295.

Lauzon, P., D. Roger-Achim, A. Achim, and R. Boyer. "Emotional distress among couples involved in first trimester induced abortions." *Canadian Family Physician* 46 (2000): 2033-2040.

Lee, Henry K. "Pastor Arrested for Oakland Anti-Abortion Acts." *SFGate*, March 21, 2009. http://www.sfgate.com/bayarea/article/Pastor-jailed-for-Oakland-anti-abortion-acts-3247604.php

Levin, Sam. "Brock Turner laughed after bystanders stopped Stanford sex assault, files show." *The Guardian,* August 26, 2016. https://www.theguardian.com/society/2016/aug/26/brock-turner-stanford-sexual-assault-victim-testimony-laugh

Lidegaard, Øjvind, Ellen Løkkegaard, Aksel Jensen, Charlotte Wessel Skovlund, Niels Keiding. "Thrombotic Stroke and Myocardial Infarction with Hormonal Contraception." *New England Journal of Medicine,* June 14, 2012. http://www.nejm.org/doi/full/10.1056/NEJMoa1111840

Littlejohn, Reggie. "Stop Forced Abortion – China's One Child Policy." *Women's Rights Without Frontiers.* YouTube. November 21, 2010. https://www.youtube.com/watch?v=JjtuBcJUsjY

Loftis, Leslie. "Florida Governor Rick Scott Ignores Families, Protects Disastrous Divorce Law." *The Federalist,* April 18, 2016. http://thefederalist.com/2016/04/18/florida-gov-rick-scott-ignores-families-protects-disastrous-divorce-law/

Lubman, Stanley. "After the One-Child Policy: What Happens to China's Family-Planning Bureaucracy?"

Wall Street Journal, November 12, 2015. http://blogs.
wsj.com/chinarealtime/2015/11/12/after-the-one-child-
policy-what-happens-to-chinas-family-planning-bureau-
cracy/

Maag, Elaine and Gregory Acs. "The Financial Consequences of Marriage for Cohabiting Couples with Children." *The Urban Institute,* September 8, 2015. https://
www.urban.org/research/publication/financial-conse
quences-marriage-cohabiting-couples-children

MacPherson, Ryan C. "From No-Fault Divorce to Same-
Sex Marriage: The American Law Institute's Role in
Deconstructing the Family." *The Family in America* 25.2
(2011): 125-140.

Mainwaring, Doug. "Gay Republican attacked, sent to hospital." *American Thinker,* October 25, 2012. http://www.
americanthinker.com/blog/2012/10/gay_republican_
attacked_sent_to_hospital.html

Mainwaring, Doug. "I'm a gay man, happily married to
a woman. And I'm not the only one." *Life Site News,*
March 27, 2017.

Major, Brenda and Catherine Cossarelli. "Psychosocial
Predictors of Adjustment to Abortion." *Journal of Social
Issues* 48.3 (1992): 121-142.

Major, Brenda, Mark Appelbaum, Linda Beckman, Mary
Ann Dutton, Nancy Felipe Russo, and Carolyn West.
"Abortion and Mental Health: Evaluating the Evidence."
American Psychologist 64.9 (2009): 863-890. DOI: 10.
1037/a0017497 http://204.14.132.173/pubs/journals/
features/amp-64-9-863.pdf

Margolin, Leslie. "Child Abuse by Mothers' Boyfriends: Why the Overrepresentation?" *Child Abuse and Neglect* 16.4 (1991): 541-551.

Martin, Nina. "Behind the Supreme Court's Abortion Decision, More Than a Decade of Privately Funded Research." *Propublica*, July 14, 2016. https://www.propublica.org/article/supreme-court-abortion-decision-more-than-decade-privately-funded-research

Maslow, A. H. and J. Sakoda. "Volunteer error in the Kinsey study." *Journal of Abnormal Psychology* 47.2 (1952): 259-62.

Mattson, Daniel. *Why I Don't Call Myself Gay.* San Francisco: Ignatius Press, 2017.

McIntyre, Alastair. *Dependent Rational Animals: Why Human Beings Need the Virtues.* Chicago: Open Court, 1999.

McManus, Michael J. "Confronting the More Entrenched Flow: The Disaster of No-Fault Divorce and its Legacy of Cohabitation." *The Family in America* 25.2 (2011): 157-172.

"Meet the Blended Families We've Featured in the Past." *Huffington Post* video. http://www.huffingtonpost.com/entry/the-blended-family-motto-this-mom-swears-by_us_55fb25fce4b0fde8b0cd9012?slideshow=true#gallery/559ee9b3e4b05b1d02900b90/0

Miller, John J. "Home Economics." *National Review Online,* September 25, 2012. http://www.nationalreview.com/home-front/328429/father-daughter-dance-banned/jennifer-roback-morse

Miller, Leila. *Primal Loss: The Now-Adult Children of Divorce Speak*. LCB Publishing, 2017.

Miller, W. B., D. J. Pasta, and C. L. Dean. "An empirical study of the psychological antecedents and consequences of induced abortion." *Journal of Social Issues* 48 (1998): 67-93.

Minear, Tom. "Mother of 13 arrested in East Melbourne clinic protest." *Courier-Mail*, August 4, 2016. http://www.couriermail.com.au/news/mother-of-13-arrested-in-east-melbourne-clinic-protest/news-story/a90d71765491cd1189348579a4f98a0b

Moloney, Daniel Patrick. "Forcing the Poor to Stop Having Children." *The Public Discourse: Ethics, Law and the Common Good*. The Witherspoon Institute, May 1, 2009.

Morabito, Stella. "The Trans Lobby hates this man for proving sex change regret is real," *The Federalist,* January 9, 2018. http://thefederalist.com/2018/01/09/walt-heyer-proves-sex-change-regret-real-thats-trans-lobby-hates/

Mosher, Steven W. *Population Control: Real Costs, Illusory Benefit*. New Brunswick, NJ: Transaction Publishers, 2009.

Mota, Natalie, M. Burnett, and J. Sareen. "Associations between Abortion, Mental Disorders, and Suicidal Behavior in a Nationally Representative Sample." *The Canadian Journal of Psychiatry* 55.4 (2010): 239-247.

"MPE Research." *Alexandra Rowan Foundation*. http://www.alexrowanfoundation.org/mpe-research/

"Nebraska Judge Tells Man He Must Speak English to Visit His Daughter," Associated Press, October 14, 2003.

Newman, Alana, ed. *Anonymous Us.* Broadway Publications vol. 1, 2013, vol. 2, 2016.

Nock, Steven L. and Christopher J. Einolf. "The One Hundred Billion Dollar Man: the annual public cost of father absence." *The National Fatherhood Initiative*, June 30, 2008. http://portal.hud.gov/hudportal/documents/huddoc?id=100_billion_dollar_man.pdf

Nolan, Patrick. *The Value of Family: Fiscal Benefits of Marriage and Reducing Family Breakdown in New Zealand.* Wellington, New Zealand: Family First New Zealand, 2008. https://irp-cdn.multiscreensite.com/64484987/files/uploaded/NewZealandReport.pdf

Nollet, Roel. "Nathan—Free as a Bird." *IDFA,* 2014. https://www.idfa.nl/en/film/a9a2b9b7-9c9b-4407-b195-1c6f374babdd/nathan-free-as-a-bird

"North Dakota Parental Rights Initiative, Measure 6 (2014)." *Ballot Pedia* https://ballotpedia.org/North_Dakota_Parental_Rights_Initiative,_Measure_6_(2014)

Obergefell v. Hodges, 135 S. Ct. 2071 (2015).

O'Hara, Mary Emily. "Minnesota Mom Sues Her Trans Child Over Gender Reassignment." *NBC Out*, November 17, 2016. http://www.nbcnews.com/feature/nbc-out/minnesota-mom-sues-her-trans-child-over-gender-reassignment-n685266

"Orgastic Potency." *Wikipedia.* https://en.wikipedia.org/wiki/Orgastic_potency

Orozco, Jeremy. "Pregnancy: A Migraine Cure?" *Migraine Key.* http://www.3dayheadachecure.com/blog/pregnancy/

"Outsourcing Embryos." *VICE on HBO*. YouTube. January 19, 2016. https://www.youtube.com/watch?v=GED9r YPkAlQ

Paschal, Kenneth. "On Wednesday night, May 4, 2016 another legislative session ended." *Alabama Family Rights Association*. http://us10.campaign-archive1. com/?u=5977883b4792901a0d405fabc&id=f07950ca3e

Pazol, Karen, Andreea A. Creanga, and Denise J. Jamieson. "Morbidity and Mortality Weekly Report, Table 17." *Centers for Disease Control and Prevention*. http://www.cdc.gov/mmwr/preview/mmwrhtml/ss6410a1. htm#tab16

"Personal Responsibility Education Program." *Advocates for Youth*. http://www.advocatesforyouth.org/publications/1742-personal-responsibility-education-program-prep

Pfeffer, Leo. *God, Caesar and the Constitution: The Court as Referee of Church-state Confrontation*. Boston: Beacon Press, 1975.

"Physical Ability Tests for Police Departments and SWAT Teams: Know Your Rights in the Workplace." *ACLU*. https://www.aclu.org/sites/default/files/assets/kyr_physi calabilities-rel1.pdf

Pitts, Jonathan M. "Little Sisters of the Poor approve Trump order on religion." *Baltimore Sun,* May 4, 2017. http://www.baltimoresun.com/news/maryland/politics/bs-md-little-sisters-trump-exec-order-20170504-story. html

Planned Parenthood v Casey, 505 U.S. 833, 856 (1992).

Pogarksy, Greg, Terence P. Thornberry, and Alan J. Lizotte. "Developmental Outcomes for Children of Young Mothers." *Journal of Marriage and Family* 68 (May 2006): 332-344.

Polikoff, Nancy. "Who says a child's two parents have to be a 'couple'? Not Canada." *Beyond (Straight and Gay) Marriage*. http://beyondstraightandgaymarriage.blogspot.com/

Pope Benedict XVI. "Letter to the Bishops of the Catholic Church on The Collaboration of Women and Men in the Church and in the World." Boston: Pauline Books and Media, 2003.

Pope Francis. *Amoris Laetitia*. March 19, 2016.

Pope Pius XI. *Casti Connubii*. December 31, 1930.

Pope Saint John Paul II. *Familiaris Consortio* (The Role of the Christian Family in the Modern World). Boston: Pauline Books and Media, 1981.

Pope Saint John Paul II. *Love and Responsibility*. San Francisco, CA: Ignatius Press, 1993.

Pope Saint John Paul II. *Male and Female He Created Them: A Theology of the Body*. Boston: Pauline Books and Media, 2006.

Pope Saint John Paul II. *Mulieris Dignitatem* (On the Dignity and Vocation of Women). August 3, 1988. http://www.vatican.va/holy_father/john_paul_ii/apost_letters/documents/hf_jp-ii_apl_15081988_mulieris-dignitatem_en.html

Pope Saint John Paul II. *The Theology of the Body: Human Love in the Divine Plan*. Pauline Books and Media, 2012.

Posavac, E. J. and T. Q. Miller. "The psychological complications of therapeutic abortion." *British Journal of Psychiatry* 160 (1990): 742-749.

"Prop. 8 Standing Oral Arguments before California Supreme Court." *American Foundation for Equal Rights,* September 6, 2011. YouTube. https://www.youtube.com/watch?v=Mmmy1fqeF0Y&feature=youtu.be

"Proposition 8: who gave in the gay marriage battle." *Los Angeles Times.* http://projects.latimes.com/prop8/

PR Newswire. "National Survey Uncovers Potential Barrier to Better Intimacy Connections for Couples." *MultiVu,* February 9, 2016. http://www.multivu.com/players/English/7749151-k-y-the-touch-initiative-survey/

Rand, Spencer. "The Real Marriage Penalty: How Welfare Law Discourages Marriage Despite Public Policy Statements to the Contrary—and What can be done about it." *University of the District of Columbia Law Review* 18.1 (2015): 93-143. https://papers.ssrn.com/sol3/papers.cfm?abstract_id=2685206

Ranjit, Nalini, Akinrinola Bankole, Jacqueline E. Darroch and Susheela Singh. "Contraceptive Failure in the First Two Years of Use: Differences Across Socioeconomic Subgroups." *Family Planning Perspectives* 33.1 (2001): 19-27. https://www.guttmacher.org/sites/default/files/article_files/3301901.pdf

Rector, Robert. "How Welfare Undermines Marriage and What to Do About it." *The Heritage Foundation,* November 17, 2014. http://www.heritage.org/research/reports/2014/11/how-welfare-undermines-marriage-and-what-to-do-about-it

"Reference Values During Pregnancy." *Perinatology.com.*
    http://perinatology.com/Reference/Reference%20
    Ranges/Estradiol.htm

Regnerus, Mark. *Cheap Sex: The Transformation of Men,
    Marriage, and Monogamy.* New York: Oxford University
    Press, 2017.

Reich, Wilhelm. *The Sexual Revolution: Toward a Self-Reg-
    ulating Character Structure.* New York: Farrar, Straus and
    Giroux, 1986.

"Rhode Island bans father daughter dances: says they
    break the law." *NBC News,* September 18, 2012. http://
    usnews.nbcnews.com/_news/2012/09/18/13938087-
    rhode-island-school-bans-father-daughter-dances-says-
    they-break-the-law?lite

Ribar, David, Seth Sanders, and Claire Thibout. "Dissolu-
    tion, Conflict and Australian Children's Developmental
    Outcomes." *Melbourne Institute of Applied Economic and
    Social Research,* July 2017.

Riben, Mirah. "End the Witch-hunt: In Defense of Rob-
    ert Oscar Lopez." *Huffington Post,* November 13, 2015.
    https://www.huffingtonpost.com/mirah-riben/end-the-
    witch-hunt-in-def_b_8539402.html

Ringback Weitoft, Gunilla, Anders Hjern, Bengt Haglund,
    and Mans Rosen. "Mortality, severe morbidity and
    injury in children living with single parents in Sweden: a
    population-based study." *The Lancet* 361:9354 (2003).

Roback Morse, Jennifer. *Children and Donor Conception
    and Assisted Reproduction.* San Marcos, CA: The Ruth
    Institute, 2016. http://www.ruthinstitute.org/store/

ruth-survivor-series/children-and-donor-conception-and-assisted-reproduction

Roback Morse, Jennifer. "Euthanizing the Unhappy: The Urgent Need for Love." *The Public Discourse*, November 7, 2013. http://www.thepublicdiscourse.com/2013/11/11113/

Roback Morse, Jennifer. Forward to *Primal Loss: The Now-Adult Children of Divorce Speak*. Edited by Leila Miller. Phoenix, AZ: LCB Publishing, 2017.

Roback Morse, Jennifer. "Gay Activist Elites at Fault: Why I am Not Angry at Lesbians Who Sue the Sperm Bank." *Christian Post,* October 9, 2014. https://www.christianpost.com/news/gay-activist-elites-at-fault-why-i-am-not-angry-at-lesbians-who-sue-the-sperm-bank-127822/

Roback Morse, Jennifer. "Getting Zapped for a Good Cause: a review of *Home Economics*." *Ethika Politika,* August 8, 2013.

Roback Morse, Jennifer. "Here's What's Fishy about Al Franken's Resignation and Selective Outrage." *Clash Daily,* December 13, 2017. https://clashdaily.com/2017/12/heres-whats-fishy-al-frankens-resignation-selective-outrage/

Roback Morse, Jennifer. "In an Industry that makes people, what could possibly go wrong?" *The Blaze*, April 20, 2016. http://www.theblaze.com/contributions/in-an-industry-that-makes-people-what-could-possibly-go-wrong/

Roback Morse, Jennifer. "Kinsey is Dead: Long Live Kinsey." *National Catholic Register,* July 15, 2005. http://

www.ncregister.com/site/article/kinsey_is_dead_long_
live_kinsey/

Roback Morse, Jennifer. *Love and Economics: It Takes a Family to Raise a Village*. San Marcos, CA: Ruth Institute Books, 2008.

Roback Morse, Jennifer. "Marriage and the Limits of Contract." *Policy Review,* April 1, 2005. http://www.hoover.org/publications/policy-review/article/6909

Roback Morse, Jennifer. "Padres, please, tell us the whole truth." *Ruth Speaks Out* blog, February 14, 2017. http://www.ruthinstitute.org/ruth-speaks-out/padres-please-tell-us-the-full-truth

Roback Morse, Jennifer. *Smart Sex: Finding Life-long Love in a Hook-up World*. Dallas, TX: Spence Publishing, 2005.

Roback Morse, Jennifer. "The Toxic Ideas that Enabled Weinstein and Others." *Crisis*, October 26, 2017. http://www.crisismagazine.com/2017/toxic-ideas-enabled-harvey-weinstein-enablers

Roback Morse, Jennifer. "Why Everyone should oppose surrogacy." *The Blaze,* May 4, 2016. http://www.theblaze.com/contributions/why-everyone-should-oppose-surrogacy/

"Rockefeller Foundation." *Wikipedia.* https://en.wikipedia.org/wiki/Rockefeller_Foundation

Rockefeller, John D III. "Population Growth, the Role of the Developed World." *Population and Development Review* 4.3 (1978): 509-516.

Rogers, Lois. "Have 800 women been killed by the Pill?" *Mail Online,* February 12, 2014. http://www.dailymail.

co.uk/femail/article-2558029/Have-800-women-killed-
Pill-The-alarming-dangers-called-generation-contracep
tives.html

Rosen, Christine. *Preaching Eugenics: Religious Leaders and
the American Eugenics Movement.* Oxford: Oxford University Press, 2004.

Rosik, Christopher. "Sexual orientation change efforts and
the campaign to ban them." *Mercator Net,* July 17, 2015.
https://www.mercatornet.com/articles/view/sexual-
orientation-change-efforts-and-the-campaign-to-ban-
them/16522

Ross, Chuck. "Clinton's Billionaire Donors Could Fund
Planned Parenthood for the Next 120 Years." *The Daily
Caller,* August 2, 2016. http://dailycaller.com/2016/08/
02/clintons-billionaire-donors-could-fund-planned-par
enthood-for-the-next-120-years/

Ruse, Austin. "Real Victims of the Gay Bullyboys." *Crisis,* October 10, 2014. https://www.crisismagazine.
com/2014/real-victims-gay-bullyboys

Savin-Williams, Ritch. *Mostly Straight: Sexual Fluidity
among Men.* Cambridge, MA: Harvard University Press,
2017.

Scafidi, Benjamin. *The Taxpayer Costs of Divorce and Unwed
Child-bearing: First Ever Estimates for the US and all 50
States.* New York: Institute for American Values, 2008.
http://americanvalues.org/catalog/pdfs/COFF.pdf

Scharf, Stephanie A. and Roberta D. Liebenberg. "First
Chairs at Trial, More Women Need Seats at the Table: A
Research Report on the Participation of Women Law-
yers as Lead Counsel and Trial Counsel in Litigation."

American Bar Foundation, 2015. http://www.americanbar.org/content/dam/aba/marketing/women/first_chairs2015.authcheckdam.pdf

Scarlett Milloy, Christin. "Don't Let the Doctor Do This to Your Newborn." *Slate*, June 26, 2014. http://www.slate.com/blogs/outward/2014/06/26/infant_gender_assignment_unnecessary_and_potentially_harmful.html

Schnitzer, Patricia G. and Bernard G. Ewigman. "Child Deaths Resulting from Inflicted Injuries: Household Risk Factors and Perpetrator Characteristics." *Pediatrics* 116.5 (2005).

Schuppe, Jon. "NBA Tells North Carolina Changes to LGBT Law HB2 Aren't Enough," *NBC News,* July 1, 2016. http://www.nbcnews.com/news/us-news/nba-tells-north-carolina-changes-lgbt-law-hb2-aren-t-n602411

Seamans, Barbara. *The Doctors' Case Against the Pill: 25th Anniversary Edition*. Atlanta: Hunter House Publishers, 1995. Originally published in 1969.

"Secularism in the General Crisis of Capitalism." *American Journal of Jurisprudence* 42.1 (1997): 195-210.

SEICUS, Sexuality Education and Information Council of the United States, Fact Sheet. http://siecus.org/document/docWindow.cfm?fuseaction=document.viewDocument&ID=07E5A0647538BFBAE5887831506AF85D88976995AD3CC0C6D329D0B0ADB5CF140E44FC566087638521D737023E39E8C6

Sex Change Regret. http://www.sexchangeregret.com/

"Sexual Orientation and Homosexuality." *American Psychological Association.* http://www.apa.org/topics/lgbt/orientation.aspx

Shackelford, Todd K. and Jenny Mouzos. "Partner Killing by Men in Cohabiting and Marital Relationships: A Comparative, Cross-National Analysis of Data from Australia and the United States." *Journal of Interpersonal Violence* 20.10 (2005): 1310-1324.

Shackelford, Todd K. "Partner-Killing by Women in Cohabiting Relationships and Marital Relationships." *Homicide Studies*, 5.3 (2001): 253-266.

Shapiro, Julie. www.julieshapiro.wordpress.com/

Sharp, Deborah, Dale F. Hay, Susan Pawlby, Gesine Schmucker, Helen Allen and R. Kumar. "The Impact of Postnatal Depression of Boys' Intellectual Development." *Journal of Child Psychology and Psychiatry* 36.8 (1995): 1315-1336.

Slade, P., S. Heke, J. Fletcher, and P. Stewart. "Psychological responses following medical abortion (using mifepristone and gemeprost) and surgical vacuum aspiration: A patient-centered, partially randomized prospective study." *Acta Obstetrica et Gynecologica Scandinavica* 73 (1998): 812-818.

Smith, Rebecca. "'Contraceptive Pill is outdated and does not work well', expert warns." *The Telegraph*, June 25, 2008. http://www.telegraph.co.uk/news/uknews/2193112/Contraceptive-Pill-is-outdated-and-does-not-work-well-expert-warns.html

"Social Indicators of Marital Health and Well-Being, 2012, Figure 5." *The State of our Unions*. http://www.stateofourunions.org/2012/social_indicators.php#divorce

"Social Indicators of Marital Health and Well-Being, 2012, Figure 13." *The State of our Unions*. http://www.stateof ourunions.org/2012/social_indicators.php#si-fig13

Sonfield, Adam, Casey Alrich, and Rachel Benson Gold. "Public Funding for Family Planning, Sterilization, and Abortion Services, FY 1980–2006." *Occasional Report No. 38*. New York: Guttmacher Institute, 2008.

Sopelsa, Brooke. "Major Corporations Join Fight Against North Carolina's 'Bathroom Bill.'" *NBC News*, July 8, 2016. http://www.nbcnews.com/feature/nbc-out/major-corporations-join-fight-against-north-carolina-s-bath room-bill-n605976

Stahl, Lesley. "Sex Matters: Drugs can affect the sexes differently." *CBS News*, May 25, 2014. http://www. cbsnews.com/news/sex-matters-drugs-can-affect-sexes-differently-2/

Stark, Rodney. *The Triumph of Christianity: How the Jesus Movement Became the World's Largest Religion*. New York: Harper Collins, 2011.

Strandskov, Herluf H. and Henry Bisaccia. "The Sex Ratio of Human Stillbirths at each month of uterogestation and at conception." *American Journal of Physical Anthropology* 7.2 (1949): 131-144.

Suk, Jeannie. "Criminal Law Comes Home." *Yale Law Journal* 116.2 (2006).

Sullivan, Sean. "Meet the billionaire hedge fund manager quietly shaping the GOP gay marriage debate." *Washington Post*, May 3, 2013. https://www.washingtonpost.com/news/the-fix/wp/2013/05/03/

meet-the-billionaire-hedge-fund-manager-quietly-shap-
ing-the-gop-gay-mar
riage-debate/?utm_term=.36e34a0d1dcd

Sundaram, Aparna, Barbara Vaughan, Kathryn Kost,
Akinrinola Bankole, Lawrence Finer, Susheela Singh,
and James Trussell. "Contraceptive Failure in the United
States: Estimates from the 2006–2010 National Survey
of Family Growth." *Perspectives on Sexual and Reproductive Health* 49.1 (March 2017): 7-16. http://onlineli
brary.wiley.com/doi/10.1363/psrh.12017/epdf

Sunstein, Cass and Richard Thaler. *Nudge: Improving
Decisions about Health, Wealth and Happiness.* New York:
Penguin Books, 2009.

Taylor Jr., Stuart. "Why Feminist Careerists Neutered Larry
Summers." *The Atlantic*, February 2005. http://www.
theatlantic.com/magazine/archive/2005/02/why-femi
nist-careerists-neutered-larry-summers/303795/.

"Teach Kids, not Stereotypes." *ACLU.* https://www.aclu.
org/womens-rights/teach-kids-not-stereotypes

"Teen Pregnancy Prevention Program." *Office of Adolescent
Health.* http://www.hhs.gov/ash/oah/oah-initiatives/
tpp_program/

Tjaden, Patricia and Nancy Thoennes. "Prevalence, Inci-
dence, and Consequences of Violence Against Women:
Findings from the National Violence Against Women
Survey." *National Institute of Justice, Centers for Disease
Control and Prevention,* November 1998. https://www.
ncjrs.gov/pdffiles/172837.pdf

Tobin, Kathleen A. *The American Religious Debate over Birth Control, 1907 to 1937*. Jefferson, NC: McFarland and Company, 2001.

Torcaso v. Watkins, 367 US 1961, 488. https://supreme.justia.com/cases/federal/us/367/488/case.html

Towers, Hilary. "Shared parenting hurts many victims of marital abandonment." *Institute for Family Studies*, June 1, 2017. https://ifstudies.org/blog/shared-parenting-hurts-many-victims-of-marital-abandonment

Trussell, James and Barbara Vaughan. "Contraceptive Failure, Method-Related Discontinuation and Resumption of Use: Results from the 1995 National Survey of Family Growth." *Family Planning Perspectives* 31.2 (1999): 64-72, 93.

Turner, Dan. *Letter from Brock Turner's Father*. https://www.documentcloud.org/documents/2852614-Letter-from-Brock-Turner-s-Father.html

Twenge, Jean. "The Age of Anxiety? Birth Cohort Changes in Anxiety and Neuroticism, 1952-1993." *Journal of Personality and Social Psychology* 79.6 (2000): 1007-1021.

Twenge, J. M., R. A. Sherman, and B. E. Wells. "Sexual Inactivity During Young Adulthood is More Common Among U.S. Millennials and iGen: Age, Period, and Cohort Effects on Having No Sexual Partners After Age 18." *Archives of Sexual Behavior* (2016): 1-8. doi:10.1007/s10508-016-0798-z

"U.S. Departments of Justice and Education Release Joint Guidance to Help Schools Ensure the Civil Rights of Transgender Students." *United States Department of Justice*, May 13, 2016. https://www.justice.gov/opa/pr/

us-departments-justice-and-education-release-joint-guid
ance-help-schools-ensure-civil-rights

Vaden-Kiernan, Nancy, Nicholas S. Ialongo, Jane Pearson, and Sheppard Kellan. "Household Family Structure and Children's Aggressive Behavior: A Longitudinal Study of Urban Elementary School Children." *Journal of Abnormal Child Psychology* 23.5 (1995): 553-568.

Volokh, Eugene. "A gag order on parents." *LA Times*, February 6, 2007. http://www.latimes.com/news/la-oe-volokh6feb06-story.html

Volokh, Eugene. "You can be fined for not calling people 'ze' or 'hir,' if that's the pronoun they demand that you use." *Washington Post*, May 17, 2016. https://www.washingtonpost.com/news/volokh-conspiracy/wp/2016/05/17/you-can-be-fined-for-not-calling-people-ze-or-hir-if-thats-the-pronoun-they-demand-that-you-use/?utm_term=.0bdaa7b58345

Vrangalova, Zhana. "Mostly Heterosexual and Mostly Gay/Lesbian: Evidence for New Sexual Orientation Identities." *Archives of Sexual Behavior* 41.1 (2012): 85-101.

Walberg, Rebecca and Andrea Mrozek. *Private Choices, Public Costs: How failing families cost us all.* Ottawa, Canada: Institute for Marriage and Family, Canada, 2009. https://irp-cdn.multiscreensite.com/64484987/files/uploaded/CanadaPrivateChoicesPublicCostsFinal.pdf

Wallerstein, Judith S., Julia M. Lewis, and Sandra Blackslee. *The Unexpected Legacy of Divorce: The 25 Year Landmark Study.* New York: Hyperion, 2000.

Walther, Stephen T. "United Nations Declaration of the Rights of the Child." *Unicef* 2003. https://www.unicef. org/malaysia/1959-Declaration-of-the-Rights-of-the-Child.pdf

Wardle, Lynn D. "Beyond Fault and No-Fault in the Reform of Marital Dissolution Law." *Reconceiving the Family: Critique on the American Law Institute's Principles of the Law of Family Dissolution.* Edited by Robin Fretwell Wilson. New York: Cambridge University Press, 2006.

Waterfield, Bruno. "Belgian killed by euthanasia after a botched sex change operation," *UK Telegraph,* October 1, 2013. http://www.telegraph.co.uk/news/worldnews/ europe/belgium/10346616/Belgian-killed-by-euthanasia-after-a-botched-sex-change-operation.html

Welling, Lisa L.M. "Psychobehavioral Effects of Hormonal Contraceptive Use." *Evolutionary Psychology* 11.3 (2013): 718-742. http://evp.sagepub.com/content/11/3/14 7470491301100315.full.pdf

"What Does Transgender Mean?" *GLAAD.* http://www. glaad.org/transgender/transfaq

"What is Intersex?" *ISNA: Intersex Society of North America.* http://www.isna.org/faq/what_is_intersex

Whelan, Robert. *Broken Homes & Battered Children: A study of the relationship between child abuse and family type.* Oxford: Family Education Trust, 1994.

White, Ron. "Offshore Jobs That Hire Women." *The Nest.* http://woman.thenest.com/offshore-jobs-hire-women-20337.html

Whole Women's Health v Hellerstedt. https://www.docu
   mentcloud.org/documents/2916939-Whole-Womens-
   Health-Scotus-Ruling.html

Wilcox, Stephanie. "Building a Better Wall Street: Training
   Female Traders." *The Glass Hammer: Smarter Women in
   Numbers*, February 22, 2011. http://theglasshammer.
   com/2011/02/22/building-a-better-wall-street-
   training-female-traders/

Wilcox, W. Bradford, Joseph P. Price, and Angela Rachidi.
   "Marriage, Penalized: Does Social-Welfare Policy Affect
   Family Formation?" *American Enterprise Institute and
   Institute for Family Studies*, 2016. https://www.aei.org/
   wp-content/uploads/2016/07/IFS-HomeEconReport-
   2016-Final-072616.pdf

"Wilhelm Reich (1897-1957)." *The Institute for Orgonomic Science.* http://www.orgonomicscience.org/
   wilhelm-reich/

Williams, Joan. *Unbending Gender: Why Family and Work
   Conflict and What We Can Do About It.* Oxford: Oxford
   University Press, 2000.

Williams, Rhiannon. "Facebook's 71 gender options come
   to UK users." *UK Telegraph*, June 27, 2014. http://www.
   telegraph.co.uk/technology/facebook/10930654/Face
   books-71-gender-options-come-to-UK-users.html

Wolfers, Justin and Betsy Stevenson. "The Paradox of
   Declining Female Happiness." *American Economic Journal* 1.2 (2009): 190-225.

"Women in STEM." *White House Office of Science
   and Technology Policy.* https://www.whitehouse.gov/
   administration/eop/ostp/women

Wootson Jr., Cleve R. "Judge in the infamous Brock Turner case explains his decision — a year later." *Chicago Tribune,* July 2, 2107. http://www.chicagotribune.com/news/nationworld/ct-brock-turner-stanford-sex-assault-judge-20170702-story.html

Wotyla, Karol. *Love and Responsibility.* San Francisco: Ignatius Press, 1993.

Yen, Hope. "As cohabitation gains favor, shotgun weddings fade." *Yahoo News,* January 6, 2014. http://news.yahoo.com/cohabitation-gains-favor-shotgun-weddings-fade-202031925.html

Yenor, Scott. *Family Politics: The Idea of Marriage in Modern Political Thought.* Waco: Baylor University Press, 2012.

Yoder, Katie. "Warren Buffett: The Billion Dollar King of Abortion." *Media Research Center.* http://www.mrc.org/articles/warren-buffett-billion-dollar-king-abortion

Zubrin, Robert. *Merchants of Despair: Radical Environmentalists, Criminal Pseudo-Scientists, and the Fatal Cult of Antihumanism.* New York: Encounter Books, 2012.